Advance Praise for
AFTER ESCOBAR

After Escobar is a high-octane thriller I couldn't put down! This incredible, first-hand account about bringing down the infamous Cali cartel reads like a Tom Clancy novel, except *this* story is 100% true.

—**Derek S. Maltz**, Acting DEA Administrator

Learn the truth about how elite DEA operators Chris Feistl and Dave Mitchell risked their lives on a daily basis, battled systemic corruption, and overcame numerous challenges to help dismantle the infamous Cali mafia. This epic adventure will keep you on the edge of your seat. It's a *must-read* for anyone one who loves True Crime stories!

—**Steve Murphy**, Retired DEA Special Agent in Charge
and co-author of *Manhunters: How We Took Down Pablo Escobar*

After Escobar is an absolute must-read for anyone with an interest in the drug war and Colombian cartels—wow, what a page turner! Straight out of a Hollywood movie. The most detailed first-hand account I have ever read regarding the take down of the Cali cartel. Well done, warriors!

—**Dave Gaddis**, Former DEA Chief of Global Enforcement Operations
and author of *The Noble Experiment*

AFTER ESCOBAR

TAKING DOWN THE NOTORIOUS CALI GODFATHERS AND THE BIGGEST DRUG CARTEL IN HISTORY

CHRIS FEISTL & DAVE MITCHELL
with Jessica Balboni

POST HILL PRESS

A POST HILL PRESS BOOK

ISBN: 979-8-88845-396-4
ISBN (eBook): 979-8-88845-397-1

Cover design by Cody Corcoran
Interior design and composition by Greg Johnson, Textbook Perfect

This book does not reflect the views of the Drug Enforcement Administration (DEA) or Colombian government. It is not endorsed by the DEA nor does it reflect the facts and opinions of the DEA, the Department of State, or the Department of Justice.

After Escobar represents the author's point of view, taken from their direct participation and insider knowledge of events that occurred during that time. In no way is it meant to suggest that others, especially within Colombia's security services, did not play a part in any operation to help take down the Cali cartel.

Although this is a true story, some names have been changed to protect the identities of U.S. sources and assets, intelligence officers, and victims of the Cali cartel.

Post Hill Press
New York • Nashville
posthillpress.com

Published in the United States of America
2 3 4 5 6 7 8 9 10

Dedicated to the memory of
Ruben Prieto and Jerry Rinehart,
who always managed to make us laugh
even in the most dangerous of times.

To all the men and women of Colombia's armed services
who dedicated their lives to combatting
drug trafficking and terrorism.
No nation on Earth has made more sacrifices
in the fight against drugs than Colombia.

"Blessed are the meek, for they shall inherit the earth."
—MATTHEW 5:5

Part of Chris and Dave's story was told in
Season 3 of the highly acclaimed Netflix series
Narcos: Rise of a New Empire, The Cali Cartel.
Now, they tell it for themselves.

"If my mind can conceive it, and my heart can believe it,
I know I can achieve it."

—JESSE JACKSON

Contents

Foreword xiii

Prologue: The Head of the Serpent 1

Chapter 1: Bienvenidos a Colombia! 5

Chapter 2: The Godfathers of Cali 15

Chapter 3: The Cartel Wars: Cali vs Medellín .31

Chapter 4: The Cali KGB 49

Chapter 5: The Supercomputer 57

Chapter 6: The Narco-Cassettes 62

Chapter 7: The Accountant 70

Chapter 8: Behind Enemy Lines 76

Chapter 9: A Narco-Democracy 84

Chapter 10: The Caravelle Capers 90

Chapter 11: Unilateral Action 96

Chapter 12: Targets of Opportunity 104

Chapter 13: Money Talks 113

Chapter 14: Pardo's Letter 117

Chapter 15: Checkmate 123

Chapter 16: Hunting Don Miguel 135

Chapter 17: The Domino Effect 142

Chapter 18: Down Goes Chepe 147

Chapter 19: Field of Dreams 155

Chapter 20: A Gold Mine 166

Chapter 21: Lights Out 176

Chapter 22: Cease and Desist 182

Chapter 23: You Wanna Do What? 196

Chapter 24: The Boys Are Back in Town 204

Chapter 25: Coming Out Party 210

Chapter 26: Our Big Break 216

Chapter 27: One Last Shot 223

Chapter 28: The Accountant's Wife 239

Chapter 29: Defection 246

Chapter 30: Please Don't Go 257

Chapter 31: Now What? 264

Chapter 32: A Dangerous Time 273

Chapter 33: The Shadow 284

Chapter 34: The Great Escape 290

Chapter 35: The Last Don 297

Epilogue: After Cali 310

Author's Note 321

Bibliography 322

About the Authors 334

Foreword

AFTER ESCOBAR ISN'T JUST ANOTHER BOOK about taking down a drug cartel—and believe me, I should know. After thirty years of service with the DEA, it's no surprise that any new account about a renowned—and even not so renowned—drug cartel never fails to capture my attention. But when the story in question is written by someone I worked with and know well, I take special notice.

Several things set *After Escobar* apart from the rest. Written by retired DEA agents Chris Feistl and Dave Mitchell, the book takes you on an adrenaline-filled roller coaster ride through some of Colombia's most turbulent, violent, and politically unstable times. It also gives the reader a rare behind-the-scenes look into the onslaught of challenges and obstacles the US government faced in Colombia in the mid-1990s during the epic operation to help bring down the savage Cali cartel, an organization former head of the DEA Robert Bonner once called "the most powerful criminal organization in the world." It's the most comprehensive work I've read about this time and also one of the most unique, given its first-person perspective.

I didn't know Chris and Dave when they arrived in Bogotá, Colombia in July 1994, and I was tasked with picking them up from the airport. For the two "new guys," their assignment was about as intimidating as it gets: help Colombian security forces bring down the infamous, vicious leaders of the Cali drug cartel. It was a challenge I understood, since Steve Murphy and I had been assigned a similar mission to help take down Pablo Escobar and his Medellín cartel not long before. Steve already knew Chris and Dave, and described them both as aggressive, motivated young agents with stellar reputations. When I asked Steve how I'd recognize them, he just laughed and said, "Don't worry. You'll know them the second you see them."

He wasn't wrong. As soon as Chris and Dave deplaned, I spotted the pair immediately. Chris looked like a card-carrying member of the World Surf League, while Dave could easily have been mistaken for a professional football player. In the early 1990s, Colombia was an extremely hostile environment for American drug agents, particularly for young, blond ones standing over six feet tall. The sheer impossibility for them to be inconspicuous made me concerned about how they'd fare operating in the hermitic, perilous city of Cali. And I wasn't alone. Just months earlier, two agents had been compromised in Cali when they were betrayed by one of their assets, a cartel double agent. Many senior DEA managers in Washington, DC had their concerns, fears echoed by a number of officials in the American Embassy.

I'd seen a lot of agents come and go during my years in Colombia. Some were successful, but many others failed, unable to adapt, and as a consequence, inevitably swallowed up in the mercurial political landscape they had to navigate. What fate had in store for Chris and Dave, I really didn't know.

As time passed and I was preparing to depart Colombia, my six-plus year tour nearly complete, I found myself consistently impressed with how adept Chris and Dave were when it came to debriefing sources and planning and coordinating enforcement operations with their police and military contacts. It didn't take long for me to see, and feel, that this pair was different. They were highly motivated, thought outside the box, and, perhaps most importantly, they were fearless. They weren't afraid to fail. I understood then why they were selected for the assignment: their passion to succeed, coupled with their refusal to let fear dictate their narrative, was the combination they needed to prove their detractors wrong.

As you read *After Escobar*, you'll be captivated by not just the history of the Cali Mafia and their bloody six-year war with Pablo Escobar and the Medellín cartel, but by Chris and Dave's own backstories and the daily struggles the two faced while trying to battle the systemic corruption within the country's armed forces. You'll have a ringside seat into the state of political affairs in Colombia during the 1990s, and learn about the inhospitable environment in which they had to operate. As Chris and

Foreword

Dave take on one dangerous challenge after another, they have to work unilaterally to accomplish their goal. Throughout their quest they come up against unending setbacks, shocking betrayals, and life or death decisions that change the course of not just their lives but the lives of countless others, as well.

The story of their journey itself is riveting, but it's Chris and Dave's unwavering commitment and their willingness to take extraordinary measures to further their objective—even having to bribe government officials to escape a potentially deadly situation—that stands out. *After Escobar* not only chronicles their time helping to bring down the Cali cartel, it also shows us the traits and qualities that often prove so critical to our own real life, day-to-day challenges—examples of courage, leadership, loyalty, overcoming adversity, and, most importantly, never, ever giving up. Their unrelenting perseverance against all odds is inspiring.

After Escobar is a thrilling read. It's as action-packed, heart-wrenching, and enthralling as any Hollywood movie, and nearly impossible to put down once you've started. So sit back, and enjoy the ride. I know you're going to enjoy it!

—**Javier F. Peña**, Special Agent in Charge (retired)
Drug Enforcement Administration

The Head of the Serpent

"Do whatever you need to do, but we can't get taken!"

—HIGH-LEVEL DEA ASSET and Cali Cartel Double Agent

Sugarcane field, Palmira, Colombia, August 1, 1995

IT WAS ANOTHER BRUTALLY HOT DAY in the Valle del Cauca, and we were operating in Cali, Colombia, almost two hundred miles to the southwest of our headquarters at the American Embassy in Bogotá. Cali was then a city of about 1.8 million people—the third largest in Colombia—and had long been famous for its salsa dancing, sugarcane, and, most recently, cocaine. It was also infamous, best known as the home to the notorious Cali cartel, a group the former head of the Drug Enforcement Administration (DEA), Thomas Constantine, once referred to as "the biggest and most powerful crime syndicate in history." In July of 1994, the DEA sent my partner Dave and me from Miami with one goal: bring down the biggest drug cartel in history. The task felt insurmountable for two fledgling agents barely out of their twenties and only six years removed from the DEA Academy.

After over a year on the ground in Cali, the head of the Cali cartel, Miguel Ángel Rodríguez Orejuela, was still at large. Commonly known as "Don Miguel" or "El Señor," his capture was the ultimate prize. If the entire cartel was ever to fall, the head of the serpent had to be cut off—and that meant Miguel. But it didn't take long to realize that Cali wasn't your typical beast. Cutting off the head wouldn't just be difficult, it would be a Herculean task. Our sole advantage at that point in the mission was one man, a man who'd already risked his life numerous times simply by choosing to meet with us.

For the man in question, the walls had recently begun to close in. A handful of critical cartel operatives openly distrusted him, while others questioned his abilities, some going so far as to believe *he* might be the one primarily responsible for the DEA's recent successes against Cali. My partner and I knew one thing for sure: from now on there could be no more mistakes, no more bad breaks, and no more compromises.

We also knew that even the most minor of errors on our part—or his—would almost certainly mean swift justice for him and his family. And justice in Cali meant only one thing: death. There would be no trial, no defense, no explanations. Instead, there would be plastic bags closed tightly over their heads until they desperately gasped for air, then suffocated.

The risks were high, and we all knew it. The safety of our asset was paramount: lives depended on it. So it went without question that this rendezvous some thirty miles north of our Cali safe house needed to be brief, thorough, and, above all, flawless.

We'd chosen to meet in this particularly remote sugarcane field because it was so isolated, far away from the prying eyes of the countless cartel spies who controlled every single inch of Cali.

In law enforcement we always talk about Murphy's Law and how it always seems to rear its head at the worst possible time. In its simplest form, Murphy's law states: if anything can go wrong, you can bet it will. We didn't know it at the time, but our imminent undercover meeting was no exception.

We parked just off a gravel thruway a few hundred yards from one of the lightly traveled local roads. The sugarcane towered at least fifteen feet over our heads, providing ample cover. We got down to business, discussing the plan in detail—and the dire consequences for our asset if it didn't succeed. We also made sure to review his extraction strategy, the one that would come into play after what we hoped would be Miguel's arrest.

That's when our friend Murphy came calling.

It was pitch-black by the time we were wrapping up when a marked Colombian National Police (CNP) patrol car raced past us on the nearby road, lights flashing. That was followed by several taxis, another patrol car, then another. I looked at Dave, then back over to our source. "Time to go," I said. Neither of them said a word.

Just then a marked CNP patrol van turned abruptly down the gravel road and accelerated toward us. "Get rid of your weapons," our insider said. I grabbed the 9mm Glock 17 pistol from the small of my back and flung it deep into the cane field, along with all my identification and credentials. Dave did the same, hurling his fanny pack holding his Glock, extra magazines, and identification cards into the sugarcane. Under no circumstances could we be identified as DEA agents. The lives of our asset—not to mention his entire family—depended on us hiding our identities.

As the CNP patrol unit approached, we found ourselves unarmed, vulnerable, and worried for our safety. We knew that these police were likely corrupt: widespread police corruption in Colombia was a well-known fact, one on which the cartel prided itself. They could, and did, infiltrate, influence, and control the vast majority of Colombian security forces and politicians throughout the country. Also, the reality was that Dave and I were a couple of young, blond gringos in a city where most residents rarely, if ever, saw an American in person. We also knew that if the cartel's intelligence network—commonly referred to as the Cali KGB—discovered our spy's identity, he'd be dead within minutes. Our spy, no doubt thinking the same, turned to us and said, "If we get arrested, I'm a dead man. I can't be compromised! Do whatever you need to, but we can't get taken!"

The van skidded to a stop, and two burly, uniformed officers got out, weapons drawn. Clearly, they meant business. But…why? Why were they here, in the middle of a remote sugarcane field, pointing weapons at us? Had we been exposed? Had the cartel learned of our plan and our asset's betrayal? And if so, were they going to kidnap and torture us, or kill us right here? Every DEA agent had heard all about the brutal abduction, torture, and murder of fellow agent Enrique "Kiki" Camarena at the hands of Mexican cartel thugs in Guadalajara, Mexico, in 1985. Our minds were racing.

The two cops sauntered over, their Israeli-made Uzis leveled directly at us. One of the officers barked at us in Spanish, "Hands up!" while the other asked for identification. "Identification?" I asked, staring at the Uzi he kept pointed in our direction. The second cop patted us down for weapons. It was obvious that we were now—as we like to say in the DEA—in the *shit* and needed to go to plan B, whatever that was. We were certain of only two things: One, we needed to protect our asset, no matter the cost. And two: that cost could mean our lives.

CHAPTER 1

Bienvenidos a Colombia!

"You and Dave don't exactly blend in."

—RUBEN PRIETO,
DEA Bogotá Group Supervisor

Twenty months earlier...

"Viva Colombia! We just killed Pablo Escobar!" It was December 2, 1993, and CNP Major Hugo Aguilar was ecstatic, shouting into his radio transmitter in Medellín's Los Olivos neighborhood. His words were met with cheers, euphoria, and an overwhelming sense of relief by millions of Colombian citizens. It was a sentiment shared by the countless brave men and women of Colombia's security forces who'd spent the last seventeen months of their lives hunting the world's most wanted narco-terrorist.

Escobar had long reigned as the number one enemy of the state, and his legendarily vicious Medellín cartel was responsible for the savage murders of thousands of Colombia's own. For many years he'd seemed untouchable, almost immortal. But times had changed, and Pablo's time was now officially over.

In June 1991, Escobar surrendered to government authorities after repeated assurances from Colombian officials that he wouldn't be extradited to the United States. Just a little over a year later, he walked out of the back gate of the "prison" he had agreed to transfer to, in reality his own

5

lavish, self-designed living quarters, a luxurious estate overlooking the city of Medellín famously referred to as "La Catedral." He'd just tortured and killed two of his top associates: Gerardo "Kiko" Moncada and Fernando "El Negro" Galeano, a horrific double murder that triggered a nationwide manhunt. Now, just a year and a half later, Pablo was also gone.

Two hundred miles to the southwest, louder cries of celebration echoed throughout Miguel Rodríguez Orejuela's mountainside mansion near the Versailles district of Cali, Colombia. Miguel—along with his older brother, Gilberto—were two of the four dynamic, elusive leaders of the powerful Cali cartel. After a fierce six-year war with Escobar, they'd finally emerged victorious. The celebration had been a long time coming, and the men were beside themselves, delirious with success.

For the past several years, the Cali godfathers had remained largely unchecked by Colombian security forces, as nearly every resource in the country had been devoted to eradicating Pablo Escobar. As a result, the Cali cartel was able to fester in the shadows, quietly building an empire that now threatened to become a more powerful force than their rivals to the north had ever been. After Escobar's death, celebrations erupted not just within the Cali inner circle but throughout all of Colombia, many of which lasted for days. For the godfathers, there was more to savor than just their former enemy's demise. With Escobar gone, they were positioned to take total control of the worldwide cocaine trade. It was exactly what they'd been preparing for, and they were ready.

Back in South Florida, the news of Escobar's demise reverberated through the halls of the DEA's Miami Field Division office, where Dave Mitchell and I had recently been selected by DEA Headquarters for a new assignment in Colombia. After the fall of Escobar, we knew that the full force of the US government—along with the government of Colombia—would be utilized in a joint effort to take on Cali. It was the opportunity of a lifetime, and we knew it.

Both Dave and I grew up in small town America, worlds away from the cacophony and hectic pace of the big city. Dave was born in Louisville, Kentucky, and raised in a rural community near Fort Knox. Like many young men with big ambitions and even bigger imaginations, he became interested in law enforcement as a child after reading about Eliot Ness and the Untouchables' legendary battle against Al Capone. Each year at the state fair he'd breeze past all the games and head directly to the Kentucky State Police welcome trailer, where he'd stare at the poster bearing the words burned into his mind: *ONE RIOT, ONE TROOPER*. In a way, he saw DEA as the modern-day version of the Untouchables, with that same One Riot, One Trooper mindset. Whereas other agencies were responsible for enforcing hundreds of crimes, DEA concentrated on only one. "We're like Kentucky Fried Chicken," one of his DEA Academy instructors once told him. "We do one thing, and we do it well."

After graduating from Eastern Kentucky University with a major in criminal justice, Dave was commissioned as a second lieutenant in the US Army and assigned to Athens, Greece, where he was responsible for the security of Nike Hercules surface-to-air missiles (SAMs) and other special weaponry. Later, he joined the elite 82nd Airborne Division at Fort Bragg, North Carolina.

Like Dave, I was competitive and ambitious in my youth—but with less of an Eliot Ness bent and more of a tenacious one. I grew up an only child in Forty Fort, Pennsylvania, with a strict, whip-smart academic father who worked as a high school teacher before going on to obtain both master's and doctorate degrees. He was a huge influence, instilling in me a work ethic that I carried throughout my entire life and career. He always pushed me to be the best I could be no matter what I did, constantly motivating me with his signature phrase, "No matter what you do in life, do it well. If you're a janitor, be the best janitor you can be."

I lived for sports, setting various high school and district records in track and field and becoming a first-team all-conference basketball player, amassing over one thousand career points. I also played basketball at King's College, starting as a guard all four years surpassing the one thousand point plateau once again—placing me eighth on the college's all-time scoring list by the time I graduated.

I'd planned on attending law school after graduating from college, but an internship as a seasonal police officer in the resort city of Wildwood, New Jersey, changed all that. I was barely twenty-one when I worked my first undercover assignment on the hectic Wildwood boardwalk, and that was the final push I needed to officially pursue a career with the DEA. To work my way toward it, I worked as a full-time police officer (and part-time surfer) in Virginia Beach, where I waited patiently for DEA to call.

AFTER ESCOBAR

Dave and I were hired in early 1988 and reported to the DEA Academy just six weeks apart. Back then DEA didn't have its own training facility, so we shared space with the FBI on the Marine Corps base in Quantico, Virginia. Although Dave was one class ahead, we routinely passed each other in the halls and sometimes caught up over pizza and beer at the academy's main dive, the Boardroom.

After graduating from the academy in the summer of 1988, Dave and I were both assigned to the Miami Field Division. Dave was assigned to Group 14, a maritime smuggling group and part of the vice president's South Florida Drug Task Force. Established in 1982 by President Ronald· Reagan, it had built a stellar reputation and was subsequently placed under the purview of Vice President George H. W. Bush. Its main objective was to slow the tidal wave of cocaine that was flooding South Florida via the Caribbean corridor, alongside a host of other federal agencies and military components. I was sent to Enforcement Group 4, better known as the Clandestine Laboratory Group. It wasn't quite on the level of Group 14, but it was an impressive squad.

Dave and I were lucky. Both groups had a good reputation, respected supervisors, and hard-nosed agents working high-level investigations. And there was no question that Miami was ground zero for the drug war in the 1980s—hell, it was home to *Miami Vice* and the legendary Cocaine Cowboys. For two ambitious young agents it wasn't just a great place to learn the ropes, it was *the* place. Miami was everyone's number one choice for an inaugural assignment, and not just because of its reputation or unparalleled level of opportunity: it also came with warm weather, pristine beaches, abundant fishing and diving spots, and countless nightlife options. It didn't have the surfing conditions I'd become accustomed to in Virginia Beach or the breathtaking beauty of North Carolina's Outer Banks, but it had plenty of ideal locations close by for quick weekend excursions.

But by far, one of the greatest advantages of being based in Miami was its international culture and flavor. It was referred to by many in law enforcement as "Medellín north" due to the large number of Colombians who lived there. It had also become home to a host of other immigrants from all over the world, particularly Central America, South America, and the Caribbean—a true melting pot. That mix created an environment rife with outstanding restaurants, beautiful women, and a unique Latin vibe that put Miami on the map as a popular tourist playground. But it was equally attractive to Colombian cartels, who saw it as the ideal entry point into the US for their cocaine. Because of its geographical proximity to myriad drug producing and transshipment countries, along with Florida's 1,350 miles of coastline, it was a veritable smuggler's paradise.

The cocaine arrived in go-fast vessels, fishing vessels, and coastal freighters transporting containerized cargo by sea; commercial and private aircraft; overland from Mexico; and numerous other ways. Cocaine was then so prevalent on the streets of Dade County we used to joke that it was falling out of the sky—and sometimes, in fact, it literally was.

But for us, the sheer number of high-level investigations waiting to be worked was the real draw. Smuggling cases, controlled deliveries, wiretaps, and complex conspiracies were the norm. These cases oftentimes resulted in leads that needed to be pursued in international destinations throughout Central and South America, and as a result of the travel and experience, agents from Miami were often sought after for foreign assignments in Latin America. The Bogotá Country Office was the main landing spot for Miami agents who'd proven they had what it took to work in Colombia, the epicenter of the drug trade.

I remember reading the article that would alter the course of my career and life: the July 1, 1991, edition of *Time* magazine. Its headline stopped me in my tracks: "Cocaine Inc. The New Drug Kings. Cold-blooded and efficient, Colombia's Cali cartel has cornered the market. Can these men be stopped?" Written by journalist Elaine Shannon, the article was a game changer for me. Though I was already well versed in the topic, her research on the power and wealth amassed by the Cali cartel—along with the massive drug seizures made by the DEA and other law enforcement agencies—left me in awe. Our then DEA administrator Robert Bonner stated, "The Cali cartel is the most powerful criminal organization in the world. No drug organization rivals them today or perhaps any time in history."

It was that exposé that marked the beginning of my path toward working in Colombia. By that point, I was focusing almost exclusively on maritime smuggling cases directly linked to Cali—but we were only scratching the surface in Miami. I knew that if I wanted to become a truly successful DEA agent and authority on Cali, I needed to be on the ground in the heart of it all. I wanted—*needed*—to go to Colombia to help bring down the biggest, baddest drug cartel on the planet.

Dave's path to Colombia was a little different. As a result of his military background, in 1991 he was recruited for Operation Snowcap, a DEA-sponsored operation in which DEA special agents, the US Border Patrol Tactical Unit (BORTAC), and other specialized military personnel conducted counternarcotics and search-and-destroy operations on cocaine manufacturing laboratories and clandestine airstrips in the jungles of South America. After serving three Snowcap tours in Bolivia, Dave returned to Miami and was assigned to Enforcement Group 10, where he focused on targeting Colombian smuggling organizations using the Bahamian islands and Caribbean Sea as a springboard to flood South Florida with cocaine. But Dave missed the excitement of being abroad. Soon after his return, he began to explore opportunities in South America.

In May 1993, I was at a club in Fort Lauderdale when someone tapped me on the back and said, "Hey, know where I can buy two keys of coke?" I immediately segued into my undercover alter ego, though I'd come a long way since my rookie undercover days on the Jersey Shore years ago. I'd since worked on scores of undercover assignments, from small street-level drug deals in Dade and Broward Counties to multi-hundred-kilogram loads of cocaine and marijuana in the Florida Keys, the Bahamas, Jamaica, Panama, and elsewhere.

I had blond hair stretching all the way down to the middle of my back and prided myself on the fact that I hadn't had a real haircut since graduating from the academy. I was tan, sported the then prerequisite five-day facial growth, wore three earrings, and, last but not least, rocked a Rolex watch paired with a full set of gold chains straight out of a Mr. T costume starter kit. People would have been more likely to mistake me for an extra from *Point Break* than a DEA agent, undercover or not. The cherry on top was my G-ride, or Official Government Vehicle, a navy-blue four-door Mercedes-Benz 300E with limo smoke-tinted windows.

When I turned around to lay down my best undercover rap, I saw Dave doubled over with laughter. It was not the first—or last—time that I had fallen victim to one of his pranks.

I told Dave that I'd applied for a spot in Colombia and suggested he do the same. We discussed the pros and cons and reviewed our qualifications,

Chris, undercover in Miami before his arrival in Colombia.

agreeing that our chances were pretty good. While we weren't fluent Spanish speakers, we both knew enough to get by—a couple months of language school and we'd be good to go.

Two weeks later, word trickled out that the vacant position in Colombia had been filled…but not with me. I was floored. How could I have been passed over? I had outstanding evaluations, had already worked a slew of high-level Colombian cases, and knew all the main Cali players.

I called Steve Murphy in Bogotá—the one and only Steve Murphy from the Pablo Escobar case—whom Dave and I knew from Miami and respected.

"Murph. How could I not be selected?" He laughed and said, "Dude, you gotta get that hair cut. Toft was probably picturing you rolling in here with your board shorts and surfboard. The American Embassy is a far different environment than Miami, believe me."

The Mr. Toft who Murph was referring to was *the* Joe Toft, the DEA Country Attaché and main man in Colombia. He'd been stationed in Bogotá since 1988 and had built an exceptional reputation leading the DEA's efforts against Escobar and the Medellín cartel. Still, I was pissed.

11

"That's bullshit," I said to no one in particular. But I knew what I had to do. Toft wasn't just a boss, he was *the* boss. He made the rules, and if I wanted to get in the game, I had to be ready to play by them. So I headed over to a local barber shop, took a deep breath, and asked the barber to lop off twelve inches of my beloved flaxen tresses.

Just like that, the result of over five years of growing my hair was erased in a few seconds. Though it was still long by most standards, to me it may as well have been a buzz cut. When I returned to the office, I felt like a zoo animal. People were staring, pointing, and asking me if everything was okay.

"Why on earth did you do that?" one of the assistants asked me.

"Um, I'm not really sure" was all I could muster.

A few days later, I got a phone call from Toft himself. "So, I heard you got your hair cut?" Word had traveled fast.

"Yes, sir. I did." I held my breath and waited for his reaction.

"Just be patient, Feistl. Things will work out for you." Click.

A month later, Dave and I received the news we were waiting for: we'd both been selected for foreign reassignment to Colombia. Not only that, but we were both being assigned to shore up operations exclusively against the Cali cartel.

This was a privilege *and* a challenge. At the time, the vast majority of DEA and Colombian resources were still being deployed to Medellín in the hunt for Escobar, and the smaller Cali-focused DEA contingent was in serious need of support. When Dave and I celebrated the news with a few beers at a nearby bar, some Miami supervisors and colleagues expressed their fear for our safety and questioned our ability to blend in. How effective could two obvious Americans be in the wildly dangerous environment that was Cali?

Over the last several years, Colombia's reputation as the most violent country in the world had only gotten worse. The war waged against the Colombian government by Escobar and the Medellín cartel helped contribute to the loss of roughly 78,000 people from 1991 through 1993. In Cali, alone, there were 2,695 reported homicides in less than a year and a half.

Kidnappings were another serious problem. From 1990 through 1992, Colombia averaged 1,450 a year, by far the highest in the world (and also inaccurate, as many abductions went unreported). Most of the kidnappings were carried out by drug cartels, organized criminal groups, and Marxist guerrillas like the Fuerzas Armadas Revolucionarias de Colombia or Revolutionary Armed Forces of Colombia (FARC) and the Ejército de Liberación Nacional or National Liberation Army (ELN). So Dave and I understood the concern, and the risks. But we weren't letting that stop us.

After a few months of Spanish language school, Dave and I were chomping at the bit to leave. By this point it was mid-1994, and things had changed dramatically: Escobar had been killed a few months earlier, and the Cali cartel was now public enemy number one. We were Colombia-bound at the best—or worst—possible time.

As soon as our flight touched down in Bogotá, Dave and I heard *"Bienvenidos a Colombia!"* over the intercom, sending chills down my spine. We deplaned and headed toward immigration, where a fellow DEA agent named Javier Peña was there to greet us. Dave and I knew Javier by reputation only; our agent friend Steve Murphy was his partner, and together they'd been critical in the quest to take down Escobar.

When we arrived at the US Embassy, we met with DEA Country Attaché Joe Toft and Assistant County Attaché Jerry Rinehart. Our assignment: work with host-nation counterparts to take down the leaders of the notorious Cali cartel—the same cartel that had been operating with total impunity in Colombia for over twenty years. Though Dave and I were assigned to work together, we were each sent to a different group. I was also given the collateral duty as Colombia's fugitive and extradition coordinator and liaison to the US Marshals Service in Washington, DC.

My new supervisor was an agent named Ruben Prieto. He was a kind, soft-spoken man and immediately made me feel welcome. He knew about my experience working investigations targeting the Cali cartel, and when I asked him when Dave and I could head there, as I already had some promising leads from my old group in Miami, Ruben shook his head. "I'm sorry. We're not sending anybody to Cali right now. It's too dangerous."

I almost fell out of my chair. "Are you kidding?"

Apparently, two veteran Hispanic DEA agents had recently been photographed in Cali, betrayed by one of their sources, a cartel double agent. The photograph made its way back to the embassy, where it was viewed by the US ambassador and DEA management as a perceived threat against

13

any American agents operating in Cali. The cartel knew the agents' identities, where they stayed, where they ate, even where they rented their cars. From that point on, no agents had been given the green light to return.

"How are we supposed to investigate the cartel if we can't go to Cali?" I asked.

"You'll have to do it from Bogotá," Ruben said. "Besides, you and Dave don't exactly…blend in." As I got up to leave, he handed me a DEA pager, a cell phone, and a Motorola SkyPager, courtesy of the Marshals Service. This way they could contact me anytime and anywhere regarding high-profile fugitives.

For two newcomers looking to make a name for themselves, the formidable mission to take down the Cali cartel had just gotten much harder. "*Bienvenidos a Colombia!*" It wasn't exactly the welcome we expected.

CHAPTER 2

The Godfathers of Cali

"To know your enemy, you must become your enemy."

—**SUN TZU**, Ancient Chinese General,
Military Strategist, and Author of *The Art of War*

The Genesis

THOUGH THOUSANDS OF YEARS have passed, Sun Tzu's words are still relevant: if you want to predict the actions of your enemy, you must first put yourself in his place. Do it and you have some chance. Ignore it, and you have none.

Resigned to the fact that Dave and I had no other option but to attempt our takedown of the Cali cartel from Bogotá, that philosophy became our mantra. But to give ourselves a fighting chance, we'd need to learn every single thing we could about the Cali godfathers.

Gilberto José Rodríguez Orejuela and his younger brother, Miguel Ángel Rodríguez Orejuela, were born near Mariquita, Colombia, in the Department of Tolima: Gilberto on January 30, 1939, and Miguel on August 15, 1943. A third brother, Jorge Eliécer Rodríguez Orejuela, was born on July 9, 1947, in Popayán, a city eighty-five miles south of Cali. The three boys grew up alongside their three sisters in Cali, where they'd moved when the brothers were toddlers. Their father Carlos, a painter, had relocated the family in the hopes that a bigger city would offer better job opportunities, while their mother, Ana Rita, was a protective stay-at-home mom.

Like their father, Gilberto and Miguel were motivated by money. When Gilberto was a child, he sold flowers to earn extra cash. As a teenager, he got a job as a delivery boy in a local pharmacy, using his bicycle to drop off the medications. A few years later, Miguel also found work in a drugstore, but the brothers soon realized that even a dual income wasn't enough. Frustrated with their limited options, they turned to crime in order to supplement their meager wages. Pharmacy deliveries soon gave way to car theft, counterfeiting, stealing and reselling medical supplies, and anything else they could get away with to make a few extra pesos.

As their lust for wealth grew, so did their propensity for crime. In the late 1960s, Gilberto and Miguel teamed with their childhood friend, José Santacruz Londoño (known as "Chepe"), and formed their first criminal clique, "Los Chemas," headed by another friend, Luis Fernando Tamayo García.

Chepe Santacruz was born on October 1, 1943, in Cali, Colombia, and befriended Gilberto and Miguel during middle school. He attended the Universidad del Valle and later the Universidad de los Andes in Bogotá, where he studied engineering, earning him one of his many nicknames, "the Student." During his time in Bogotá, Chepe was implicated in the kidnapping of two individuals for whom he received a decent ransom, which he used to purchase several taxis. The small step into the kidnapping business quickly led Gilberto, Miguel, and Chepe on the path straight into the world of drug trafficking.

As Los Chemas grew and the men focused their efforts on the more profitable business of kidnapping and extortion, the three (now without Tamayo) found success via securing large ransoms from their victims or the victims' families. In 1969, Los Chemas was said to have kidnapped a pair of Swiss citizens—a diplomat and a student—netting the group $700,000.

Not long after, the trio met someone who would alter the course of their lives: Benjamín Herrera Zuleta. An Afro-Colombian smuggler known as "the Black Pope of Cocaine," Zuleta was one of the early pioneers of cocaine trafficking, widely known not just in the Valle del Cauca region but all throughout Colombia. The Black Pope introduced Los Chemas into the world of drug trafficking and forever changed their destiny.

With substantial cash in hand, the three fledgling entrepreneurs branched out into marijuana trafficking but found it problematic—bulky, pungent, challenging to conceal, and difficult to transport. Sizable quantities needed to be smuggled into the US in large ships or planes, posing a higher risk of interception and seizure by law enforcement. More importantly, their resources were limited, and they were only capable of moving smaller loads. They decided it wasn't worth it: marijuana was never going to produce the return on investment the group wanted.

In the early 1970s, Gilberto realized that if they were to be *really* successful, their future lay with a far more lucrative commodity: cocaine. So they shifted strategies, opting to smuggle coca paste and cocaine base from Peru and Bolivia into southern Colombia with a small airplane they'd purchased with some of the profits made during their stint in the kidnapping business. After it was refined in Colombia, the cocaine was smuggled into the United States.

The business had humble beginnings but an extravagant payoff, with Gilberto himself driving a kilo or two of cocaine from Panama to New York City via the Pan-American Highway in an old, beat-up car in early 1973. The 4,500-mile trip took a few weeks, but the reward was astounding: their initial investment of $1,000 to $1,500 in Colombia, plus another thousand dollars or so in transportation costs to the States, yielded between $50,000 to $60,000 per kilogram of cocaine on the streets of New York. The end result: a hefty profit of $48,000 to $57,500 per brick. With that, the Cali cartel was born.

Soon thereafter, a steady flow of couriers and mules began arriving on commercial flights to both Miami and New York with a few pounds of cocaine strapped to their bodies or concealed in shoes or album sleeves, quickly followed by concealing larger kilogram quantities of cocaine in double-sided suitcases. At the time it was surprisingly easy, as no one was worried about cocaine in 1970s New York—or anywhere else, for that matter. The New York Drug Enforcement Task Force (NYDETF), the New York State Police, and the Bureau of Narcotics and Dangerous Drugs (BNDD), which would later become the DEA, were focused on a much more serious threat: heroin.

For some time, heroin shipments had been smuggled into New York from southwest or southeast Asia, often transiting through Marseilles,

France. By 1972, a staggering 95 percent of those treated in New York for drug addiction were heroin related. Understandably, law enforcement officials focused their efforts on taking down major international heroin traffickers along with equally significant dealers in Harlem like the legendary Nicky Barnes and Frank Lucas, with little to no attention being paid to cocaine.

Most people considered cocaine to be a harmless party drug associated with celebrities, musicians, and high rollers at decadent parties. But it gained a foothold in a drove of diverse New York bars and discos, including the world's most famous nightclub, Studio 54. While cocaine use spread throughout New York, making it the city that *literally* never sleeps, Gilberto—and later Chepe—flew under the radar of authorities, raking in more money than they'd ever imagined.

With the textile industry on the brink of collapse and Colombia's economy in decline, many Colombians sought refuge and work in New York's garment industry and other service industry–related jobs. This mass exodus played perfectly into Gilberto's long-term vision. But as the demand for cocaine grew, so did the need for increased production and distribution. That posed a problem—the three men couldn't transport the cocaine to the US or repatriate the proceeds to Colombia fast enough. By 1975, Gilberto started sending larger loads of cocaine concealed inside mahogany lumber planks from the Port of Buenaventura on Colombia's Pacific coast to America's Eastern Seaboard. Boxes of money began to pile up inside the cartel's various New York apartments, but they were elated. There were far worse problems to have.

Initially tasked with overseeing their emerging franchise in the Empire State, Chepe soon realized he needed help. He thought back to a young, laid-back, but eager man in Cali, whom Chepe knew was looking to become part of something special. Chepe also knew that the man desperately wanted to fit in and would do anything to make that happen. That young man was Francisco Hélmer Herrera Buitrago, better known as "Pacho" Herrera.

Herrera was born on August 24, 1951, in Palmira, Colombia, just east of Cali. Widely rumored to be the illegitimate son of Benjamín Herrera, the Black Pope of Cocaine, Pacho was easygoing, affable, and openly gay and, like so many of his fellow Colombians, lived for soccer. He jumped at the chance to join Chepe in a new city, and together they expanded Cali's footprint in New York while also working part-time jobs: Chepe in construction and Pacho as a mechanic and part-time jewelry dealer. But their pedestrian moonlighting gigs wouldn't last long.

From the beginning, Gilberto called the shots. Nicknamed "the Chess Player" due to his exceptional long-term vision and talent for making strategic business decisions, he was always two steps ahead of everyone else. His brother Miguel, "Don Miguel" or "El Señor," remained in Colombia. A well-educated lawyer, Miguel was more intense, methodical, and obsessive about detail. Initially more content behind-the-scenes, Miguel deferred to his older brother to helm the business. Meanwhile, Chepe and Pacho wreaked havoc on the streets of the Big Apple, flooding it with cocaine and reveling in the decadence.

Both Chepe and Pacho were arrested during their tenure in New York: Chepe in 1976 for possession of a false passport and 1977 for weapons violations, and Pacho for cocaine possession in 1975 and 1978. Since cocaine was still largely ignored as a potential problem, possession wasn't considered a serious offense. Pacho breezed through two short stints in jail and emerged unfazed.

The Business Model

In 1978, Medellín cartel co-founder Carlos Enrique Lehder Rivas (nicknamed "Crazy Charlie" by his cartel associate Pablo Escobar) devised a scheme that revolutionized cocaine smuggling. During this time, small aircraft carrying several hundred pounds of cocaine weren't able to complete the long journey from Colombia to the US without refueling. Lehder discovered Norman's Cay, a small, strategically perfect island in the Exuma island chain 210 miles southeast of Miami. It was remote, sparsely populated, and known mostly for its exclusive private resorts. Lehder recognized it as the ideal place to establish his smuggling headquarters and went on a real estate spending spree, and by 1980 he owned and/or controlled nearly all of the island.

After chasing out most of the residents, Lehder constructed a 3,300-foot paved runway, built airplane hangars, and turned the once tropical Bahamian paradise into a transshipment and refueling mecca for cocaine-laden aircraft. Wealthy vacationers were replaced by armed cartel gunmen there to protect the operations and product. Lehder also bribed Bahamian officials and politicians, all of whom were happy to look the other way for huge payoffs. For the next four years, the Medellín cartel bombarded the southeastern US seaboard with tens of thousands of kilograms of cocaine, air-dropping the bales to awaiting speedboats in the Florida Everglades or landing on remote dirt roads and clandestine airstrips.

The Cali cartel also flew thousands of kilos of cocaine from Norman's Cay into secluded ranches in Alabama and the southeastern US, where it was picked up and driven to New York, then distributed by Chepe, Pacho, and other Cali operatives. At that time, the Colombian cocaine business was more collaborative then combative, with the Cali and Medellín cartels working together whenever it was mutually beneficial.

There was still competition, of course. In the drug trade there are no secrets, and Lehder's Caribbean conquest was something Gilberto and Miguel yearned to emulate. If Lehder and the Medellín cartel controlled the sky, then Cali would control the sea. The brothers looked to the Caribbean corridor and began sending thousands of kilos of cocaine into Florida hidden inside containerized cargo or transferring them from fishing vessels directly onto high-powered speedboats. Flush with cash, Cali began looking for more outlets into which they could funnel their profits.

To better disguise and launder the source of their money, the brothers made one of their savviest moves by branching further out into legitimate business. They made a string of enormous purchases, including Grupo Radial Colombiano (a network of over thirty radio stations), Drogas La Rebaja (a leading pharmacy chain), the concession for Chrysler Motors, and later, a controlling interest in two banks: Banco de los Trabajadores and the First InterAmericas Bank in Panama. But the jewel in the crown was the acquisition of their beloved soccer team, América de Cali. That wasn't just good business, it was a dream come true for the brothers and their top two associates.

As the brothers continued to expand their corporate empire, they created a credible façade as upstanding entrepreneurs and perfected their image as legitimate tycoons. They paid great attention to detail, wearing expensive but understated suits and rubbing elbows with top executives, politicians, government officials, and elites from Colombian society. They passed out money like candy, using it to curry favor with countless powerful men and women throughout the country. They soon became known as "the Gentlemen of Cali" or, even more reverentially, "the Godfathers of Cali."

To the average Colombian, their success in transforming the city into a thriving business and economic center was impressive, but in reality, it was all smoke and mirrors. Every bit of it was achieved using drug money.

Still, their reputation remained unsullied. Whereas the Medellín cartel relied primarily on violence, threats, and intimidation, Cali's weapon of choice was the bribe, which proved to be just as effective. Cali preferred to *buy* officials in key positions, not kill them. Of course, they were hardly pacifists—far from it. But when the cartel felt they had no choice but to resort to violence, they did it quietly. Better to have their problems "disappear," they thought, than to leave a trail of bodies behind.

Cali ran their illegal affairs with the same discipline as they did their legal ones. They established compartmentalized drug and money-laundering cells and ensured that each one operated wholly independently from the other. If a member of any cell was arrested or the entire group taken down, only that one cell was jeopardized. Cali's New York structure was so regimented and insular, in fact, that it most resembled that of an international terrorist organization like al-Qaeda.

The New York–based operatives communicated via pay phones, pagers, and faxes, and always in heavily coded language, making it nearly impossible to intercept and decrypt. They dealt only with other Colombian nationals whose family members were known (or those who'd been recruited by other operatives), making it even more difficult for law enforcement to crack the trafficking cells.

But despite Cali's foothold in New York, the men and women of the NYDETF and DEA were among the finest investigators in the country, and painstakingly and patiently, they began to slowly infiltrate the Cali cells. Key operatives were identified and arrested, and cocaine loads were seized along with millions of dollars and enormous caches of weapons. Much of the evidence pointed to one man: Victor Crespo. Crespo, they'd later discover, was one of Chepe Santacruz's many aliases.

In one 1979 raid alone, the task force seized a staggering forty-four pounds of cocaine and stacks of financial records that revealed the cartel had collected almost $7 million in under three weeks. "Nobody had *ever* seen 44 pounds of cocaine in New York City before," Kenny Robinson, a member of the NYDETF, said in Ron Chepesiuk's book *The Bullet or the Bribe.*

That record was crushed the following year when the task force seized 285 kilos stashed in a Florida warehouse. It was the biggest cocaine seizure ever made and, like the one before it, led straight back to Chepe. Investigators soon became so obsessed with arresting Chepe that they referred to themselves as the "Chepe Chasers."

As a result of increasing pressure from the US, in mid-1982 the Bahamian government shut down Lehder's Norman's Cay operation, forcing him to flee to Colombia. But even with Lehder gone, the Caribbean corridor remained the preferred smuggling route into the US, with a staggering 75 percent of Colombian cocaine entering the States via the Caribbean, thanks in large part to Crazy Charlie. A joint drug interdiction initiative called Operation Bahamas Turks and Caicos (OPBAT) was launched in April 1982 to help interdict drug shipments and prosecute smugglers.

Meanwhile, the Cali godfathers were busy looking for alternative smuggling routes. Armed with enhanced law enforcement interdiction capabilities and additional resources, Cali turned to other countries to send their cocaine shipments. To defer suspicion, well-camouflaged drug loads on coastal freighters started originating from Venezuela, Panama, Chile, and other Central and South American countries. With millions of containers arriving every year in South Florida and other Gulf Coast seaports, identifying drugs hidden in legitimate cargo without any prior intelligence was practically futile.

As law enforcement pressure continued to increase, Gilberto looked to more virgin territory into which to expand Cali's empire: the European markets. Cali began to forge alliances with other powerful criminal groups and organized crime families all throughout Europe, especially Spain, as its shared history and language with Latin America made it easy for Colombians to blend in. Better yet, Colombian nationals didn't need a visa there. But, as with everything else, the real draw was the money. In Madrid, just one kilo of cocaine could fetch up to $70,000, sometimes more.

But one problem was becoming impossible to ignore: how to handle the cash. Cali was generating so much money, it was stacking up—literally. Along with his brother Ramiro, Pacho was tasked with laundering the money made in New York and repatriating the proceeds back to Colombia. But they couldn't get it there fast enough—there was simply too much.

As a work-around, Cali began smuggling money out of the US the same way they brought cocaine in: with couriers and mules. Back then, airport security was far more lax, even on international flights. Cash was stuffed into suitcases, electronics, or other appliances, then sent through Mexico. It was flown in private aircraft to offshore banking havens like the Cayman Islands or Aruba or smuggled into Mexico, then flown *back* to Colombia on private aircraft. Cartel operatives also purchased thousands of money orders in New York and sent them to Colombia in maritime shipping containers.

In the late 1970s and early 1980s, large amounts of cash were carted into US banks for deposit, and no one batted an eye. Though legally required to report cash deposits of more than $10,000, banks rarely did. When authorities increased pressure on the banks to comply, the cartel found better ways to circumvent law enforcement.

The Black Market Peso Exchange (BMPE) also played a significant role in the cartel's money-laundering operations. A trade-based money-laundering system, it allowed the cartel to receive pesos (in Colombia) in exchange for their drug dollars located in the US. It remains an indispensable tool not just for Colombian and Mexican cartels but countless other criminal organizations.

By the early to mid-1980s, all the Cali godfathers had multiple outstanding US federal indictments for drug-trafficking and money-laundering crimes. For Chepe and Pacho, the risk was simply too great. They had no choice but to abandon the excitement of New York and return to Colombia.

The Boom

When Chepe returned to Cali, Gilberto and Miguel gave him a new task: establish and expand distribution outlets in a number of other major American cities. He was more than up to the challenge and before long had a foothold in pivotal markets all over the US, including Los Angeles, San Francisco, Las Vegas, Dallas, Atlanta, Philadelphia, Chicago, and Detroit—even across the northern border into Montreal. Chepe had an advantage he lacked in the States: in Cali the capos flew freely, even fragrantly, under the government's radar.

Cali continued to refine their routes, with Mexico soon becoming the next Norman's Cay. Thanks to its size, proximity to the US, and preexisting smuggling routes, it was the natural next step. Mexico quickly became the new and improved Norman's Cay.

Initial alliances were formed with Honduran national Juan Ramón Matta Ballesteros, then Mexican traffickers from the Guadalajara cartel or the Federation, including founders Miguel Ángel Félix Gallardo, Rafael Caro Quintero, and Ernesto Fonseca Carrillo. The Federation transported Cali cocaine through Mexico and smuggled it across the border into the US, where Cali operatives would retake possession and distribute the drugs throughout the States. For their services, Mexican transporters were paid up to $1,000 for each kilo smuggled, a price that would steadily increase over time.

In February 1985, Félix Gallardo, Caro Quintero, Ernesto Fonseca, and a handful of others were involved in the abduction, torture, and brutal murder of DEA agent Enrique "Kiki" Camarena in Guadalajara, Mexico. Quintero and Fonseca were arrested soon after, and the US and DEA wasted no time making their reaction clear: if you dare harm one of our own, you *will* pay the price.

Which they did. They demanded that Mexico immediately bring everyone involved to justice—or whatever it was that Mexico considered justice. In 1987, in an effort to protect his remaining empire, Félix Gallardo divided up the cartel and assigned specific leadership to individual, newly created territories (also known as plazas.) Amado Carrillo Fuentes, a.k.a. "the Lord of the Skies," was awarded the Juárez corridor, and Cali forged a powerful alliance with Amado that transformed Colombian cocaine air-smuggling operations entirely. Félix Gallardo was later arrested by Mexican authorities in 1989.

In late 1987, Pacho become embroiled in a major dispute with Escobar and sought the protection of Gilberto, Miguel, and his old friend Chepe. Pacho had been an unwaveringly loyal operative—not to mention successful—and had spent most of his adult life making the cartel hundreds of millions (if not billions) of dollars. At thirty-six, his time had come.

He was awarded a position on Cali's board of directors, a promotion that essentially made him the cartel's fourth godfather. His first order of business was to fully support Cali in its inevitable war against Escobar and the Medellín cartel. His second task was equally critical: continue to expand Cali's smuggling alliance with Mexican traffickers and the Lord of the Skies.

Later, massive cocaine shipments as large as fifteen tons were flown into dry lake beds in Todos Santos, Baja California, Sombrerete, Sonora, and other remote areas of Mexico. The Medellín cartel followed in Cali's footsteps, joining in the exploitation of Mexico as the preferred trans-shipment destination. Cali utilized old Boeing 727s and French-made Caravelle jet aircraft to transport the multi-ton loads of cocaine.

Meanwhile, the Mexican contingent proved to be just as savvy as their Colombian counterparts. The more product Cali moved into Mexico, the more Mexican traffickers charged to transport it across the border and into the States. By the late 1980s, Mexican cartels were charging several thousand dollars per smuggled kilo. But Cali's payments were often late, and sometimes they failed to pay at all. Medellín was even worse. As a result, a dispute arose, and Mexican smuggling groups began holding back cocaine shipments until they were paid in full. They continued to move cocaine for both cartels into the US, but not as they had been, refusing to release large portions of it to Colombian cells for subsequent distribution to American cities.

It took just one incident in September 1989 to change everything. Acting on a tip, DEA, along with other state, local, and federal agencies, raided a warehouse in Sylmar, California, and seized a whopping 47,300 pounds of cocaine along with $12 million in cash. It became the new largest cocaine seizure in American history—made in a sleepy suburban California community, no less. The real score, however, was the staggering amount of information found, including records and documents showing exactly how the product was smuggled: north through Mexico to Juárez, across the border into El Paso, Texas, then into the Los Angeles area via tractor trailers.

The seizure sent shock waves throughout DEA and the US government. By most accounts, it had a street value of over $7 billion—nearly as much as the gross domestic product (GDP) of Nicaragua at the time. But it was the documents that mattered most: stacks of ledgers revealed that during the three months leading up to the bust, Mexican smuggling groups had received over seventy-seven tons of Cali and Medellín cocaine and repatriated over $80 million in cash. Those seventy-seven tons had a reported street value of over $25 *billion*. And $25 billion, in 1989, was an unheard-of amount for *any* business, criminal or otherwise.

With no end in sight to the dispute between the Colombians and Mexicans, a new mode of compensation was agreed on, with Cali offering to pay Mexican-based smuggling organizations a percentage of each cocaine shipment moved to the US in product instead of cash. The offer was unanimously accepted, and everyone benefited. By the mid-1990s, Mexico-based smuggling organizations were receiving as much as 50 percent of each load in product—half of every shipment. As massive loads of cocaine continued to arrive in Mexico via 727 and Caravelle jet aircraft, hundreds of millions of dollars were repatriated back to Colombia on return flights. Without question, this was the key development that set in motion the Mexican cartels' ascension to power.

While several other large seizures were made, Cali considered them to be minor inconveniences, a drop in a bottomless bucket. DEA estimated that *maybe* 10 percent (and probably less) of the cocaine that entered the US was seized. For Cali, that was a damn good success rate.

But DEA persisted. In April 1988, 3,270 kilos hidden inside Brazilian cedar planks (just like the ones Gilberto was sending to the US back in 1975) were seized aboard the coastal freighter *Amazon Sky* in Tarpon Springs, Florida.

In June 1988, 2,270 kilos were found sealed in 1,200 blocks of chocolate, of all things, at a Long Island warehouse after arriving on a cargo vessel from Ecuador.

And in November 1989, close to 5,000 kilos were seized inside drums of potentially lethal sodium hydroxide at a warehouse in Queens. The markings on the kilos of cocaine found buried in the drums of lye in New York bore the same markings as some of the packages found in the Sylmar seizure—ultimately those markings were linked back to Cali and, of course, the self-proclaimed King of New York himself, Chepe Santacruz.

Law enforcement was also hitting Cali where it hurt the most: their wallet. In January 1989, New York agents seized a Mexico-bound truck loaded with $19 million. Soon after, another $14 million was found on Long Island, tucked inside heavy cable spools. All of the $33 million led back to Chepe and had its own paper trail, this one showing more bulk cash shipments of an additional $100 million during a nine-month period.

Along with the booming demand, several other world events helped give Cali more of an advantage to dominate the world cocaine trade. The fall of the Berlin Wall in 1989 and subsequent collapse of the Soviet Union in 1991 led to Cali's total control of European cocaine markets and their expansion into Russia and other Baltic countries. In February 1992, the Maastricht treaty was signed—officially creating the European Union—going into effect twenty-one months later. With newly open borders and unrestricted European travel, Cali was able to introduce massive cocaine shipments into ports all throughout Europe. Italian, Russian, and scores of other organized crime groups and families were free to follow suit, moving their own product to various European destinations with very little effort.

By late 1992, large shipments of cocaine were being recorded in less expected countries like Czechoslovakia, Poland, and Hungary. In February 1993, Russian authorities seized over a ton of cocaine hidden inside cans of corned beef hash. The shipment had originated in Cali and had been destined for the Netherlands via St. Petersburg.

Cali's ingenuity when it came to smuggling was impressive and infuriating. There was no question that only a fraction of the cocaine smuggled was being seized, and at times it seemed as if their creative methods would mean endless torment for US authorities. But major seizures and arrests in Miami would soon pose a serious threat to Cali's global operation.

In January 1994, the implementation of the North American Free Trade Agreement (NAFTA) became a milestone event in world history and a godsend for Cali. Signed by President Bill Clinton, NAFTA opened the door for the cross-border trade of legitimate goods between the United States and Mexico. But Cali—in conjunction with Mexican trafficking organizations—took advantage, smuggling *hundreds* of tons of cocaine across the border and into the US. "Mexico became the FedEx of the cocaine business," observed the *Wall Street Journal*. Almost 2.8 million trucks crossed the border into the US in 1994, many of them carrying large cocaine loads deftly camouflaged with legitimate goods.

In barely a decade, the Cali cartel had evolved into a behemoth, a massive conglomerate run with the precision of a Fortune 500 company. They had over ten thousand employees managing their countless legitimate business—and criminal—interests; they'd become a sleek, stealthy, finely tuned machine—the Ferrari of organized crime organizations. To further streamline things, they divided their criminal enterprise into five compartmentalized divisions: trafficking, financial, military, legal, and political.

Trafficking was responsible for the production, transportation, storage, distribution, and sale of cocaine in the US and all throughout the world. Independent cells were established in numerous countries, with each reporting directly to a cell head, or regional manager, who in turn reported directly to Miguel or Gilberto Rodríguez back in Colombia.

The financial division was tasked with laundering most of the drug proceeds through financial institutions, as well as hundreds of legitimate and shell companies established by the cartel. They also smuggled bulk US currency back into Colombia and Panama and took advantage of the Colón Free Zone (CFZ), the largest free-trade zone in the Western Hemisphere, to exploit the BMPE.

The military division was the most critical. They dealt with threats not just from rival trafficking groups but a host of hostile law enforcement entities. The military wing was also responsible for the personal security of cartel leaders and their families, contract murders, physical and electronic surveillance of potential adversaries, and continued corruption of government forces—police, military, prosecutors, judges, or anyone else who could aid (or harm) the business.

The legal division handled criminal proceedings against cartel operatives in Colombia, the US, and around the world. Scores of Colombian and high-profile, costly American lawyers also worked to secure favorable outcomes for the cartel on matters such as extradition, illicit enrichment, and asset forfeiture.

The political division was also paramount. They were responsible for establishing loyalties (through bribes, blackmail, whatever it took) and maintaining contact between Colombian politicians and the Cali godfathers. It was imperative that the cartel keep key political figures on the payroll in order to secure the required number of votes for the passage— or defeat—of legislation of interest to the organization.

What had started as the lofty pipe dream of two brothers had become a global force. The Cali cartel was more of a phenomenon than a mere success: the largest drug cartel and organized crime syndicate in history. By the mid-1990s, the Cali godfathers were responsible for 80 to 85 percent of the cocaine that reached US soil and 90 percent worldwide, dominating the cocaine trade on six continents. The DEA estimated their annual profits in 1995 alone were over $8 billion, but by some accounts that figure was actually as high as $10 to $15 billion. In reality no one really knew, not even the US government. All Dave and I needed to know was that the money "Cocaine Incorporated" was generating was approaching mythic proportions. And nothing was slowing them down.

To put $8 billion in perspective: "The annual revenues from Colombia's largest legal export, oil, were approximately $1.5 billion in 1995; the DEA's annual budget reached $1 billion for the first time in 1997; Coca-Cola's total sales were approximately $8 billion (with profits of $120 million); and General Motors and Walmart's *combined* profits were just less than $8 billion. If the Cali cartel were a corporation, it would rank number one in gross profits, beating out Exxon ($7.5 billion), General Electric ($7.3 billion), Philip Morris ($6.3 billion), and IBM ($5.4 billion)."[*]

Still, when Dave and I arrived in Colombia in mid-1994, the godfathers remained at large and worry-free, thanks in no small to part to the millions of dollars used to keep the loyalties of the thousands of corrupt officials who didn't hesitate to accept Cali's dirty money. Morals were a commodity, just like anything else. Everyone was for sale.

Ultimately, the Cali cartel would prove to be the single most formidable adversary in the history of international drug law enforcement. I still think back to that *Time* article, all these years later: *"Can these men be stopped?"*

Back then, we didn't pretend to know the answer. But ever since the extradition of Colombian nationals to the US was prohibited in July 1991

---

[*] Source: *The Wall Street Journal Almanac 1988* (Random House, 1997).

by a new Colombian constitution, Dave and I knew that the Cali leaders would probably never see the inside of a US prison. The only way they *could* be stopped, if at all, was to partner with Colombian security forces to capture or kill them on their home turf. We would have to use their feelings of omnipotence against them, to act while they felt the most invulnerable. But considering their sophisticated security, intelligence networks, and scores of corrupt allies, that was essentially a real-life David vs. Goliath. And we weren't even allowed to step foot in Santiago de Cali, the mystical and maddening city they controlled with an iron fist.

CHAPTER 3

The Cartel Wars: Cali vs Medellín

"None of you fucking Cali spies will ever be welcome here."
—MEDELLÍN CARTEL

Adversaries

BOTH THE CALI AND MEDELLÍN CARTELS can trace their roots all the way back to the early 1970s, when they got their start by smuggling marijuana from Colombia into the United States. Each got their names from the cities in which they were formed: Medellín, Colombia's second largest city, and Santiago de Cali, the country's third largest city. Although they were just 210 miles apart, the two cartels coexisted amicably and without conflict for well over a decade.

In fact, the two were often collaborators. In November 1981, Marta Nieves Ochoa—sister to the powerful trio of brothers who led the Ochoa Vásquez clan—was kidnapped by members of the 19th of April Movement (M-19), a Marxist left-wing revolutionary group known for their ongoing war with the Colombian government. In the late 1970s, the M-19 guerrilla movement had segued from extremist activism into kidnapping, choosing to focus on drug traffickers and their families in order to net enormous ransoms. After Marta was seized outside the University of Antioquia, Medellín leaders including Escobar and Jorge Luis Ochoa

Vásquez immediately responded by arranging a meeting at Las Margaritas restaurant in Medellín. What followed was a rare display of narco-solidarity, with scores of drug traffickers from all throughout Colombia coming together to create a powerfully equipped paramilitary group called Muerte a Secuestradores (MAS), or "Death to Kidnappers," in response.

MAS received millions of dollars in financial support from nearly all major drug barons throughout Colombia—including Miguel and Gilberto Rodríguez and Chepe Santacruz—to help put a stop to the kidnappings fronted by M-19 and other guerrilla groups. The money was used to fund a death squad threatening the immediate execution of any M-19 members involved in the kidnapping of Marta Ochoa and to provide a 25,000,000.000 peso reward (roughly $12 million USD) for any information leading to her safe return. That was the same amount the M-19 had demanded as ransom, a sum the Ochoa family vowed never to pay.

MAS garnered support not just from the majority of cartel leaders but from countless wealthy landowners, businessmen, politicians, prominent families, and rogue members of Colombia's armed forces. All had grown weary of the left-wing guerrilla groups' antics and were determined to put a stop to it, no matter the cost. One month after Marta's kidnapping, MAS dropped hundreds of leaflets from a small plane during a Medellín vs. Cali soccer match. The shower of flyers promised the public execution of any leftist guerrillas involved in Marta's—or other—kidnappings.

MAS kept their word. Not long after, dozens of suspected M-19 members were murdered, their battered bodies left in public venues or parks for everyone to see. The payback was delivered with a brutally clear message, with the initials "MAS" carved deep into the victims' chests and their bodies left hanging from trees or disemboweled and dumped on the side of the road. The message was received loud and clear. It wasn't meant to be subtle.

Three months after Marta's kidnapping, the M-19 released her unharmed and without any ransom money received. By that point they'd suffered devastating losses at the hands of MAS, who, in turn, had evolved into a commanding right-wing paramilitary death squad that went on to torment Colombia throughout the 1980s.

MAS was also indirectly responsible for cementing a new alliance, a syndicate made up of affiliated drug traffickers including Pablo Escobar and co-founder José Gonzalo Rodríguez Gacha (a.k.a. "El Mexicano" or "the Mexican"), Carlos Lehder, and brothers Jorge Luis, Juan David, and Fabio Ochoa. Thanks to the evolution and success of MAS, this collection of traffickers would officially become known as the Medellín cartel.

To ensure equitable distribution of the rapidly expanding cocaine market in the US, MAS decided early on to grant each cartel exclusive access to one major city. Miami went to the Medellín cartel, New York to Cali. The move was designed to maximize profits and—of equal importance—eliminate competition and the threat of turf wars. In actuality, Medellín and Cali were already firmly entrenched in their designated markets. The rest of the US, however, was considered fair game. As such, all remaining cities were considered open markets—both cartels were free to operate in any or all of them as they pleased. The cartels' equivalent of a gentlemen's agreement, it was cemented by the longstanding friendship between Jorge Ochoa and Gilberto Rodríguez. Close since childhood, they'd managed to sustain their bond even as each cartel broadened their respective domains.

To help move the hundreds of millions of dollars both cartels were generating, Cali and Medellín took full advantage of Colombia's and Panama's lax money-laundering regulations and strict bank secrecy laws. They worked with myriad banks, including the Banco de los Trabajadores (of which Gilberto owned 67 percent and served as its chairman of the board), making it possible for both cartels to establish massive money-laundering operations and move millions through the bank unquestioned. They also used a multitude of shell companies throughout Colombia and Panama to camouflage and launder the illicit proceeds.

Cali and Medellín also used the First InterAmericas Bank S.A. in Panama. Truckloads of cash, checks, and international wire transfers from the US and myriad European countries flooded First InterAmericas consistently, with no one ever raising any concerns. And why would they? To question the bank directly connected to the two most powerful cartels would be foolish, if not dangerous. Corporate records publicly listed the bank's official majority shareholder as Gilberto Rodríguez, with Miguel as a fellow executive board member. Joining the two brothers on the board was Cali's resident financial wizard, Edgar Alberto García Montilla, who oversaw their entire global money-laundering operation.

Both cartels worked with First InterAmericas until mid-1985, when the Panamanian government dissolved the bank amidst growing international pressure and rumors it was being used to facilitate large-scale money-laundering operations for Cali and Medellín.

When needed, Cali also acquired cocaine from production laboratories operated by their colleagues in Medellín. Although Cali had access to their own labs, they occasionally purchased from Medellín's lab known as Tranquilandia. This "super lab" was located deep in the jungles of Caquetá, Colombia, some 350 miles south of Bogotá.

On March 10, 1984, the DEA and CNP launched a massive enforcement operation against Tranquilandia, seizing 13.7 metric tons (30,200 pounds) of cocaine, then worth an estimated $1.2 billion. It was, by far, the largest cocaine laboratory ever seized.

Less than a month later the Medellín cartel declared an all-out war on the Colombian government, beginning with the assassination of Minister of Justice Rodrigo Lara Bonilla. The minister was murdered while being driven home from work, struck with a shower of gunfire from a .45-caliber MAC-10 machine pistol fired by a Medellín *sicario* perched on the back of a motorcycle. The order had come from Escobar himself.

After the assassination, Colombian president Belisario Betancur's government immediately implemented the extradition of Colombian traffickers wanted on drug charges in the US. As a result, a slew of Medellín cartel members went into hiding in Colombia or escaped to Panama.

Escobar, Rodríguez Gacha, and the three Ochoa brothers all fled to Panama to seek refuge with their friend, notorious Panamanian ruler General Manuel Antonio Noriega. After a short stint there, Jorge Ochoa traveled to Madrid in June 1984, as did Gilberto Rodríguez. Relaxed and refreshed in their new hideout city, both gave serious thought to permanently relocating and quietly living off the millions they'd earned from their illicit ventures. Others theorized that they'd actually traveled to Spain in order to explore new European cocaine trafficking routes and partners, sick of the US government crackdown on the Caribbean corridor.

Their visions of a peaceful life in Madrid came crashing down on November 15, however, when Ochoa and Gilberto Rodríguez were arrested by Spanish authorities based on US-issued provisional arrest warrants and drug-trafficking indictments. It was an ironic twist: two of

Colombia's most powerful drug lords had fled to Spain out of fear of extradition to the US, only to be arrested a few months later on charges that could send them to prison—an American prison, no less.

But in another twist, during their time in a Spanish prison they began an alliance with Galician smugglers, paving the way for further expansion of the cocaine trade not just in Spain but all throughout Europe. More relationships were soon formed with various Italian Mafia families and European organized crime organizations, and the lust for cocaine spread almost as quickly throughout Europe as it had in New York.

Of course, the US wasn't the only country that wanted Ochoa and Gilberto. Colombia also filed extradition requests with the Spanish government to force the two cartel heads back home to face charges: Ochoa for trafficking in fine cattle and illegally importing bulls from Spain, and Gilberto for drug trafficking. Once again Cali and Medellín worked closely together—legally and financially—to ensure they were sent to Colombia. Anywhere but the United States.

During Gilberto's incarceration in Spain, Miguel took over as the CEO of Cocaine Inc., seamlessly transitioning into a role he'd hold for over a decade. In 1986, a Spanish judge ruled that Ochoa and Gilberto be returned to their native country to stand trial on the blatantly fabricated charges. It's not a stretch to assume that various players in the Cali and Medellín cartels bribed Spanish officials to ensure Ochoa and Gilberto weren't extradited to the US.

In June 1986, Gilberto was extradited to Colombia and confined to the Villahermosa prison in Cali until July 1987, when he was acquitted due to a lack of evidence—despite the fact that the state of Louisiana had provided *more* than enough evidence proving Gilberto's involvement in large-scale drug trafficking.

In July 1986, Ochoa was also extradited to Colombia but released from prison a month later after a judge suspended his sentence and released him on bond with the caveat that he attend future court proceedings—which, of course, he ignored. In both cases "friends" of the cartel had intervened, working behind-the-scenes to ensure the two men's freedom. But that was the norm, just another example of the power Cali and Medellín wielded in the mid-1980s, even when it came to currying favor with government officials and judges.

The cartels' honeymoon phase didn't last long. Relations between the two began to deteriorate during the latter part of 1987: Cali was busy expanding their footprint in South Florida, while Medellín was making flagrant efforts to gain market share in the off-limits New York area. Several kidnappings and murders by Medellín operatives in Jackson Heights and Queens escalated the tension between the cartels, and before long they'd become competitors once again.

During one of Pacho's two prison stints in New York, he befriended a Colombian by the name of Alejo Piña. The two grew close and remained so even after Pacho was released from prison. Alejo soon became a trusted employee of Herrera's organization.

While Alejo was still serving time in the US, he befriended another trafficker and assassin named Jorge Pabón (also known as "El Negro" or "Negro Pabón") who worked for Escobar and the Medellín cartel. Alejo and Negro made a pact: whomever got released from prison first would look after the other man's family until the second man was released. Alejo was the first to go and, vowing to keep his promise, returned to Colombia to check on Pabón's family.

Neither man could have anticipated that their pact would lead to Colombia's very own Trojan War. Most unfortunately for Negro, the Colombian Helen of Troy (the face that launched a thousand ships and, in this case, the battle between the Cali and Medellín cartels) was his own wife. Alejo's role as temporary protector led to an illicit romance, and when Negro was finally released from prison the following year, he rushed home to Medellín to see his wife, oblivious to the affair.

As he drove through the streets of Medellín after a soccer match a short while after returning from the US, two assassins pulled up alongside on a motorcycle and ambushed him, shooting him multiple times. Miraculously, he survived, but the question was: Who would have the balls to attempt the assassination of a Medellín operative (and close friend of Escobar)—on their home turf? After what must have been a particularly brutal interrogation with one of the found assassins, they got their answer. The mastermind behind the assassination was none other than Alejo Piña.

When Escobar heard the news, he was irate. He called Gilberto Rodríguez and demanded that Pacho either kill Alejo or turn him over to face justice in Medellín—a far worse fate. Pacho refused, saying, "I don't turn over my people." No demand—no matter who from—would make him say yes.

But Pablo wasn't used to being told no. He gave Pacho an ultimatum: kill Alejo, or *both* Pacho and Alejo would be considered military targets by the Medellín cartel, hunted down, and murdered. Any Cali leaders who dared interfere would suffer the same fate.

Gilberto, Miguel, and Chepe met in Cali to discuss Pablo's decree. They told Escobar that they refused to hand Pacho over, nor did they have any intention of sitting idly by and allowing him to be killed. For his part, Pacho was steadfast in his commitment to protect Alejo, pledging countless millions of dollars as well as the use of his powerful military wing to help fight Escobar not if, but *when* war came to Cali's doorstep. Together, the men decided that a united front was their best defense against an increasingly erratic Escobar and further cemented their standby, officially naming Pacho the cartel's fourth godfather. When Gilberto ignored Escobar's incessant stream of calls, he declared war against the Cali cartel.

Meanwhile, in November 1987, Jorge Ochoa was arrested at a police roadblock just north of Cali driving a Porsche registered to a Honduran diplomat. Ochoa was held on the outstanding bull-smuggling charges for which he'd been extradited from Spain, and rumors quickly spread that his detention was orchestrated by the Cali godfathers. Now, Ochoa once again faced potential extradition to the US, which worried Escobar and the Medellín cartel. Just nine months earlier, Medellín cartel leader Carlos Lehder was captured, extradited to the States on drug-trafficking charges, convicted, and sentenced to life in prison plus 135 years. It was every Colombian drug trafficker's worst nightmare, and Escobar was no exception. He wasn't joking when he'd proclaimed, "Better a tomb in Colombia than a jail cell in the United States."

Within days of Ochoa's arrest, "the Extraditables" (a group created by Colombian drug traffickers in the early 1980s for the purpose of intimidating the Colombian government into banning the extradition of Colombian nationals) forwarded a communiqué threatening a declaration of war against the government if Ochoa was extradited to the United States. On December 30, 1987, Ochoa was released under "questionable" circumstances. Once again, he'd managed to avoid extradition to the US. The back and forth between the traffickers and US government was fast approaching the frenzied levels of a Colombian soccer match, and it was Medellín 2, US 0.

The damage between the cartels was irreparable. Cali had defied Escobar by refusing to turn over Pacho and Alejo, and they were now suspected of playing a part in Jorge Ochoa's arrest. With that, a full-blown war was inevitable. Someone just had to strike first.

War

Just before dawn on January 13, 1988, Cali assassin Andrés Vélez (also known as "Pecoso" or "Freckles") parked a car loaded with over 175 pounds of dynamite outside the luxurious eight-story Mónaco building in the exclusive El Poblado section of Medellín. Colombia's first officially documented car bomb explosion, it caused extensive damage to the heavily fortified building, but Escobar escaped injury. Fortune had favored him yet again: he'd left with his bodyguards just minutes before the bomb was detonated.

The explosion left a twenty-foot-deep crater outside the building, shattered windows in a four-block radius, and badly compromised the structural integrity of the armored fortress. It also took the lives of three people (including two security guards), seriously injured ten, and left Escobar's three-year-old daughter Manuela with permanent hearing loss. Escobar's wife, María Victoria Henao, and their son, Juan Pablo Escobar, were also sleeping in the penthouse apartment but miraculously managed to avoid injury.

The concept of using remote-controlled car bombs stemmed from Gilberto and Jorge Ochoa's stint in the infamous Carabanchel prison. While there, they'd forged alliances with members of the Spanish Basque separatist terrorist organization known as Euskadi Ta Askatasuna (ETA), or "Basque Homeland and Liberty," who shared everything they knew about the technology behind the most powerful car bombs with both the Cali and Medellín cartels.

After the attempt on his life, Escobar was beside himself. Crazed, his first act of vengeance was to order the detonation of a car bomb at one of the Drogas La Rebaja stores owned by the Rodríguez Orejuela brothers in Medellín, followed by several more at a handful of the chain's other locations throughout Cali. By mid-1988, over forty of the Cali-owned stores in Colombia, along with ten Grupo Radial Colombiano radio stations (also owned by the brothers), were hit. The war escalated quickly, and violence consumed the nation, affecting scores of innocent residents.

In March 1988, the Cali godfathers sent a highly trained five-man military infiltration team to Medellín to gather intelligence on Escobar's whereabouts. Their bodies were sent back in boxes a few weeks later, dismembered and chopped up into tiny pieces. The ghastly delivery was dumped outside one of the Drogas La Rebaja stores with a note reading, in essence, *"None of you fucking Cali spies will ever be welcome here."* A new low had been reached.

In late 1988, when a massive two-hundred-pound car bomb ripped through Ciudad Jardín, one of Cali's most luxurious neighborhoods, it was, literally, far too close to home. The blast—which destroyed three houses and killed two key Medellín operatives—was intended for Miguel Rodríguez, who was staying nearby. Once again it was pure luck that saved the target's life, as the car bomb exploded before it could be deployed, killing the two spies sent to carry out the mission. Still, that was enough of a close call for Miguel. Cali needed Escobar gone. Immediately.

At this point, both cartels were at a heightened state of alert, and security for the leaders and their families had reached unprecedented levels. In January 1989, Luis Mario del Vasto Cerón, head of security for the Cali cartel (who'd come to work for the cartel after a stint as a highly decorated Colombian Army major), proposed a bold plan. It was straight out of a Hollywood movie, but it was also the best option they'd heard. Del Vasto knew a man who had connections to a group of British mercenaries and international soldiers of fortune—an elite team ideally suited to tracking down and killing Escobar. The man with the connections was Jorge Salcedo Cabrera, a.k.a. "Richard."

Salcedo, forty-two, was highly regarded and well educated, with degrees in mechanical engineering and industrial economics. He spoke perfect English and had an enviable pedigree as the son of a retired, revered military general who del Vasto knew from his time as a captain in the Colombian Army reserves. Salcedo considered following his father into the military but opted to join the army reserves as a commissioned officer, where del Vasto commanded his Cali-based reserve unit. The two men worked closely together and became good friends.

Salcedo's history with the mercenary group began in mid-1988, when the Colombian military wanted to have them lead a clandestine operation to attack the FARC at Casa Verde, their mountain headquarters. A left-wing Marxist-Leninist insurgent group, FARC is the oldest, most significant guerrilla group in the Western Hemisphere, fighting against inequity and the Colombian government since 1964. The mission took months to plan but was ultimately canceled, so the mercenaries returned home and waited patiently for their next gig.

The Cali leaders were impressed with Salcedo. He was a rare find: erudite, accomplished, and an expert in communications, counterintelligence, weapons, explosives, and guerrilla warfare. His mercenary contacts and background as an army reserve officer just added to his appeal. At the direction of the godfathers, del Vasto lured him to Cali on the pretense of a potential business deal. He knew that if he'd told him the real reason, Salcedo likely wouldn't even step foot on a plane.

Once in Cali, Salcedo was shocked to discover that the meeting was actually an intimate gathering with the four godfathers, who welcomed him magnanimously into one of Pacho's homes and unveiled their plan to use the mercenaries to kill Escobar. Salcedo could barely hide his surprise—it wasn't just unexpected, it was outrageous. As the men waited for his answer, Salcedo couldn't help but think of *The Godfather*—except this was real life. The godfathers—the *real* Cali godfathers—had just made him an offer he couldn't refuse. Salcedo had always stayed far away from any illegitimate dealings, but he knew enough to realize that telling the cartel no was not an option. And telling them no to this particular offer— if you could even call it that—to kill the most infamous cartel leader of all time? Forget his career: that would be risking his life. If he wanted to leave that room alive, he had no choice but to accept. So he agreed, but with one condition: after the mission was complete and Escobar was dead, he'd be free to return to his civilian life.

The godfathers agreed and prep began immediately. One month later, a dozen mercenaries arrived in Colombia, led by two men: Scotsman Peter McAleese, a former British Special Air Service (SAS) sergeant and paratrooper, and David Tomkins, a British arms dealer and explosives expert.

Both were the best in their field: experienced, highly trained, and with remarkable military résumés, having previously served in armed conflicts in Angola, Rhodesia (now Zimbabwe), and South Africa. Their price for killing Escobar: $5,000 per month plus expenses, in addition to a substantial bonus of $1 million.

In late May, Cali spies confirmed that Escobar was planning a party at Hacienda Nápoles, his 7,400-acre mega-estate in Puerto Triunfo, to celebrate his soccer team, Club Atlético Nacional de Medellín, who'd just pulled off a huge win at the prestigious Copa Libertadores de América soccer tournament. It was the perfect opportunity, and after three months of intense training, the mercenaries were ready. The mission was given the code name Operation Phoenix.

Initially, Operation Phoenix called for two Huey helicopters to land at Hacienda Nápoles. The idea was that the mercenaries would land, infiltrate the grounds, find Escobar, and kill him along with anyone else who got in their way. But one of the Hueys they'd acquired was still undergoing repairs and wasn't even close to being airworthy. They couldn't let this opportunity pass, however, so they decided they'd make do with a smaller, less powerful helicopter, the Hughes 500.

On June 3, 1989, the Huey and the Hughes 500, both painted to resemble CNP helicopters, departed for Hacienda Nápoles. They were jam-packed with the team of mercenaries, many of whom had previously served in the French Foreign Legion or the elite SAS. Weather conditions were extremely poor that Saturday afternoon, but the men were determined.

Then tragedy struck. During their final leg of the mission and with no warning, the Hughes 500 clipped the top of a tree and slammed into the mountainside. Of the five men aboard only three emerged with minor injuries. But the pilot was killed, and McAleese suffered five broken ribs, a sprained back, and other injuries.

What had started as an ideal plan had ended in disaster. Meanwhile, the celebration went on at Hacienda Nápoles, with Escobar and his crew oblivious to the news of the assault until the following day. A few months later, the operation was officially shut down. Once again, the mercenaries returned home without completing their mission. Back in Colombia, the war continued.

AFTER ESCOBAR

In August 1989, Liberal Party presidential candidate Luis Carlos Galán Sarmiento was assassinated by Medellín cartel gunmen in Soacha, a city on the outskirts of Bogotá. That evening, President Virgilio Barco Vargas declared a state of internal commotion, imposed martial law, and—in his boldest move—reestablished the extradition of Colombian nationals to the US. With that, a second major offensive against the Medellín cartel was launched. In response, Pablo and the Extraditables again declared war on the Colombian government. This led to a string of terrorist acts that killed hundreds of innocent people and devastated the nation for months.

In early 1989, the Cali leaders hired assassin Jorge Enrique Velásquez, better known as "El Navegante" ("the Navigator"), to infiltrate the organization of Medellín cartel leader José Rodríguez Gacha. Gacha was previously implicated in the 1984 murder of Justice Minister Lara Bonilla and, like Escobar, deemed an enemy of the state. El Navegante's proposed cost for serving up Gacha was exactly the same as the mercenaries had been: $1 million.

In just ten months, El Navegante had gone from overseeing a fleet of speedboats delivering Medellín cocaine loads to being placed in charge of one of Gacha's security details. During a trip to Colombia's north coast in December 1989, he gave Gacha's location to the national police, who mounted a massive operation. But Gacha was tipped off and escaped via speedboat with his son Freddy and five bodyguards.

In his haste, Gacha didn't think twice about telling El Navegante that he was headed to a series of nearby beach cabanas followed by a ranch outside the small resort town of Tolú. The following afternoon, CNP gunships descended on the ranch. A firefight ensued, Gacha and his henchmen fought back, and when the barrage of gunfire finally ceased, Gacha, his seventeen-year-old son Freddy, and five bodyguards were left dead.

Now it was Escobar's move. Everyone knew that Gacha's death, the Mónaco car bomb attack, and the failed attempt at Hacienda Nápoles would be avenged, and on September 25, 1990, Medellín struck. While Pacho was busy enjoying his favorite pastime, a weekly pick-up game of soccer at his *finca* "Los Cocos" ("the Coconuts") in Candelaria, east of Cali, assassins were setting up camp at a nearby farm. As dusk fell, twenty heavily armed *sicarios* disguised as national police officials boarded two covered trucks and drove toward the world-class soccer pitch.

Pacho's security detail was taken completely by surprise. The *sicarios* were ruthless, methodically chasing down and slaughtering Pacho's men and bodyguards under the bright stadium lights that illuminated the field. It was a typically hot and humid night, and the men had been relaxed and dressed casually in shorts and T-shirts, their weapons left in their vehicles or scattered across the pitch.

When the massacre was over, nineteen people had been murdered and eight wounded. Escobar had delivered a devastating blow to Pacho's inner circle, but it wasn't the success he'd hoped: his two main targets—Pacho and his brother William—had survived. They'd escaped by fleeing into the sugarcane fields surrounding the pitch, then hid and waited out the brutal assault listening to the gunfire and screams of the men as they fell.

In the merciless underworld of Colombian drug cartels, justice is carried out swiftly. Two of the *sicarios* were arrested by Colombian police while trying to return to Medellín, and when interrogated they gave up the entire operation. The men were sent to prison, where they were murdered by men loyal to Pacho a short time later.

For cartel members, guilt by association is often viewed with as much disdain as guilt itself, and such was the case with the family of the man who'd rented his farm to the Medellín assassins. The farmer, knowing what fate would have in store for him, vanished. But the three innocent relatives he'd left behind were forced to suffer his wrath in his stead. All three were executed by Pacho's henchmen, and Pacho scoured the countryside for the farmer. The Cali cartel had a long memory, and they never forgot an act of betrayal.

Almost two and a half years later, the owner was found and taken to Pacho's ranch, "El Desierto ("the Desert")—an apt moniker, as many who went there never returned. As Cali operatives arrived for the "show," screams could be heard coming from behind one of the ranches many structures. They were the result of Pacho and his crew taking out two and a half years of revenge fantasy on the farmer via perhaps the most abhorrent torture: being drawn and quartered. After tying the farmer's arms to one SUV and his legs to another, the men signaled for both drivers to rev their engines. They inched forward in opposite directions, pulling the man apart at an excruciatingly slow pace. The farmer begged and begged, until the torture reached a point where he couldn't beg anymore. Pacho and his men stood idly by, taking swigs of their beer and whiskey as they watched and cheered. The scene was nothing new to them. It was simply justice, served up the cartel way.

In an attempt to quell the escalating violence gripping the republic, in September 1990 Colombian President César Augusto Gaviria Trujillo proposed a deal to drug traffickers: surrender, and you'll be promised a reduced prison sentence—in Colombia—and no extradition to the US Over the next few months, brothers Jorge Luis, Juan David, and Fabio Ochoa—three of the leaders of both the Medellín cartel and the Extradit-ables—all took the offer and turned themselves in. Jorge and Juan David served roughly five years in prison, while Fabio served five years and nine months. The sentences were lenient and the brothers had avoided extra-dition to the US, where they were wanted on a variety of drug-trafficking charges. Their punishment in the States, they knew, would have been far worse.

Escobar didn't give the deal much thought at the time. He was still embroiled in a two-front war: the ongoing battle with the Colombian government and the conflict with his Cali adversaries, once his allies. But now, he had to go it alone. Carlos Lehder was in prison in the US, the Ochoa brothers were in jail in Colombia, and Rodríguez Gacha was dead. As his level of protection and support dwindled, government secu-rity forces intensified their operations to capture (or kill) him, forcing him further underground. The fact that he was harder to locate made him even more dangerous.

The Cali leaders had changed locations as well, reluctantly leaving the comfort of their mansions and downsizing to smaller, more secure apartment buildings and complexes. They were terrified of more Esco-bar-ordered military-style assaults and feared for the safety of their families, their properties, and themselves. At that point, eighty-five phar-macies from the Rodriguez's massive drugstore chain had been blasted by Escobar. But the brothers' belief was that their success was indestructible, the business version of Hydra. Blow up one drugstore and two more shall take its place. Besides, Escobar was no Hercules. He was a bitter fugitive, on his own and on the run.

To further protect themselves from Pablo's wrath, Cali purchased a state-of-the-art IBM mainframe computer to help analyze and store intelligence on suspected Medellín operatives. Chepe reportedly paid over $1 million to obtain the sophisticated hardware—then nearly impossible to acquire—which could cross-reference telephone calls, track airline passengers and flight manifests, and access Colombia's motor vehicle records. It was so advanced for the time, in fact, that many deemed its existence a ruse, nothing more than an elaborate rumor spread by the godfathers in an effort to unnerve Escobar and his remaining *sicarios*. Either way, it was a smart move. Mental warfare, especially in times of great strife, was just as effective as any other kind.

Though Escobar would surrender to authorities in June 1991 (after being given assurances he wouldn't be extradited), the war continued. La Catedral, Pablo's self-built extravagant fortress, was more of a luxury resort than a prison. The idea was to keep Escobar's enemies out, not the Medellín cartel leader in. Still, at least the Cali cartel knew where he was.

In late 1991, Pacho proposed another elaborate plan, this one absurd enough to be the cinematic sequel to the failed helicopter mission to Hacienda Nápoles. In lieu of a copter full of mercenaries, this time the cartel would simply drop a five-hundred-pound bomb on La Catedral. The war had now reached a point where nothing seemed impossible, let alone ridiculous.

Jorge Salcedo, whose reputation had only grown since he was first hired, was chosen to helm the mission. Despite his reservations about the logistics and feasibility of the plan, he set off to El Salvador to negotiate the sale and purchase of four US-made MK-82 five-hundred-pound bombs. Sourced from Salvadoran Air Force Lieutenant Colonel Roberto Antonio Leiva Jacobo, the price was $500,000. Cheaper than the mercenaries, the godfathers figured. Why not?

First, an aircraft capable of delivering the bomb needed to be found. Salcedo contacted his old mercenary pal and arms dealer David Tomkins, who located an ideal aircraft in Opa-locka, Florida: a Cessna A-37 Dragonfly, a counterinsurgency aircraft developed during the Vietnam War. When the two traveled to South Florida to inspect it, however, something seemed off to Salcedo. Sensing a possible law enforcement sting operation, he decided to abandon the deal and begin another search.

In February 1992, Salcedo returned to El Salvador to coordinate the transfer of the four MK-82 bombs to Colombia. A gutted Beechcraft King

Air 200 was dispatched from Cali to handle the transport, but even with the passenger seats removed the King Air 200 was capable of carrying only three of the bombs. The fourth bomb was left in El Salvador, hidden in a nearby river to be picked up a few days later.

Salvadoran authorities later discovered the discarded bomb and arrested Lieutenant Colonel Leiva along with several others. The arrests and seizure of the five-hundred-pound military ordinance in El Salvador made headlines around the world, compromising Salcedo's identity and exposing his role as a key Cali cartel operative. Cali's second elaborate plot to assassinate Escobar was officially failure number two.

Criminal investigations followed in Colombia as well as El Salvador, with Salcedo being declared a person of interest. He went into hiding—not just from Colombian authorities but from Escobar and the Medellín cartel, who'd declared him a military target for his role in the attempted bombing. Salcedo, who'd primarily accepted his role within the cartel out of fear for his own safety, had now gone from respectable businessman to accused criminal. He lost his commission as a captain in the army reserves, along with much of his self-respect. Still under the thumb of the cartel, he began working to enhance their communication and counterintelligence programs.

After Escobar killed associates Fernando Galeano and Gerardo Moncada at La Catedral in July 1992, he chose to leave, casually walking out of the back of the complex. Enraged, a new, ruthless group emerged from the shadows with the mission shared by many: kill Pablo Escobar and anyone associated with him. This latest vigilante group was known as "Los Pepes " or "People Persecuted by Pablo Escobar." As the name implied, the group consisted of a host of Escobar's enemies—his victims, rival drug traffickers, and paramilitary fighters. All sought revenge.

The leaders of Los Pepes were former Medellín cartel associates and brothers Fidel and Carlos Castaño Gil, along with Diego Fernando Murillo Bejarano, or "Don Berna." Fidel Castaño—often referred to as "Rambo"—had an added incentive: he'd been invited to the same meeting with Escobar where friends Galeano and Moncada were shot, cut into pieces, and incinerated. After Escobar killed Galeano—Berna's former boss—he'd turned against him. For Berna, this was personal.

By February 1993, the Pepes were busy carrying out targeted extra-judicial killings, bombings, kidnappings, and public displays of violence, all designed to intimidate Escobar. They made attempts on the lives of his wife, children, and other family members with car bombs and orchestrated attacks on his bodyguards, lawyers, money launderers, accountants, and anyone else close enough to him to weaken his infrastructure. Some days as many as six bodies would turn up dead on the streets of Medellín—all victims of the Pepes. Much like MAS did in the early 1980s, the Pepes often sent communiques or left markings on their casualties proudly claiming responsibility. They weren't just out to kill Escobar, they were out to humiliate him as well.

Needless to say, the Pepes counted the Cali cartel among their allies. Cali's contribution to the manhunt wasn't just limited to sharing intelligence; they also provided more than enough funding to support their campaign against Escobar and his inner circle, giving millions of dollars to the cause. Pacho Herrera alone contributed at least $30 million during the war.

And there was yet another group hunting Escobar: the Medellín "Bloque de Búsqueda" ("Search Bloc"). Created in late 1989 after Escobar declared war against the Colombian government, the Search Bloc was a special operations group within the national police, tasked with capturing or killing the most dangerous of narcos. When Escobar escaped—rather, chose to leave his "prison" in mid-1992—a second iteration of the Search Bloc emerged, this time with over 650 members. With three distinct entities now pursuing the same monster, "the enemy of my enemy is my friend" became their shared mantra.

After the three formed their solid (unofficial) alliance, Cali supplied the Pepes with intelligence regarding Escobar's activities, which, in turn, was shared with select members of the Search Bloc. Sometimes the Pepes used Cali's intelligence for their own exclusive use—the extrajudicial killing of Escobar's associates. The Pepes maintained an open channel of communication with the Search Bloc throughout 1993 during the hunt for Escobar. For the Search Bloc, the Cali capos supplied much of the same: intelligence, equipment, money, and even bonuses to the most loyal of officers.

Over the next ten months, the bloodthirsty triumvirate of crooks, cops, and vigilantes decimated Escobar's infrastructure. The Pepes alone killed well over fifty Escobar confidants and destroyed countless holdings belonging to his family members and associates. A slew of Escobar loyalists targeted for execution by the Pepes ultimately waved the white flag and defected, denouncing their allegiance to the drowning drug lord as they scrambled to make their way off the sinking ship.

And if that wasn't enough, the US assigned their best operators from the DEA, CIA, and other government entities to assist the Search Bloc. Even the US Joint Special Operations Command (JSOC), Delta Force, and the secretive Centra Spike—an elite Tier 1 intelligence-gathering unit specializing in signals intelligence (SIGINT)—were on the ground providing training, equipment, and logistical support.

In the end, the unholy alliance proved to be fatal for the cartel legend. On December 2, 1993, heavily armed police connected to the Search Bloc shot and killed Escobar as he made one final desperate attempt at escape. After so many years of extravagance and power, Escobar's death was far from glamorous. Frantic and alone, he was shot to death as he stumbled his way across the rooftop of a three-story house in Medellín's Los Olivos neighborhood.

At long last, the mission was accomplished: Pablo Escobar was dead, and the war was finally over. It was Cali's time now.

CHAPTER 4

The Cali KGB

"If we can't buy him, we can always ruin him."
—MIGUEL RODRÍGUEZ OREJUELA

AFTER ESCOBAR WAS KILLED, the celebrations went on for days—especially in Cali. The godfathers' greatest threat had been eliminated, and they stood poised and ready to inherit the throne. The *real* hunt for the Cali leaders, however, didn't begin until January 1994. Incredibly, not all of the godfathers had drug charges pending against them in Colombia, and any other existing indictments lacked the amount of evidence needed to detain them for any meaningful amount of time. With US officials breathing down their necks, Colombian authorities had their work cut out for them.

Many in the government were reluctant to start a new battle with another powerful syndicate so soon after finishing off Medellín. Colombian security forces were drained, along with the rest of the country.

In fact, the previous decade had set a precedent when it came to battle fatigue. The country had suffered through the April 1984 assassination of Justice Minister Lara Bonilla, the November 1985 siege of the Palace of Justice by M-19 guerrillas (which took the lives of 98 people), the August 1989 assassination of Liberal Party presidential candidate Luis Carlos Galán, the November 1989 bombing of Avianca Flight 203 that killed 110, and the December 1989 truck bombing of the headquarters of Colombia's secret police, the Department of Administrative Security (DAS), which literally tore open the entire front of the eleven-story building, killing 57 people and wounding over 2,200. That was, by far, the biggest narco-terrorist attack in Colombian history. It was unthinkable to expect the people of Colombia to be able to live through much more.

More than a few people thought the godfathers deserved a pass— amnesty, even—since they'd given the Colombian government so much help in their effort to eliminate Escobar. After all, they were the *Gentlemen of Cali*, legitimate businessmen who kept a low profile, avoided any conflict with the government, and openly socialized with politicians and the upper echelon of Colombia's most elite.

But there was one man who wasn't buying any of it. Sick of Cali's propaganda, Colonel Carlos Alfonso Velásquez Romero was on a personal crusade to take them down. Velásquez was a decorated officer with years of experience and specialized training (including time spent at the prestigious US Army Command and General Staff College at Fort Leavenworth, Kansas), and he'd just been appointed commander of the army's elite Search Bloc at the 3rd Brigade. Dave and I knew him as our first real contact and partner in our war against Cali.

Ever since his appointment in December 1993, Velásquez's military unit had produced immediate results. The previous commander had refused to take any action against the Cali cartel, wary of upsetting the godfathers and jeopardizing his career, not to mention his life. But Velásquez was different. He was an honest man, a hardworking career soldier who'd dedicated his life to the fight against narco-trafficking and serving his country. His lifelong dream had been to become a general, and taking down the godfathers would almost certainly propel him to that rank.

Dave and I always enjoyed working with Colonel Velásquez and the military. They had more resources than the national police, better equipment, better intelligence, and were trained and supported by—well, let's just say another US government agency. Key members of the Search Bloc were polygraphed and drug tested, weeding out potentially corrupt cartel spies from the very beginning of the colonel's tenure. He also offered us the use of living quarters at the military base and always invited us to assist in enforcement operations.

Despite our eagerness to work with Colonel Velásquez and the Search Bloc, the fact was that Dave and I were doomed before we even began. Cali had been preparing for this moment for well over a decade, during which time they'd paid off hundreds, if not thousands, of cops, military officials, and politicians.

Unsurprisingly, Colonel Velásquez had his own brush with such offers. Days after his arrival in Cali, he was offered a $300,000 bribe by a gentleman well connected in political and military circles who'd taken on the role of emissary for the Cali godfathers that day. Colonel Velásquez turned down the offer, drove back to his office, and reported the encounter to his superiors in Bogotá. That would be the first of at least three bribes the cartel would offer Velásquez during his time as commander, all of which he refused and reported. His sense of morality was infuriating to the cartel. "How *dare* he turn down such generous offers!" Chepe fumed.

Cali continued on regardless, further fortifying their infrastructure by recruiting highly skilled retired military and police officials to head their security, communication, and counterintelligence programs. Retired army major Mario del Vasto and reserve captain Jorge Salcedo were two of the Cali operatives armed with specialized military training and experience. All were able to easily infiltrate government institutions in order to ensure that the godfathers were well protected from Colombian and US law enforcement actions.

Cali operatives set up manned around-the-clock strategic observation posts (OPs) near the bases to monitor when police and military raiding parties arrived and departed, and did the same with American agents. The operatives communicated via radio back to cartel security, who then surveilled the targets to determine if there was any potential threat. Dave and I were often followed whenever we left military or police installations—not because they wanted to cause us harm (yet), but because they wanted to identify our sources. Identifying and eliminating any and all DEA assets or contacts deemed a possible risk for the cartel was a top priority.

Listening posts (LPs) were also established. Overlooking the bases, these posts made it possible to intercept communications from the Search Bloc command staff. The cartel was able to wiretap Colonel Velásquez's office phone and even plant electronic listening devices capable of recording conversations in and around his entire office and reception area. The surveillance produced hours of recordings Salcedo and his operatives would listen to and analyze. They often proved to be intelligence gold, giving the cartel countless details and advance notice of any impending actions against the godfathers. A trusted aide to the colonel, Sergeant Humberto Valencia, was also secretly on the cartel payroll—making surveillance all the more effective. The price for betrayal to his own government was reportedly $1,000 a month, plus periodic bonuses of $20,000.

Valencia had worked with the previous colonel as well, making his experience invaluable to Velásquez when he took over. Although Sergeant Valencia had been polygraphed, the cartel had long ago figured out a way to lure in newly vetted military and police officials. Cali always knew in advance when the polygraphs were happening, so they had a routine: immediately after an officer was polygraphed, the cartel approached them with a huge bag of money. Those who accepted were welcomed into the group of turncoat spies on the cartel payroll, with about twelve to eighteen months passing before they were polygraphed again. It was a simple yet genius move, and also perfectly represented the times: wait until the officials were "proven" to be honest, then corrupt them the very next day. As always, all it took was money.

Cali's counterintelligence capabilities were so advanced that the CIA began referring to them as "the Cali KGB"—a comparison to the notorious Russian security agency. Yet despite all these obstacles, the Search Bloc made steady progress. Through their own interception of radio communications, pager messages, and a female source code-named "Diana," Velásquez gleaned enough intelligence to launch a series of enforcement operations in early 1994 that caught the cartel off guard. Although Rodríguez had been tipped off by Sergeant Valencia, giving him just enough time to escape before the raid team arrived, valuable intelligence was still recovered. It was near impossible for cartel operatives to move large volumes of documents or files within such a short period of time.

Even though Cali had no shortage of corrupt officials, the information that Diana was providing concerned Miguel. The data gathered revealed numerous details about Cali's security and counterintelligence infrastructure, as well as their legitimate financial holdings and payoffs of public officials. The newfound information prompted the Colombian Attorney General's Office to begin new legal proceedings against the Rodríguez

Orejuelas for illicit enrichment, *testaferrato* (using strawmen to hide businesses and real estate), and money laundering. Other inquiries were also opened against Chepe, Pacho, and a number of government officials for their alleged ties to the cartel.

The Cali godfathers now had two major problems: Colonel Velásquez, who could not be bought, and Diana, who continued to leak damaging details. In an attempt to slow Velásquez down the cartel threatened his sister, the not-so-subtle implication being that if they couldn't get to him, they'd get to his family. They also made sure the colonel knew that if one of the Cali leaders were to be arrested, it would be a declaration of war—not against the military, but against Velásquez himself. Still, the threats had zero effect. He reported them to his superiors in Bogotá and continued his pursuit.

After weeks of intelligence work, a raid targeting Miguel looked promising—until it was compromised by Sergeant Valencia. Although the godfather and his fourth wife, Marta Lucía Echeverry Trujillo, narrowly escaped capture, the operation wasn't a total failure. Once again key documents were discovered, including plans regarding the upcoming wedding of one of the Rodríguez Orejuela children.

That gave Velásquez an idea: What if they arrested a Cali capo at the wedding? The very idea was thrilling. But once again, Sergeant Valencia proved his mettle. He alerted Miguel, who, incensed, shared the news with Gilberto. Both were outraged that Colonel Velásquez would have the audacity to target family members—ones with no charges or open investigations against them, no less—let alone at a wedding. The irony was of course lost on the men that they, too, routinely took action against innocent families related to their own targets. Actions far more violent than the mere disruption of a celebration.

Optimistic, Velásquez set his plan in motion. While hundreds of people partied late into the evening at a Jamundí ranch, soldiers in military fatigues and black hoods set out in covered transport trucks from the 3rd Brigade in southern Cali. Their departure was spotted by the cartel spies manning the OPs outside the military base and confirmed by Valencia.

As the convoy approached the ranch, they saw scores of cars lining the entrance, heard laughter and loud music, and watched the guests dance and mingle. Then they spread out, quietly surrounding the ranch.

In moments, at least one of the Cali godfathers would be in handcuffs, thought Velásquez. Followed by the others.

As the soldiers were rounding up the tipsy, startled partygoers, they got their own surprise: the gathering wasn't a wedding at all. In fact, no major narcos—let alone *any* cartel figures—were present. To make matters worse, the majority of the guests who *were* present were influential members of Cali's highest of society. And they were all predicably appalled by the military's disruption of their private soirée.

The "wedding" turned out to be an elaborate counterintelligence hoax dreamt up by the cartel, designed to embarrass Colonel Velásquez and the military. The actual wedding was moved to a different location after Miguel and Gilberto learned of Velásquez's plan, and it was, by all accounts, a celebration for the ages.

After the debacle, it was the cartel's turn to be audacious. Lawyers representing the Rodríguez Orejuela family complained to the attorney general (as well as several high-ranking military leaders in Bogotá) that the army was persecuting innocent members of their family. The accusations brought even more scrutiny on Colonel Velásquez and the Search Bloc, with the colonel's judgment being called into question.

Cali's investigation into the identity of the colonel's source, meanwhile, was progressing. After listening to several conversations between Diana and Velásquez, Salcedo began to suspect that their professional relationship was evolving into something very unprofessional. Velásquez's hunt for the godfathers, it seemed, was also turning into a romance. While his dinner meetings with Diana may have appeared platonic to the outside observer, their calls conveyed a very different tone—and not one of a faithfully married man. When Salcedo briefed Miguel on the budding affair, Cali went straight to the blackmail section of their cartel playbook. "If we can't buy him, we can always ruin him," Miguel said.

Thanks again to intel from Sergeant Valencia, Diana was eventually identified as Dolly Buendiá de la Vega, an attractive, forty-something divorcée who mingled with the city's elite, including some close to the Rodríguez family.

Once Diana/Dolly was exposed, Chepe set up a meeting with her— brokered through mutual friends—during which he "convinced" her to work for the cartel as a double agent. Not that she needed much convincing: she knew what rejection would lead to: a plastic bag being pulled over her head followed by a slow suffocation. She told them yes. Immediately.

Along with the sparing of her life, Dolly also got a handsome payoff from the godfathers—so handsome, in fact, that it made the monthly stipend she received from Colonel Velásquez look like minimum wage.

Salcedo was the logical choice to oversee the operation, as he already knew Dolly (albeit not very well) from when they'd lived in the same apartment building a few years prior. Salcedo was surprised when Dolly told him that she and the colonel often met for drinks at Tangos y Rancheras, followed by the occasional tryst at the not-so-subtly-named Motel Campo Amor ("Field of Love"). He couldn't believe the colonel was so obvious with his choice of meeting spots, but it made his job easier: Tangos y Rancheras was a popular bar with strong drinks and loud music, the perfect spot for Salcedo and cartel operatives to covertly take compromising photographs of Velásquez and Dolly. Campo Amor was nothing more than a cheap, seedy motel in southern Cali. The rooms were rented by the hour, and the decor gave it the look of a smuttier Bates Motel. Even better, it was owned by a trafficker loyal to the cartel, so gaining access was easy. Salcedo couldn't have dreamt up a better setup.

Miguel's plan was simple—lure Colonel Velásquez into a compromising situation at Campo Amor, then blackmail him. But the cartel didn't want to just tarnish his reputation, they wanted to destroy his career entirely. Surely their salacious blackmail material would be more than enough to bring down the one officer they couldn't bribe.

When Dolly and the colonel arrived at Tangos y Rancheras for drinks, they made themselves cozy at a table near the bar, while Salcedo and a female cartel operative sat close by and snapped photographs of the two kissing and embracing. The camera was well hidden, and the two just looked like another couple on a romantic date.

After finishing their cocktails, the pair headed to Campo Amor. Salcedo had stopped by earlier to prepare, selecting the perfect room in which to install the hidden video camera inside the air-conditioning vent. He also rented out the adjoining room so he could monitor and record everything that went down next door. It was a flawless layout, and ultimately the cartel got exactly what they wanted: a good old-fashioned raunchy sex tape.

On a Saturday afternoon in mid-May 1994, twelve days after the recorded romp at Campo Amor, a retired army captain walked into Colonel Velásquez's office at the 3rd Brigade and told Velásquez that he'd been stopped on the street by several men who threatened him harm unless he delivered a package on their behalf. When the colonel opened the package, his heart dropped. Inside was a photograph of him and Dolly, locked in a passionate embrace. And there was more: a stack of incriminating photographs of them at the bar, a copy of the video from the motel, and a letter outlining exactly what would happen to him—and his career, reputation, and family life—if he didn't immediately resign.

Velásquez sat in shock as he watched the tape. The cartel now had the upper hand, and for the next few hours he did nothing but curse his own choices and ponder his next move.

Ultimately, the colonel decided to do the opposite of what the cartel expected: come clean. Taking a cue from his favorite offensive principles of war, the adage "the best defense is a good offense," he called his superiors in Bogotá—including Hernando Camilo Zúñiga Chaparro, deputy commander of the army—and fell on the sword. "It's very possible they will send you a similar package aimed at discrediting the institution," Velásquez said, humiliated. "When I come to Bogotá next week, I'll explain everything."

His longtime dream of becoming a general in the army now shattered by the Cali KGB, he faced the very real possibility of being transferred or, worse, court-martialed or fired. He had only a few days until his meeting in Bogotá, and if he had any hope of saving his job, he needed to make something happen, and soon.

CHAPTER 5

The Supercomputer

"Not even NASA can get one of these."
—DEA INFORMATION TECHNOLOGY SPECIALISTS
(Reston, Virginia)

FROM THE VERY BEGINNING, Dave and I spoke often with Colonel Velásquez about the best ways to take down the Cali cartel, and one thing we always agreed on was the idea of attacking their communication, intelligence, and security networks. We needed to conduct enforcement operations specifically designed to degrade Cali's infrastructure, forcing them to alter their routines. With the clock ticking, the army intel team scrambled to identify potential raid locations. While their efforts did lead to several enforcement actions against cartel properties, nothing of significance was recovered. Disappointed, Velásquez returned to the 3rd Brigade and continued rehearsing his presentation to the military high command.

On May 18, as Velásquez headed to the Cali airport, the army unit developed last-minute information regarding an apartment in Edificio Kris, a building in downtown Cali. The multistory property—owned by Chepe Santacruz—was suspected of being a cartel communications center. Velásquez immediately authorized a raid on the apartment and continued to the airport.

When Search Bloc special operators made their way into apartment 101, they didn't find anyone—cartel spies had alerted security operatives to the raid just minutes prior. But even with the advanced warning, valuable information was left behind.

That information prompted a call to Colonel Velásquez, who reversed course and headed back toward Edificio Kris. When he arrived and saw what was inside, he was awestruck. Spread out across the apartment was an elaborate counterintelligence center outfitted with high-tech computer networking equipment and multiple terminals, encrypted computer disks, and cutting-edge electronic machinery capable of intercepting pager messages, radio frequencies, and more. The team also recovered evidence of an equally complex radio and repeater network, a system that had provided the cartel with secure communications throughout the city. And then there was the coup de grâce: a massive state-of-the-art IBM AS/400 mainframe computer.

Seven feet high, four feet wide, and with an incalculable amount of storage, the computer cost well over $1 million and was unlike anything they'd ever seen. Nothing with that level of sophisticated technology had ever been seized from drug traffickers—not by DEA, not by anyone. The cutting-edge counterintelligence center required no fewer than six IT specialists just to process the immense amount of data it generated. Used by the cartel during their war against Escobar, it had long been rumored to exist, with many believing it was a myth. But now here it was, right in front of them.

Velásquez knew he'd hit the jackpot, but accessing the information was going to be a serious problem. The data was protected by sophisticated encryption, rendering it impenetrable—at least for Velásquez and his crew. With no other choice, he called his superiors in Bogotá to report the discovery and request that his presentation be moved to the following day. That evening, the Search Bloc worked with the Colombian Air Force to relocate the IBM mainframe computer to the military's intelligence headquarters in Bogotá for further analysis.

Within hours of the seizure, a stream of calls began to flood the Cali regional prosecutor's office, all of them regarding the whereabouts of the computer. This confirmed what they'd already suspected: the Cali Mafia desperately wanted to recover the computer and would do anything in their power to do so before any sensitive information could be retrieved.

The Supercomputer

The next day, Velásquez arrived in Bogotá for his rescheduled meeting with the army's commanding generals, but now instead of just handing over compromising photos and a raunchy sex tape, he came equipped with a bevy of photographs and a complete rundown on the IBM computer and counterintelligence center. During the three-hour meeting, the colonel confessed to everything about his relationship with Dolly, the setup, and subsequent blackmail attempt by the Cali KGB and apologized for embarrassing the institution he loved so dearly. Once he'd finished his mea culpa, he switched gears, deftly summarizing the Search Bloc's successes under his leadership and outlining the progress they'd made over the past five months. In the end, the army high command, and then minister of defense Rodrigo Pardo García-Peña, decided in the colonel's favor, and Velásquez was allowed to return to Cali and remain commander of the Search Bloc.

It didn't take long for military IT specialists and intel analysts to realize they didn't have the skill or technology to bypass the state-of-the-art security features and encryption the Cali cartel had been utilizing. The Colombian government then granted approval for the DEA to transport the equipment to DC for further analysis, hoping that their IT specialists were up to the task. But even they were blown away. "Not even NASA can get one of these," one of the tech specialists lamented.

It took almost an entire month for DEA forensic experts to finally crack the encryption, and, as expected, it revealed a treasure trove of counterintelligence information—a chilling glimpse into just how technologically advanced (and corrupt) the Cali cartel really was. Among the hundreds of files on the IBM computer were ones detailing the staggering number of bribes the cartel had made to police, military, judges, politicians, and other government officials, along with personal information and telephone numbers of dozens of Cali residents, US Embassy diplomats, and Colombia-based DEA agents. The unique data-mining software had allowed the Cali cartel to cross-reference and track telephone calls made by Medellín operatives during their war with Escobar, as well as any informants who were suspected of secretly working with the DEA. The cartel then wiretapped anyone their software revealed to be a potential security risk.

The godfathers had a point man at Emcali, the Cali telephone company: Carlos Espinosa Muñoz, also known as "Pinchadito." Along with a dozen or so other employees, Pinchadito facilitated the intervention of as many as four hundred telephone lines a month. The cartel's wiretapping capability far exceeded even that of the Colombian government, and as a result, scores of people considered threats were wiretapped and eventually killed.

Among the bounty of additional revelations gleaned from the computer was the fact that Cali had several thousand (by some estimates five thousand) taxi drivers on the payroll who doubled as their eyes and ears throughout the city. They also employed scores of workers at airports and hotels whose job it was to inform the cartel of any suspicious activity or individuals, such as the arrival of American DEA or CIA officers in Cali. Files containing lists of cartel holdings and front companies, names of key operatives, and a plethora of other intelligence was also culled from the AS/400.

And as if all that wasn't enough, Cali also had access to aviation records, tail numbers, and flight manifests, allowing them to track the exact movements of commercial airliners and passengers as well as DEA and CIA aircraft. They even had Colombia's entire motor vehicle registry, giving them instant access to ownership information on any questionable vehicles identified. During the war with Escobar, any driver spotted by the Cali KGB with Medellín license plates was immediately stopped and questioned. If the vehicle's ownership traced back to any known Medellín operative, the occupants were interrogated, and often tortured or killed.

The supercomputer had been just as useful in-house for the cartel, becoming their virtual keeper of accounting information, bank accounts, payments to corrupt officials, and other sensitive intel. Many of the files were still too heavily coded to decipher, but the discovery was a gold mine. Investigators now had thousands of leads to pursue.

Now that Pandora's box was open there was no way of closing it. No one was prepared for how explosive the discovery was, but with the excitement came frustration, as it was now so obvious that the cartel's intelligence apparatus and networks were far more revolutionary than those of most governments. How could we—not just US law enforcement but also the intelligence community (IC)—have underestimated Cali to such a degree?

The Supercomputer

Looking back, it makes perfect sense. For all six years leading up to the IBM breakthrough, every single Colombian and US resource was dedicated to bringing down Escobar and the Medellín cartel. As a result, very little attention was paid to Cali, who benefited from being able to methodically go about fortifying their infrastructure, infiltrating government institutions, and creating their vastly superior technological network.

Dave and I were both shocked by the developments. We headed out to break it down over a few beers (not an uncommon occurrence), and Dave confessed that he was beginning to question just how effective we could *really* be when investigating a cartel so sophisticated as Cali. Maybe our Miami colleagues were right: a couple of small-town American gringos could never blend in and accomplish anything in Colombia.

I ordered us another round and with my usual subtle delivery summed up my thoughts: "That's bullshit." Dave laughed.

"We'll be fine. All we need to do," I said, "is find the person who *can* crack everything that's still encrypted."

"Yeah, that should be a breeze," Dave said. "Too bad they're already dead."

After five months of ceaseless operations, Colonel Velásquez had finally delivered a significant blow to the cartel. Over the next few months, he and the Search Bloc raided cartel locations nearly around the clock, all because of intel gleaned from the IBM computer.

But the colonel knew that these were the most perilous of times for him, more so than ever before. Not only did physical danger lurk around every corner, he still hadn't confessed his indiscretions to his wife. He was consumed with worry about the cartel *and* his personal life, with no idea how his wife would react. The idea that she might not forgive him was unthinkable. It also tortured him that the Cali KGB still had the "kompromat," which he knew could be used against him at any time. The damaging material could go to his wife, the press, or the entire public. Progress or no, the Cali KGB still had all the chips, and the colonel knew it was just a matter of time before they went all in.

CHAPTER 6

The Narco-Cassettes

"Brothers, we just bought ourselves a president."
—MIGUEL RODRÍGUEZ OREJUELA

MAY 1994 BROUGHT ABOUT YET ANOTHER contentious presidential election in Colombia. The previous administrations under Presidents Virgilio Barco (1986–1990) and César Gaviria (1990–1994) were tumultuous, to say the least. The country was still reeling from the recent decade's extreme turmoil, and people prayed that a new president would usher in a more peaceful era. They had good reason to be optimistic: after Escobar's death, the overall destruction and chaos had noticeably decreased.

The two leading men vying to be Colombia's next president were Liberal Party candidate Ernesto Samper Pizano and the country's conservative candidate, Andrés Pastrana Arango. Samper, an economist and lawyer, was first elected to the Senate in 1986, served as minister of economic development from 1990 to 1991, then as the ambassador to Spain, serving from 1991 to 1993. During the final days of his tenure in the Senate, he was caught in the crossfire during the assassination of a fellow leftist politician by suspected right-wing rival extremists. Samper was shot eleven times during the attack, preventing him from running for president in the 1990 election.

Pastrana's background was equally impressive. A journalist, lawyer, and former fellow of the Center for International Affairs at Harvard

University, he served on the Bogotá city council, had the distinction of becoming Bogotá's first popularly elected mayor in 1988, and served three years in the Senate from 1991 to 1993. Like his competitor, he had his own brush with terror when he was kidnapped by the Medellín cartel in January 1988 during his mayoral campaign and held for seven days before being freed in a dramatic rescue by the national police.

The godfathers, meanwhile, saw the election as nothing more than another opportunity to increase their own power. They all agreed to pursue three projects, one of which they dubbed "the Champagne Project," designed to ensure that the next president put in Casa de Nariño (the Colombian equivalent of the White House) was sympathetic to their cause. The cartel had already corrupted upwards of seventy-five members of Congress, and they were also the actual architects behind the legislation drafts (referred to by the Cali cartel as "the Constitutional Reform Project") that, in part, led to the new constitution banning the extradition of Colombian nationals to the United States in mid-1991.

Now, with extradition off the table, they hoped for a soft landing. The godfathers assumed their contribution toward taking down Escobar had earned them even more favor with the Colombia government (referred to by Cali as "the Submission to Justice Project"). The Cali leaders offered a bold proposal to Colombian authorities: they would voluntarily surrender, on several conditions. First, that they receive prison sentences of no more than five years each (and serve no more than three) for crimes related to drug trafficking and illicit enrichment. Second, they keep all their assets. And third, they serve out their sentences in a prison in Palmira, a city close to Cali and a longtime cartel stronghold.

An army of cartel attorneys were already deep into discussions with Attorney General Gustavo de Greiff about the potential surrender, but many in the government were vehemently opposed, including President Gaviria. The memory of Escobar and the embarrassment that was La Catedral—his luxurious "prison"—was still too fresh in people's minds. Wary of history repeating itself, the talks came to an impasse. Unfazed, the godfathers figured they'd just *buy* the next president, who'd then return the favor by supporting their Submission to Justice Project.

Still, they weren't taking any chances. Instead of backing one candidate, they thought, far better to buy *both*. They assigned Alberto Giraldo, a Colombian journalist and operative in the cartel's political division, to discreetly contact representatives for each. Pastrana (whose father, Misael Pastrana Borrero, had been president of Colombia in the early '70s) reportedly refused more than a few financially substantial offers. On the other hand, team Samper was all in from the very start.

By late 1993, reliable information collected by DEA and the IC revealed that the Samper campaign and some in the Liberal Party were, in fact, accepting gifts from the cartel. During a November visit to DC, Samper was confronted by Robert Gelbard—then Assistant Secretary of State for International Narcotics and Law Enforcement Affairs—and bluntly asked if the intel was true. Samper flatly denied any and all of the allegations.

But Gelbard and others remained skeptical—they'd already seen various reports dating back to the mid-1980s about Samper's suspected ties to drug traffickers and the Cali cartel. Understandably, many bureaucrats were consumed with fear that their already precarious counterdrug operations against Cali would come to a screeching halt. It wasn't out of the realm of possibility that Colombia could be turned into a narco-democracy overnight, a thought that led to many a sleepless night in Washington.

To expand the financing of Samper's campaign, Miguel established a front company and corresponding bank account (LTD IV), shared by the four godfathers at the Banco de Colombia in Cali. The Cali leaders solicited contributions from other drug-trafficking organizations throughout Colombia, including the North Valley cartel (NVC), the North Coast cartel, and even the Medellín cartel, which were all deposited into the account. The donations ranged widely in size, from $25,000 for smaller operatives all the way up to $800,000 for each of the four Cali godfathers.

The cash was withdrawn and placed in boxes gift wrapped by Miguel, each containing roughly $500,000. The "gift" boxes were driven to airstrips or farms on the outskirts of Cali, then flown to Bogotá in aircraft owned by Pacho Herrera. Once in Bogotá, cartel operatives delivered the money to Santiago Medina, the treasurer for Ernesto Samper's presidential campaign.

The cartel also hired people to create political ads (run during airtime they purchased) and even had T-shirts made sporting Samper's name and ballot number—10—and distributed them throughout the country. Unknowingly, Colombians everywhere were wearing apparel in support

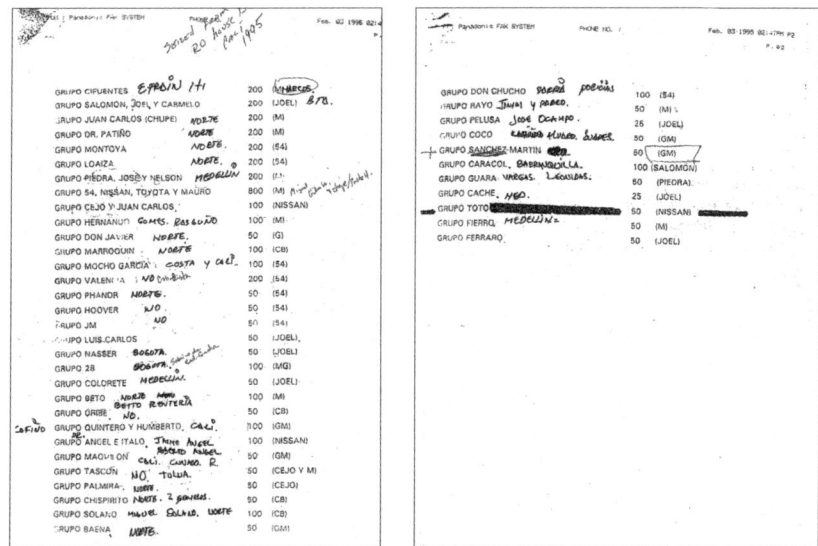

Financial donations given by the cartel in 1994 to use for the presidential campaign.

of Samper, made by and funded entirely with drug money from the Cali cartel.

Early on in the race, Samper was considered the universal favorite. But as election day neared, poll numbers revealed a much tighter race than they'd thought. Pastrana had run a stellar campaign, resonating with voters from all across the country, and was now poised to take the lead and shatter the godfathers' plans. Prior to the first round of the election, Miguel Rodríguez reportedly hosted a dinner party for Samper in Cali (which Samper denied), with three of the godfathers in attendance. That evening the godfathers expressed their undying support for Samper and stressed the importance of their Submission to Justice plan. They'd done everything in their power to make the Champagne Project a reality, and now their fate, as well as Samper's, was in the hands of the voters.

On May 29, 1994, the first round of the election concluded without one candidate garnering at least 50 percent of the vote, so a second round of voting was scheduled for June 19 to determine the winner. It had been painfully close—Samper had won 45.3 percent of the first-round popular vote while Pastrana received 44.98 percent—a difference of just over eighteen thousand votes. With the Samper campaign left reeling and their political war chest perilously low on funds, Cali arranged for the delivery of more cash. They had only three weeks until the runoff.

In the meantime, both candidates hit the campaign trail to sway any undecided voters. On June 15 during a stop in Cali, a man gave Pastrana cassette tapes with recordings of telephone conversations between Miguel and Gilberto Rodríguez and Alberto Giraldo. Also mentioned on the calls were other prominent members of society, as well as several Colombian politicians, including former senator Eduardo Mestre Sarmiento.

The calls were nothing short of explosive, containing damning evidence proving Cali had, in fact, made a number of sizable contributions to Samper's campaign. "Look, the reality is that they need five billion [pesos], of which they have two billion, and they need three from you," Giraldo was recorded telling Miguel. (At the time, five billion Colombian pesos was the equivalent of about $6 million in the US.) Later, Miguel is heard saying, "It'll probably be Wednesday when we send you some money, and then the rest would be sent Monday of next week." Before hanging up, Giraldo leaves Miguel with a somber reminder: "The presidency depends on *you*."

For Pastrana, the tapes were all the evidence he needed to prove beyond a doubt that the Samper campaign was working in concert with Cali. The next day, his team delivered copies to President Gaviria and his defense minister, Rodrigo Pardo, and additional copies to the US Embassy in Bogotá. Within twenty-four hours, Gaviria's administration certified the tapes as authentic and turned them over to Colombian attorney general de Greiff, who promptly opened an investigation. All the politicians named in the calls were now under intense scrutiny.

Despite the bombshell evidence on the cassettes, however, neither the Colombian government nor the US Embassy opted to make them public. Both feared being seen as willfully interfering with the election—there was no question that releasing the tapes forty-eight hours before the second round of voting would swing the election in Pastrana's favor.

The US State Department didn't feel much differently, wary of getting further involved with the mess that was now the Colombian election. DEA Attaché Joe Toft, however, disagreed. Toft had long been a vocal critic of corrupt politicians in Colombia and their nexus to drug traffickers, and he argued with US Ambassador Morris Busby to make the tapes public. His insistence didn't change any minds, though, and the decision by Washington officials to not release the tapes angered Toft so much that he considered taking matters into his own hands, despite what that would mean for his own future. Ultimately, he chose to remain silent. For the moment.

On June 19, Samper won the election by the slimmest margin in Colombian history, receiving 50.57 percent of the popular vote and beating Pastrana by a mere by 2.1 percent. Over 7.4 million citizens cast their votes in the runoff election, an increase of almost 22 percent from the first round. It wasn't difficult to make the case that the sole determining factor in the victory was the $6 million the godfathers had gifted the Samper campaign.

"Brothers, we just bought ourselves a president," Miguel said, elated, as the godfathers celebrated the victory back in Cali. Their dreams of a soft landing—lenient prison sentences, and the ability to keep all their ill-gotten assets—would soon be a reality. Or so they thought.

The party came to an abrupt end the very next day, when the tapes were made public: Toft had defied his superiors and leaked them to Colombian journalists. Predictably all hell broke loose, and the Narco-Cassette scandal was born. The recordings became the subject of the newest, biggest scandal in Colombia, and Pastrana, furious, publicly demanded Samper renounce his victory and step down as the president-elect, immediately.

Samper refused, indignant, and denied any knowledge of cartel drug money entering his campaign. His hubris was such that he didn't just *deny* involvement, he went so far as to call the Attorney General's Office and demand a formal investigation.

Back in Washington, the government's worst nightmare had officially come true. Assistant Secretary of State Gelbard delivered a stern statement: "If true, the allegations would have serious consequences for Colombia's relations with the United States. We take this extremely seriously, and we are investigating it very intensively right now."

The United States had invested a great deal of time and hundreds of millions of dollars into Colombia in recent years to help fight Pablo Escobar and his Medellín cartel. Despite all those efforts to slow (if not quell) the flow of cocaine to America, how could the US government continue relations with Colombia now, let alone count on President-elect Samper to help go after Cali?

In New York in early July, Samper and several members of his staff met with State Department officials involved in Colombia's antidrug campaign. The US delegation was sent as emissaries of President Bill Clinton and Secretary of State Warren Christopher with one message: Washington was deeply concerned about Samper's reported ties to Cali. After reviewing a litany of evidence, the general consensus of the US government was that there was irrefutable proof that the Cali cartel had, indeed, facilitated significant financial assistance to the campaign.

But Samper stuck to his denial, stating that if any drug money was received by his campaign, it was without his knowledge. He insisted that his administration deserved a chance, and even agreed to write an open letter to the US Congress vowing to take action against the Cali cartel.

The US wanted more. They demanded that once in office Samper remove the head of the CNP, Director General Octavio Vargas Silva, in a first step toward addressing the rampant police corruption. They also wanted Vargas Silva to be replaced with someone above reproach— someone who'd already worked with the US government—and suggested General Rosso José Serrano Cadena, a trusted ally who'd worked closely with the CIA and DEA during his time as commander of Colombia's anti-narcotics forces.

In response, Samper wanted the US to issue a public statement of support on his behalf that plainly said there was no merit to the allegations nor any basis to suggest that his campaign had received any money from the Cali cartel. US officials scoffed at the request, and negotiations came to a halt. The counterdrug policy that had once been deemed so critical now remained in limbo, and no one knew what would happen next with foreign relations between the United States and Colombia.

One thing was certain: the release of the narco-cassettes had propelled Colombia into one of its biggest political scandals ever (no easy feat, considering their past), and the press worldwide reported every single salacious detail. While Samper continued his denials, they were met with tepid reactions at best. Several Samper aides wondered if he'd actually ever assume the presidency and worried that even more allegations might come to light. One more crack in the Samper campaign could potentially collapse Colombia's already fragile government.

In an attempt to shift the narrative, on July 13 the Rodríguez Orejuela brothers signed a letter stating that neither campaign had received any donations from them. Coincidently, the Attorney General's Office suggested that the tapes had been illegally intercepted and possibly tampered with, raising questions about their validity.

By this point, the election had gone from a fierce, seemingly legitimate political battle to a total farce. The entire future of Colombia was up in the air, and no one seemed to have control.

The pressure was now on for the attorney general to conclude his investigation. For everyone else, it had come down to nothing more than a waiting game. And the godfathers were not known for their patience.

CHAPTER 7

The Accountant

*"He knows exactly what the cartel's money is spent on,
right down to the penny."*

—COLONEL CARLOS ALFONSO VELÁSQUEZ,
Commander of Colombia's Military Search Bloc

AS COLOMBIA CONTINUED TO REEL from the Narco-Cassette scandal, Velásquez and the DEA kept their heads down, choosing to focus on the leads obtained from the decrypted files of the now infamous IBM supercomputer.

But Colonel Velásquez was playing with house money. The military high command and defense minister had supported him during the cartel's blackmail attempt, and better, his wife had forgiven him for his affair with Dolly. Still, Velásquez knew his standing as the Search Bloc commander in Cali was tenuous at best. In a way, though, that made him even more of a threat to the cartel. What else did he have to lose?

In mid-June 1994, the Search Bloc conducted several operations against targets related to Miguel Rodríguez. One, on the luxurious Casa 19 in Ciudad Jardín, led to the discovery of numerous documents detailing the aliases of four retired army officials listed as part of Miguel's security detail. The estate was empty and undergoing major renovations at the time of the raid, with just one guard from the private security company Hercules Ltda. there to protect the property.

The Accountant

After extensive analysis of the intel by military intelligence officers, three of the retired army officials were identified and their homes subsequently raided. Other retrieved documents revealed that Hercules had played a key role in providing personal security to cartel family members and associates as well as cartel-owned businesses and properties.

Around the same time, human intelligence (HUMINT) was given to the Search Bloc by the CIA identifying a Chilean national known as "Reagan" as a trusted member of the cartel who performed several crucial duties for the godfathers. A thorough search of DEA and military databases came up empty, and Colonel Velásquez made it a priority to identify him.

On July 7, the Search Bloc raided Hercules Ltda. and collected evidence suggesting that Hercules was a front, established merely to provide security to the Rodríguez Orejuela brothers along with their family, associates, and vast number of businesses and real estate holdings. The evidence also included minutes from various board meetings, replete with several names and telephone numbers of cartel operatives, including Reagan and G. Pallomari.

Further analysis concluded that Reagan and G. Pallomari were, in fact, the same person. When analyzed, the numbers traced back to the phone's owner, revealing the dual moniker's true identity: Guillermo Alejandro Pallomari González. His listed work address was for Universal Link, a computer networking company in downtown Cali, and more digging revealed that Pallomari also managed an accounting and financial consulting business in the Siglo XXI building, just one block away from Universal Link.

Guillermo Pallomari was born in María Elena, Chile, and boasted degrees in both accounting and systems engineering. Originally hired to set up a computer networking system for the Rodríguez brothers' chain of Drogas La Rebaja stores, Pallomari segued into working exclusively for the Cali drug cartel in 1990, serving as an accountant, financial advisor, and assistant to Miguel.

Velásquez was thrilled with the intel. He knew that Pallomari could lead to a stockpile of incriminating evidence, and he made plans to raid his Siglo XXI office the following day.

That evening, Jorge Salcedo was reviewing a fresh batch of wiretapped calls from lines at the army Search Bloc and noticed one referencing a planned raid at an address in downtown Cali the following morning. Salcedo recognized it immediately: Pallomari's. He called and warned him, making sure to tell him not to leave *anything* even remotely revealing or sensitive behind.

The next day, an army raid team left the 3rd Brigade and headed north into the morning traffic. Cartel spies spotted their departure from an OP outside the base and alerted motorcycle surveillance units, who covertly followed the convoy as they made their way toward downtown Cali. Within minutes, the army soldiers arrived, surrounded the Siglo XXI building, and raided office 601.

Even though he'd been alerted to the raid, Pallomari appeared surprised as the swarm of soldiers burst into his office and began their search. Another cornucopia of documents exposing details of more high-level corruption within the Colombian government and security forces was recovered, along with additional connections between the Cali cartel and President-elect Samper's campaign.

Ledgers, documents, and copies of checks disclosed that a staggering 60 percent of Cali's Metropolitan Police were on the cartel payroll, and they didn't come cheap: cops on the take received north of $20,000 per month, combined. The financial ranking system was based on the quality of information someone could provide and ranged from a few hundred dollars a month to well over $1,000. An additional $60,000 a month in bribes was paid to higher ranking/key national police and military officials, and tens of thousands more was distributed among scores of prosecutors, judges, politicians, the DAS, and others. All told, the godfathers were shelling out at least $250,000 to $500,000 in monthly payments and bribes—and those were just the ones we knew about. Other ledgers were too heavily coded and impossible to decipher. In reality, who knew how much money Cali was really spending on bribes?

Checks were also found made payable to Guillermo Villa Alzate (a former prosecutor who'd left the Inspector General's Office to serve as an attorney for Miguel Rodríguez) and, among others, Alberto Giraldo and former senator Eduardo Mestre, both of whom had been previously implicated in the Narco-Cassette scandal. At a certain point, it seemed as if it would be much harder to find an official *not* in the pocket of the Cali cartel.

The Accountant

An extensive list of vehicles and motorcycles used by the army and police in their collective counterdrug efforts against the cartel was also recovered. But even with the mass identification of innumerable cartel spies, dozens more corrupt officials remained embedded in key positions throughout the government and Colombian security forces. Sergeant Valencia—along with other sources so sensitive they were known only to Miguel and Gilberto Rodríguez—continued to provide critical intelligence on all counterdrug operations in Cali. Colonel Velásquez, meanwhile, was still treading water. But the raid on Pallomari's office had been an unquestionable success, and he waited with bated breath for the godfathers' response.

When Pallomari was interviewed by Colombian prosecutors, he made a sworn, if dubious, declaration. The first question the prosecutor asked was, "Who do you work for?" to which Pallomari replied, "I work for Don Miguel Rodríguez Orejuela." He was the official business manager for the Rodríguez Orejuela family, he said, and managed their legitimate chain of drugstores, Drogas La Rebaja. Though the statements seemed harmless enough at the time, Pallomari would soon deeply regret making them.

With no official charges pending, Pallomari was released, with the caveat that he'd have to make himself available for future declarations. In the meantime, as a result of the information contained in the narco-cassette tapes and the substantial amount of evidence recovered from the raid on Pallomari's office, Colombian prosecutors opened a formal investigation: Proceso 8.000.

Though he'd managed to escape prison, Pallomari now had bigger problems to deal with. In an unbelievably foolish move, he'd violated the Mafia's most sacred code: never talk. It was common knowledge that no matter the situation, one must deny, deny, deny—wise choice, actually, since the cartel owned many of the prosecutors in the regional Cali office.

The godfathers called an emergency meeting to manage the fallout. They knew Pallomari had inexplicably admitted to working for the Rodríguez Orejuelas and that everything seized from his office linked the brothers straight back to hundreds of corrupt government officials. Gilberto gave serious consideration to giving the gift of new shoes to Pallomari (of the cement variety) but opted to keep him alive until his accounting services were no longer needed, or until he became more of a liability to the cartel.

Still of major concern to Cali, however, was the fact that Pallomari was now on the DEA's radar, and the mere possibility of a US indictment and arrest by American agents posed a threat to the cartel. Pallomari was a Chilean national and subject to extradition to the States under Colombian law if arrested. Velásquez once told me and Dave, "He knows exactly what the cartel's money is spent on, right down to the penny." In other words, he knew where all the bodies were buried—and there were a hell of a lot of bodies.

The godfathers knew that if Pallomari ever testified against the cartel, the repercussions would be devastating. Fortunately for Pallomari, Miguel and Gilberto had several American defense attorneys on their payroll who confirmed that there were no outstanding criminal indictments against him in the US.

During a series of "consultations" with the godfathers, Pallomari agreed to recant his prior statements to Colombian officials. He knew that he didn't have much of a choice—either retract his initial declaration and say he *never* worked for Miguel and Gilberto Rodríguez, or wind up disemboweled at the bottom of the Cauca River. He didn't need much time to deliberate.

After recanting his testimony, Pallomari requested to confer with his cartel-appointed legal team before making any further statements. Prosecutors allowed it, granting him a conditional release after he promised to appear for all future interviews and declarations. After leaving this time, though, Pallomari went directly into hiding. From that point on he'd be under the protection and watchful eye of the cartel.

In the wake of the Pallomari raid, numerous police officials were fired or reassigned. The evidence also sparked another round of salacious media coverage in Colombia, fueling further outrage in Washington. US State Department officials had lost whatever confidence in the national police they had left, along with whatever leverage remained of their ability to successfully attack the Cali cartel. Once again, officials lobbied behind-the-scenes for additional leadership changes. They conveyed their displeasure to President-elect Samper and demanded he take immediate action against Cali as soon as he took office. DEA officials also made their disappointment known, canceling a visit to DC they'd previously arranged for CNP Director General Octavio Vargas.

As always, Samper stuck to his declarations of innocence and support for the narco-cassette investigation. He was calm, collected, and confident—the Colombian equivalent of a Teflon President Reagan. He was also bolstered by the fact that de Greiff would be replaced by a new attorney general just after he'd be taking office—rendering the possibility of any criminal charges against him unlikely. And he also knew that as the Liberal Party candidate, he would have the support of most, if not all, of the Liberal Party–controlled congress should any charges of wrongdoing or whispers of impeachment arise.

In private, however, Samper was growing increasingly frustrated. The US government was relentless, and he was infuriated by their constant meddling into Colombian affairs. He knew what Washington wanted: for him to wage an all-out war on the Cali cartel. But Samper wasn't a DC bureaucrat; he was a savvy Colombian politician determined to survive—politically and otherwise—by any means possible. If there was one thing he'd learned in his career, it was that no one wins a war against the Cali cartel. And he'd be damned if he was going to start losing now.

CHAPTER 8

Behind Enemy Lines

"You guys need to operate like you're
behind enemy lines at all times."

—JERRY RINEHART,
DEA Assistant Country Attaché in Colombia

IN A DIMLY LIT WAREHOUSE not far from Bogotá's El Dorado International Airport, teams of DEA agents and analysts were bleary-eyed from working round-the-clock shifts. Document exploitation (DOCEX) teams were formed, in conjunction with Colombian authorities, to photocopy the mountain of files recovered from Pallomari's office. They had a brutal task: catalog, copy, and document every single last seized document.

Dave and I were among the overwhelmed, literally aching from the incessant sorting and copying—and we'd barely begun to review the files recovered from the supercomputer two months earlier. We were also receiving requests to assist other DEA offices with issues related to the godfathers, particularly from Miami and Operation Cornerstone, a joint DEA and US Customs Service (USCS) investigation targeting the Cali cartel. Attempting a takedown of the leaders of the Cali cartel from Bogotá was no longer a viable strategy (if it ever really was to begin with), and a new course of action was needed.

Dave and I met with DEA Attaché Toft and Assistant Attaché Rinehart to plead our case. With President Bill Clinton and the current administration in Washington demanding results (and contemplating the withdrawal of counterdrug funding to Colombia thanks in part to the Narco-Cassette scandal), we figured we had a shot. We made our argument, explaining that for DEA to make any meaningful progress in its fight against the Cali cartel, we needed to be much more involved. "We can't effectively investigate the cartel from the embassy," I told them. "We need to be able to coordinate directly with Colombian police and military forces in Cali... *on the ground.*"

We were met with immediate resistance: any DEA travel to Cali was still deemed too dangerous, especially after the recent reveal of just how extensive the cartel's counterintelligence capabilities were, not to mention their iron grip over Colombian security forces. And, of course, our appearance came up—again. How could Dave and I *not* be conspicuous in Cali?

We'd anticipated their reaction, but we kept on badgering for a week until DEA brass and the newly appointed US ambassador, Myles R. R. Frechette, finally approved our request. But there were several conditions: first, we had to be back by nightfall—overnight travel was out of the question. Second, under no circumstances were we *ever* allowed to leave any government installation without a Colombian police or military escort. And, lastly, there was to be *no* unilateral activity, ever. Which, in DEA speak, essentially translates to: no cowboy shit. Period.

The ambassador gave us a copy of the Mansfield Amendment, asking us to acknowledge we understood its contents. Its main point was clear: "The Mansfield Amendment to the Foreign Assistance Act provides that no officer or employee of the United States may engage in or participate in any direct police arrest action in any foreign country with respect to narcotics control efforts." 22 USC. § 2291 (c). Further, ... "It does *not* prohibit involvement of United States officers in activities that would *not* ordinarily involve arrests."

But Rinehart knew we loved to stir shit up, so he pulled us aside before we left. "While you're in Cali," he said, "you need to operate like you're behind enemy lines. On second thought, it's probably better if you just do nothing. Does the base have an officers' club?"

Ambassador Frechette was adamant that the entire "country team" in Bogotá work together, sharing any and all intelligence. He was new to the position but already understood that Cali was the single biggest existential threat to the national security of the US and required, in his words, "an all-hands-on-deck approach." This was music to the CIA's ears.

At the time, there weren't many bogeymen left in the world. Communism had fallen apart along with the Berlin Wall in 1989, and the Cold War was officially over. With Pablo Escobar dead, the CIA needed a new nemesis—and Cali fit that bill perfectly. Not everyone within DEA circles was thrilled about it, but Dave and I never gave it a second thought.

Dave called Colonel Velásquez to let him know about our travel plans and requested we meet at the 3rd Brigade the following day. That morning, Dave and I (along with two CIA case officers) bid a not so fond farewell to a cold and rainy Bogotá and headed to the airport. The CIA already had a well-established relationship with Colonel Velásquez and the army Search Bloc, having long been providing intelligence and logistical support to the unit.

A little less than an hour later, we landed at the Marco Fidel Suárez Air Base in Santiago de Cali. It was brutally hot, and I was instantly captivated by the view: massive mountains to the west fading into low-hanging clouds that reappeared and stretched even higher into the sky. When we deplaned, I saw I had a message waiting for us from Mike, a CIA case officer back in Bogotá. "They already know you boys are on your way," he said. "They" meaning the Cali cartel, and "you boys" meaning me and my fellow gringo. That was how powerful the Cali KGB was: they knew that DEA agents were about to arrive before we'd even landed. It was an unnerving feeling.

After we pulled up to the front gate, we were ushered into an armored SUV, then sped off with a pickup truck in tow. The truck was an ominous sight, with two benches inside the bed holding six heavily armed uniformed soldiers. We knew they were there to provide security, but their mere presence was yet another reminder of the possible danger ahead.

When we arrived at the army Search Bloc, we met Colonel Velásquez and his assistant, Major Martín Arango, then got down to business, discussing strategies and potential leads. When we finished, Velásquez gave us a tour of the base and briefed us on pending military operations targeting the godfathers. Dave and I were impressed with the facilities and the army personnel, who were well-trained and savvy operators of the Bloc's sophisticated electronic intercept capabilities. Velásquez had also reserved living quarters for us at the base next to ones reserved for CIA officials, a great way to help make our joint endeavors more seamless. Things were going well, but we couldn't help but notice that everywhere we went, there were stares: everyone wanted to know who the two new, lanky *monos* were. The CIA officers were both Hispanic, so they blended in perfectly. We couldn't have been more conspicuous.

Later that afternoon, Colonel Velásquez let us know that the national police were still building up their Search Bloc in the same manner that had been so effective in Medellín during the hunt for Escobar. He asked if we'd want to meet the new police colonel, adding that he was a friend and eager to work with the DEA. "Of course," Dave replied. It would be an ideal start.

Thirty minutes later, Colonel Argemiro Serna Arias arrived. A polite, quiet, and professional man, he'd been in charge of the police Search Bloc for only a few months and was still working out the kinks. But he was eager to get started and welcomed us with open arms. Much like his friend Velásquez, he aspired to be a general and had faith that with the DEA's assistance his brief tenure in Cali would end with a gold star on each of his shoulders—and a set of handcuffs on each of the godfathers. He had a perfect understanding of what DEA brought to the table: drive, intelligence, resources, and, most importantly, confidential sources and assets who could provide critical information about the possible whereabouts of the Cali leaders. Unlike Velásquez, he didn't speak English well, but Dave and I were more than proficient in Spanish by that point. It was an auspicious beginning.

Regardless, Dave and I were wary of working with the national police. The seized office documents from the Pallomari raid, along with the IBM computer, revealed the extent of corruption within the institution, with hundreds of officials being fired as a result. Still, it was near impossible to know who to trust. The CIA had cautioned us about working with the police. "That place is like Swiss cheese," one analyst told us, adding that she wouldn't dare go anywhere near the police base. But given the shared history between DEA and the national police (most notably the takedown of Escobar), we decided to give them a shot.

Colonel Serna and his security detail drove Dave and me over to the police base and gave us a tour of the grounds. He introduced us to the small team of officers and analysts who manned their electronic intercept (wire room) and intelligence programs, followed by a visit with the Colombian prosecutor embedded with the Search Bloc that week (prosecutors were on hand 24/7 at the police and military Search Blocs). We also met the young captain who would serve as our primary contact there, an enthusiastic man named Efrén Buitrago.

The military and police Search Bloc were different in many ways. The police base was smaller, housing about seventy-five troops—less than a quarter of what the military had. The base itself had once been a rundown ranch that had been converted into a mounted police unit (Carabineros) before being taken over by the Search Bloc, and the equipment was antiquated. Their analysts were inexperienced and far from well versed when it came to Cali operations. They didn't have a fraction of the actionable leads the army did. But the two garrisons did have one thing in common: the stares. Wherever Dave and I went, all eyes were on us.

The base was located in the southwestern part of the city, high up in the hills. Large trees provided ample shade but also ample cover for the Cali KGB, who established listening and observation posts much like those at the military base. Any covered assault vehicles departing the police Search Bloc en route to a raid were immediately detected by cartel spies. Worse, police trucks had to navigate a narrow one-lane road followed by a large traffic circle to get anywhere in the city. Not exactly a setup where we could fly under the radar.

It was swarming with nonpolice activity, too. The circle doubled as a park, surrounded by a host of restaurants, bars, and small food and beverage stands that attracted patrons round the clock. Dozens of cartel-controlled taxis and motorcycle surveillance units blended seamlessly into the circle. There was no way Dave and I could have known at the time, but Cali had both the army and police bases thoroughly stocked with loyal spies.

When we returned to the embassy that evening, DEA management had deemed our visit to Cali an unmitigated success. We'd established a good rapport with the military and the police, with both inviting us back to stay the night anytime. We were also offered living quarters at the air force base, where a clandestine collection site was being operated by a small number of vetted army intelligence officers under the watch of Colonel Velásquez. Because the colonel and his military unit were light-years ahead of the police, they had a huge head start. Plus, they were flush with intelligence—a result of their recent successes in a number of operations.

Dave and I began to up our visits to Cali, alternating between the three bases but usually winding up sleeping at the police Search Bloc. We hadn't forgotten the restrictions we'd sworn to abide by: no leaving the base without an official escort, and no unilateral activity of any kind. Also, we weren't exactly dealing with luxury accommodations. The barracks were so filthy we tracked more dirt *out* than we did in, the mattresses were dusty and sagging, the showers were freezing, and the food was ... well, let's just say we skipped a few meals. Still, we were happy. We were down range, miles away from the stuffy bureaucracy of the embassy halls.

Sometimes, though, our appetites got the best of us. When that happened Dave and I would request a ride to the air base, saying we had a meeting with our CIA counterparts when really all we wanted was just a hot shower and some halfway decent food. Also, by rotating our stays between the three bases, we had no discernible pattern, and only one of the security forces (army or police) would know when we were in town. Two, actually, if you counted the Cali KGB—which we did.

During one of our trips to Cali in early August, Dave and I sat down for a bite at the police chow hall before we were to head out with Captain Buitrago to check on a possible location for Gilberto Rodríguez. Samper had just taken office, and the majority of the police on hand gathered around to watch the news as we ate.

As we were finishing up, we turned our attention to *Noticiero 24 Horas*, which came on each evening at 7:00 p.m. The broadcast began with a quick intro, then segued immediately into a video—and that's when our jaws dropped. There on our TV screen—and the TV screens of nearly every home in Colombia—were Colonel Velásquez and Dolly, intertwined. The distinguished colonel the people so admired was now the unwitting star of the seediest story in ages, set at the Campo Amor motel, of all places. It was Velásquez's worst nightmare come true.

But for the Rodríguez brothers, it was a dream. In a perfectly calculated move, the brothers had cashed in their chips, releasing the blackmail tape just days after Samper was sworn in. They knew the timing would maximize the number of viewers, but really it was about payback—for the seizure of the IBM computer, the wedding debacle, the Pallomari raid, and for having the audacity to refuse their generous offers. The Cali KGB had cornered the market on kompromat, and they didn't hesitate to use it to destroy the colonel who'd dared defy them.

After the video finished, there was complete silence in the mess hall. We knew it was over for Velásquez. We were about to lose the one person who'd made any real headway against the cartel.

Dave and I checked in on Velásquez a few days later. For someone whose life was falling apart, he was admirably upbeat, even confident. He told us that he'd survive the storm and that he still had the full support of the military high command in Bogotá. "The cartel couldn't buy me, so they tried to discredit me, ruin my reputation and my career," he said. "But that didn't work either."

Dave and I weren't as optimistic. Certain his time as the Search Bloc commander was coming to an end, we continued to plan and conduct some operations with the military, but we slowly shifted more of our focus to working with the police.

Dave and I were now spending almost entire weeks at the police base, sharing intelligence with them and participating in raids against the Cali leaders. We developed a friendly rivalry with some of our CIA colleagues and military contacts at the 3rd Brigade and made bets on who would capture the first Cali kingpin. That gave us yet another reason to succeed: our pride. It wasn't long before the police base became our new unofficial home.

Most days we'd leave the base with our escort, Captain Buitrago, making sure we complied with Ambassador Frechette's directives. Our mission was twofold: investigate possible Cali target locations without revealing exactly what we were looking at to the captain (no easy feat) and to learn our way around the city as quickly as possible.

Dave and I were suspicious of Buitrago from the start. He was constantly loitering nearby, asking questions and passive aggressively monitoring our activities. We were so wary of him, in fact, that we agreed to never discuss operational details in our bunks, fearing that listening devices might have been planted there. Whenever we needed to discuss something critical, we'd head down to the soccer pitch on the Search Bloc grounds and talk as we walked around in circles. We were overly paranoid, perhaps, but we weren't taking any chances.

We also remained in daily contact with DEA offices worldwide as well as a group of cooperating sources. We used intelligence gleaned from domestic arrests and cartel-related investigations to conduct numerous raids with the police Search Bloc, but the results were negligible at best. Most—if not all—of the operations appeared to be compromised. Raid after raid yielded nothing but empty homes—sometimes we'd find unmade beds, lingering cigarette smoke, or mugs still filled to the brim with hot coffee, even though no one was there.

While we continued to seize evidence connected to the cartel, we hadn't made any significant arrests. The lack of progress due to widespread corruption was exasperating and was getting more and more challenging with every passing day. And if the task of trying to navigate and evade the Cali KGB behind enemy lines wasn't stressful enough, we had another group of powerful leaders to answer to elsewhere: our bosses. DEA was under constant pressure from Washington brass to produce results, and fast. We had the godfathers on one side and the entire US government on the other. And there were only two of us.

CHAPTER 9

A Narco-Democracy

"Colombia is a narco-democracy."

—JOE TOFT,
DEA Country Attaché in Colombia

AUGUST 7, 1994, MARKED ERNESTO SAMPER'S first day as the president of Colombia. The past weeks had been a maelstrom of controversy, and he didn't have much time to catch his breath before things got worse. The Clinton administration (along with Ambassador Frechette, who'd arrived in Colombia a few weeks earlier) continued to question his desire to fully engage the Cali cartel, for whom not much had changed. They all remained safe and comfortable in their hillside mansions, exquisite ranches, or luxury apartments, heavily protected by their vast network of corrupt officials and loyal allies. They'd come this far—they'd even gotten away with murder. Who—or what—was gonna stop them now?

When Attorney General Gustavo de Greiff suspended the investigation into the narco-cassette tapes due to a lack of evidence, the godfathers' sense of invulnerability only deepened. What was once considered to be a—*the*—smoking gun was now nothing more than a stack of illegally recorded tapes collecting dust. Ultimately, they failed to prove Samper had any prior knowledge of—let alone approved—the influx of cartel cash into his campaign. And though the decision infuriated many in Washington, it was supported by Colombia's Inspector General's Office.

Yet more good news was headed Cali's way. After nearly thirty years of government service, Joe Toft's tenure as the DEA country attaché in Colombia was coming to an end. He'd served as the agency's top man at the American Embassy in Bogotá for almost seven years and was paramount in leading the fight against Escobar and the Medellín cartel. He was also largely responsible for the influx of DEA resources directed toward filling the intelligence void regarding the Cali cartel. Along with DEA agents Javier Peña, Steve Murphy, and a few others, Toft had endured some of the most turbulent times in Colombia's history.

But Colombia was a country he cared about deeply. Toft wasn't your typical American diplomat: born and raised in Bolivia, he spoke fluent Spanish and was very open about the connection he felt to Colombia. He'd developed a real affinity for the country and its people—so when he leaked the tapes to the Colombian press, it was, for Toft, an act of solidarity.

The Colombian Attorney General's Office decision to suspend the narco-cassette investigation infuriated Toft, who'd long insisted that if Colombia had any hope of putting an end to internal corruption, the Cali leaders had to be arrested *and* sentenced to long prison terms. In his opinion, the tapes contained conclusive, indisputable evidence that Cali was not just in bed with dishonest politicians but also that the issue as a whole was being ignored and swept under the rug. He knew he wouldn't be there to see that happen, but that didn't stop him from motivating me and Dave to get better results with the police. He'd even remind us how critical our mission was during embassy pickup basketball games back in Bogotá.

"You guys just gotta keep pushing forward," he'd say during a break in the action. "Don't ever let up."

A platoon of Cali-based attorneys continued to pressure Attorney General de Greiff, hoping he'd agree to the godfathers' Submission to Justice plan. The four wanted to lock down their lenient prison sentences before de Greiff left office, giving them just a few weeks. Toft knew all about the proposal and continually sparred with de Greiff and other Colombian officials to shut it down. Ultimately, the godfathers' dreams of lush jail cells decked out with maids and personal chefs were shattered not by Toft but a man named Alfonso Valdivieso Sarmiento. When Valdivieso took over as Colombia's new attorney general in mid-August 1994, it marked the beginning of the end for the four horsemen of Cali.

Valdivieso was a cousin of Luis Carlos Galán, the former Liberal Party presidential candidate who'd been assassinated by the Medellín cartel. Like his cousin, he was a fervent anti-cartel crime fighter who'd vowed never to negotiate with the cartel. With Washington's scrutiny of the Samper administration at an all-time high, the godfathers' hands were tied, and Samper surrogates weren't much help, telling them simply: "Don't get caught." Hardly the sage wisdom Cali was hoping for.

Just nine months prior, General Octavio Vargas Silva had been on the receiving end of a chorus of accolades as he led the charge to take down Escobar. Now, in his new role as director general of the CNP, he was receiving nothing but criticism from both the US and Colombia. Several of the conversations from the narco-cassette tapes (and other recordings uncovered later) had alluded to the possible promotion of a complicit senior official, a veiled reference that sparked immediate concern for Washington. Though his name was never explicitly mentioned, some people assumed the reference was to General Vargas.

Washington continued to put pressure on Samper to remove Director General Vargas from office. Armed with the growing evidence of systemic police corruption, they also demanded additional commanding generals go as well, to be replaced with trusted officials who'd already worked with the DEA. Unfortunately for the US government, that was a very short list. And when it came to General Rosso José Serrano, there was another issue: there were other more senior generals in line for the director general position.

As the end of September drew to a close, so did Toft's tenure as the DEA chief in Colombia. He opted to retire (rather than return to a new post in the US), and on September 29 he summoned his most trusted media contacts to a surprise press conference, having decided to exit with a bang.

True to form, he didn't hold back. He'd made sure his announcement would be televised and declared Colombia to be a "narco-democracy" to reporters, adding that its current president had accepted millions in campaign contributions from the Cali cartel. Nearly *all* of Colombia's institutions had been infiltrated and compromised by drug traffickers, he continued, and people simply preferred to close their eyes and look the other way. He paused and took a deep breath before forcefully delivering his final words. "The Cali cartel, for me," he said, "is Enemy Number One." Toft's incendiary comments rocked Colombia and the US, leaving the already fragile bilateral counterdrug policy hanging by a very thin thread.

President Samper summoned Ambassador Frechette to Casa de Nariño and gave him an earful, but the ambassador kept his cool. "The guy retired last night so he's an American; he's free to do what he wants," the ambassador said. "I regret that this thing, what he had to say, was so upsetting, but the guy is gone." Frechette then suggested that had Toft not retired, he would have been immediately expelled from the country.

Samper, media savvy and aware that public perception was paramount, quickly responded. "Toft has offended our national dignity and... denigrated an entire nation which has made the most sacrifices in the fight against drugs," he declared.

But it wasn't just Samper who worried about public image—it was the entire nation. Well regarded, Toft's comments were a blow to Colombia's already damaged reputation. Between the well-publicized years of violence, drugs, cartel wars, and political corruption, they looked more like a third world banana republic than a respected country populated with educated, decent, civilized citizens. Colombia's elite was mortified.

The State Department and Ambassador Frechette were also quick to denounce Toft's declarations. They insisted Toft was speaking only for himself and stressed that he was no longer an employee of the US government.

Colombian officials were just as incensed as the rest of the country, if not more so. Several internationally famous people also weighed in to express their outrage, including the Colombian Nobel laureate Gabriel García Márquez. For those people who'd spent more than half a decade in their country fighting side by side against narco-trafficking, they saw his statement as a betrayal.

The administration's repeated denials aside, many Colombian officials believed Toft was speaking on behalf of the US government and gallantly taking the fall for it. Still, other senior Liberal Party members and conspiracy theorists went so far as to speculate that the US was actively trying to destabilize the Colombian government and topple Samper's fragile administration. It wasn't long before requests came in from current and former Colombian government officials—including key cabinet ministers—to reevaluate the future of the DEA's role in Colombia.

In truth, Samper's administration already distrusted the DEA. We were seen as an unpredictable gang of spies, illegally tapping the president's calls, intent on undermining his authority and committing political espionage. Word even got out that repercussions might not end with DEA activities possibly being restricted—it might mean expulsion from the country entirely.

Ambassador Frechette wasn't a huge fan of the DEA either, especially in light of the Toft debacle. But in private discussions with Colombian officials, he pushed back hard, never agreeing to concede an inch. He understood that the intimations against the DEA were complete nonsense and urged Colombian officials to remember the importance of their role. DEA had to be in the country to assist host-nation counterparts in their fight against the Cali cartel or they'd never bring them down. In other words, Colombia needed the DEA, not the other way around.

Back at the embassy, Ambassador Frechette and Deputy Chief of Mission (DCM) James B. Craig sang a different tune. They expressed internally how they'd lost confidence in the DEA and made it clear that under no circumstances were agents allowed to speak to the press. The ambassador also reiterated to Assistant Attaché Rinehart that all agents must continue to abide by the prohibition of undertaking unilateral enforcement action in the country and demanded he be briefed in advance on any and all DEA activities with host-nation counterparts. In a rare moment of levity, he bellowed, "And I better not hear about it for the first time on CNN!" But the moment quickly passed. He wasn't remotely amused.

There were some US officials (and even some Colombia-based DEA personnel) who thought that Toft's comments weren't just a threat to ongoing DEA operations but to the agents' own lives as well. Of course, there were dissenters: more than a few agreed and sided with Toft. For the most part Dave and I fell into that camp but regretted how it had played out. Our issue wasn't with the message, it was with the delivery.

Although Dave and I never felt our lives were in danger as a result of Toft's statements, we were frustrated by how it affected our cooperation with the Search Bloc and Colombian officials. The operational tempo against the godfathers slowed significantly, and we faced additional scrutiny from Colonel Serna and Captain Buitrago whenever we requested to leave the base. Of course, we knew that the order had come directly from the highest levels of the Colombian government.

With that in mind, Dave and I had to take even more precautions to ensure that we not draw any undue attention (let alone harm) to ourselves, lest we make a terrible situation even worse. The truth was, the last thing we wanted was for the DEA's reputation to be discredited or harmed in any way. But we had to be honest with ourselves: we had our own reputations to worry about, too. We knew that things were rapidly devolving into an increasingly vicious game of political chess, and neither of us wanted to be the next pawn.

CHAPTER 10

The Caravelle Capers

"If you don't fail, you're not even trying."
—DENZEL WASHINGTON

STILL SUFFERING THE AFTERMATH of Toft's scathing rebuke of Colombia's current state of political affairs, Dave and I spent the next two weeks taking an unwanted time-out at the police base. We thought that some end-of-year fiscal funds might have brought about some goodwill with Colonel Serna, but we also knew he had to follow orders. We tried our best to stay active, reviewing binders of intercepted cartel pager messages, joining soccer games at the pitch, and training with a handful of police commandos. But for the first time ever, we were bored.

One afternoon, Dave and I received a call at the police base from a couple of DEA agents in Phoenix, Arizona, who'd been assigned to Operation Emerald Clipper, a program designed to systemically attack Cali's covert aviation fleet. The operation was successful in tracking and inspecting Colombian aircraft suspected of smuggling cocaine, and a series of recent investigations had led to the seizure and subsequent forfeiture of dozens of cartel-owned planes. The operation's motto: "Kicking ass, taking planes."

The Phoenix agents were particularly focused on large Caravelle and 727 cargo jets that might be housed at the international airports in Cali and Bogotá. The Cali cartel had reportedly retrofitted several jetliners in their fleet to transport their largest cocaine shipments from Colombia to remote locations in Mexico.

Dave and I asked Colonel Serna for a small contingent of officers to help conduct a "routine inspection" of myriad aircraft and tail numbers at Cali's Alfonso Bonilla Aragón International Airport without revealing our true objective—we still weren't sure who we could trust. But our request seemed innocuous enough to the colonel, who assigned Captain Buitrago and a few other officers from the Search Bloc to accompany us. Although we encountered only one Boeing 727, Dave and I spent more than two hours recording over a hundred airplane tail numbers to further conceal our actual intent.

Back in Bogotá we had slightly better luck, locating a Caravelle and a 727 at El Dorado Airport. Yet again we recorded scores of tail numbers and forwarded the complete list to Emerald Clipper agents, who found that many of them were registered to sham or shell air cargo companies.

By late October, things were finally returning to normal, and Dave and I were once again coordinating enforcement operations with the police Search Bloc. More arrests and drug seizures in South Florida by agents assigned to Operation Cornerstone generated a steady stream of intel for us, and a new specialized police intelligence group in Bogotá was formed that developed target packages from information recovered during prior search operations of Cali locations. The raids produced more documents but no arrests.

At the same time, a series of law enforcement strikes in the United States, Panama, and Guatemala were disrupting Cali smuggling operations throughout the Central American corridor. This forced the cartel to redirect additional loads through Mexico while they established new cells and front companies in the region. These strikes also produced a cooperating source who had intricate details about Cali air smuggling activities in Mexico, in conjunction with "El Señor de Los Cielos" (the Lord of the Skies) Amado Carrillo Fuentes and the Juárez cartel.

We nicknamed the asset "Profe," short for Professor. He confirmed that the godfathers, along with Amado, were using old jetliners to transport massive loads of cocaine to clandestine airstrips and makeshift runways in the Baja California Peninsula and Mexican interior, some carrying as much as fifteen tons of cocaine (on a single flight), after having the seats removed and the interior completely gutted. The jets were also used to repatriate tons of bulk cash to Colombia.

In Mexico, the cocaine was off-loaded (with the help of corrupt Mexican Federal Judicial Police officials), then transported overland through Mexico via the Juárez cartel. Eventually the loads were smuggled across the border into the US and turned *back* over to Colombian cells for distribution—after doling out a hefty commission to Amado and his crew. Sometimes the jetliners were filled with stacks of cash and turned right back around for the return trip to Cali. Other times they were simply destroyed or abandoned, like the converted Caravelle discovered in a barren lake bed near the remote Baja town of Todos Santos, Mexico, in November 1995. All of them were owned by shell companies so the tail numbers were fake, often painted on or pasted over the old ones, making ownership nearly impossible to trace.

The obsolete jetliners could be likened to disposable cameras: use them once, then throw them away. Financially speaking, the approach was extremely cost effective. Each aircraft purchased for a few hundred thousand dollars ultimately netted the godfathers a whopping return of tens, if not hundreds of millions of dollars per trip. It was also the fastest and safest way to repatriate bulk currency to the homeland.

A few days before Thanksgiving, one of the cell phones I carried in my backpack rang around 3:15 a.m. Dave and I carried multiple cell phones—each one marked with a code name and dedicated to a specific asset. "Who in the hell is calling at this hour?" Dave grumbled, pulling the sheets over his head. I squinted down at the lit screen: it was Profe.

"Chris? We don't have much time. A Caravelle, en route from Mexico, fully loaded, maybe $40 or $50 million," Profe said in Spanish. "It should be landing at the Cali airport within the hour."

"Damn! That doesn't leave us much time," I responded.

"That's a shitload of money," Dave replied, now wide awake. "I'll go brief Colonel Serna," he added as I hurriedly prepped our go bags.

Even at that time of night, the airport was a good forty-five-minute drive from the Search Bloc, so time was of the essence. "I have an urgent request," Dave said to the sleepy-eyed colonel he'd just jostled awake from a sound sleep.

"Is there any other kind of request with you guys?" Serna said, rubbing his eyes. After Dave briefed him, he radioed for Captain Buitrago to have the troops ready to muster in forty-five minutes.

"Forty-five minutes!" Dave bellowed. "We need to move now!"

Colonel Serna was always very mild-mannered, but the combination of the jarring wakeup along with Dave's tone struck a chord with him.

"Agent Mitchell, per your *ambassador*, you are here strictly in a liaison capacity and to share intelligence," he said, voice slightly raised. "You're lucky I even let the DEA go out on operations!" Dave got the message, while I raced to the wire room to ask the lieutenant to monitor known cartel radio frequencies and targeted pagers in real time for any suspicious activity at the airport. Forty-five minutes later, we left the Search Bloc with Captain Buitrago and the embedded prosecutor in two covered transport trucks and a reactionary force of twenty-five troops.

We pulled into the cargo area of Alfonso Bonilla Aragón International Airport in Palmira just outside the city limits of Cali at 5:00 a.m. Our nerves were frazzled, and we were seething: we'd driven *under* the speed limit—on a deserted highway, no less—the entire way.

We searched the entire area and at first saw nothing. Then we got lucky: there it was, a Caravelle jetliner parked behind a large hangar. It was the same aircraft Dave and I had seen in Bogotá a few weeks earlier, right down to the tail number.

"Looks like bad intel," Buitrago quipped over the radio in Spanish.

"Bad intel my ass," I muttered to Dave as we cautiously approached the aircraft.

Dave was livid. "This is bullshit," he said. "The entire fucking Search Bloc is compromised."

I was equally irate. "The cartel knows we're coming before we even leave the base."

The next day, Dave and I reviewed radio transmissions and intercepted pager traffic from cartel transportation operatives sent that night of the Caravelle op. While the chatter was heavily coded, it was clearly corresponding to the early-morning time of the event and also intimated that cartel operatives were moving through the city. The idea that it might be pure coincidence was preposterous.

One week later, Profe let us know that the shipment aboard the Caravelle jetliner contained $60 million in cartel cash, and that wasn't even the kicker. He'd also learned from Cali-based transportation and logistical coordinators that the Rodríguez brothers always bought a window of time from someone assigned to the Search Bloc for every bulk currency smuggling event at the airport. Dave and I weren't surprised, but the confirmation just served to further infuriate us.

We knew that there were only a small handful of officials (along with the prosecutor) who had the ability to control events to the point where they could ensure American agents and a police raiding party didn't arrive in the middle of a currency off-load. Dave and I had our suspicions, but we had no way of knowing for certain who was on the payroll, forcing us to operate under the assumption that the *entire* police base was infiltrated with cartel spies—fairly or not. We took even more safeguards to protect ourselves and the source of our intel. Dave and I were drained from the stress of constantly fighting with one hand tied behind our backs.

Over the next six weeks, Dave and I launched two successive operations with the Search Bloc at the Cali airport to attempt to intercept the Caravelle and 727 money flights based on Profe's intel, and each time the outcome was the same. It was like a criminal version of *Groundhog Day*: each operation started with the same slow as molasses early-morning police prep time, followed by Dave and I desperately trying to control our fury, followed by a drive to the airport that took longer than if Daisy herself was driving Miss Daisy, followed by a gigantic goose egg. Dave and I estimated that between $150 and $200 million USD (conservatively) was repatriated to Colombia during our three attempted interdictions, and those were just the flights we knew about. It was a safe bet to assume there were others, and who knew how many?

We were fed up. It was then that Dave and I made a vow, one we had no idea if we could really keep.

"Whatever it takes and however *long* it takes, we are not leaving this country until every single one of those four motherfuckers are in handcuffs or dead!" I said, looking Dave directly in the eye. "You in?"

"I'm in," Dave said. "I'm in for whatever it takes."

While the vow further motivated us, it did nothing to quell our outrage. We returned to Bogotá to meet with Assistant Attaché Rinehart and Toft's newly arrived replacement, DEA chief Tony Senneca. We told them how frustrated we were with the lack of results and how hindered we were by the infiltration of the Search Bloc. Despite Washington's continued efforts to exert immense pressure on both the Samper administration to arrest the godfathers *and* the DEA to make something happen, we still hadn't made any major arrests, and there'd been no operations of real significance since the Pallomari raid, and that was five months ago.

We were failing. There was just no other way to say it.

Determined to turn things around, I told our bosses that to be truly effective, Dave and I had to leave the base—alone—to pursue leads and meet privately with the assets we'd worked so hard to cultivate. There was simply no way we could effectively continue by just relying on cryptic thirty-second phone calls from our sources, and we weren't about to risk their lives by revealing their identities. In essence, we needed to work unilaterally, and in direct violation of the embassy protocols implemented by Ambassador Frechette. It was that or continue to fail. And we'd need wheels, too. A vehicle just for Dave and me.

At first, Senneca was reluctant. He'd been in the country only a short time and wasn't thrilled about one of his first orders of business being to defy the ambassador's own orders. But he was also what we called "an agents' supervisor," someone who had our backs when it came down to it. Ultimately, Senneca approved our request with a wink, a nod, and some heavy behind-the-scenes prodding from Rinehart, who left us with one final piece of advice before we returned to Cali: "Don't screw this up," he said. "All of our asses are on the line here."

Five days later, an armored blue Toyota Land Cruiser was sent to me and Dave at the police base. It was old and beat-up with dark tinted windows and looked exactly like a narco truck. In other words, it was perfect.

We had our wheels. Now we just had to make sure we didn't crash and burn.

CHAPTER 11

Unilateral Action

"If you want a thing done well, do it yourself."
—NAPOLEON BONAPARTE

WHILE DAVE AND I WERE BUSY REVELING in our newfound freedom, President Samper and the Clinton administration remained at odds. Washington continued to badger Samper for failing to engage the Cali Mafia and wanted both Director General Vargas and the now second in command, General Guillermo León Diettes Pérez, gone—especially Diettes, who'd previously served as the police attaché at the Colombian Embassy in Washington (and head of the Metropolitan Police in Bogotá) and was long suspected of having ties to Cali.

In September 1994, Diettes was replaced as the new police attaché in Washington, DC, by General Serrano, the man the US wanted to lead the fight against Cali. The move infuriated Clinton officials, who informed Samper that it would now be more difficult—"hypothetically"—for Colombia to obtain loans from the World Bank or receive a definite outcome in their favor when it came time for their annual certification as a fully cooperative partner on anti-narcotics matters. This wasn't news to Samper, who knew that the US had him over the proverbial barrel and that Colombia stood to lose hundreds of millions of dollars as a result. His administration still hadn't produced any significant arrests of Cali cartel members, and their ongoing "investigation" into police corruption in Cali was a farce. The US had lost any remaining confidence in the national police, along with most other security services. The Colombian press, meanwhile, feasted daily on the controversies.

With the US ramping up the pressure, in late November 1994, President Samper and Defense Minister Fernando Botero Zeà (Samper's former presidential campaign manager) implemented sweeping changes across Colombia's armed forces. Vargas and Diettes were out, and General Rosso José Serrano was named the new director general of the CNP, with General Luis Enrique Montenegro Rinco as deputy director. Five other top officers from the army, navy, and the air force were also forced to retire.

When General Serrano took command in early December, he immediately cleaned house, dismissing roughly 300 officers and almost 2,500 enlisted personnel on the basis of alleged corruption or suspected ties to the Cali cartel. He expanded the Search Bloc staff, adding over 100 troops, including elite soldiers from their Special Operations Group, and made it a priority to meet with me, Dave, and DEA leadership. He wanted to hear directly from, as he put it, "the agents on the ground" and get our honest assessment of operations in Cali.

With enhanced resources now available to the Search Bloc, we suggested more aggressive enforcement operations against the four godfathers and their main lieutenants, coupled with roadblocks and mobile checkpoints in ever-changing, strategic locations. We also brought up the possibility of the Colombian government offering large cash rewards for the arrest of the major Cali leaders.

Perhaps most importantly, we expressed our concerns about the infiltration of the Search Bloc by cartel spies. Without question, no one— aside from the people—had sacrificed more in the war on drugs than Colombia's security forces. While there were, of course, many honest and hardworking officers throughout Colombia's armed forces, it took only *one* turncoat to decimate months of planning and hard work. Just *one* well-positioned corrupt official with access to sensitive information could completely subvert or sabotage any operation's chance of success.

Lastly, we briefed the general on a proposed plan to gather intelligence unilaterally as a means of potentially circumventing corruption at the base—a suggestion that made the DEA bosses visibly uncomfortable. The general, however, was fully supportive, patiently hearing us out and even requesting additional DEA agents be assigned to Cali to further support the Search Bloc. "I'm doing everything I can to root out corruption in the institution," he told us. He even gave us his personal cell phone number before we left, just in case we encountered any problems. There was definitely a new sheriff in town, and he was on our side.

Back in Cali the operational tempo continued to increase throughout December. Dave and I were back to coordinating daily raids with the Search Bloc, consistently recovering more documents revealing further political and police corruption. General Serrano's firing spree continued, and Attorney General Valdivieso expanded his Proceso 8.000 investigation, taking formal declarations from scores of politicians suspected of having ties to the cartel.

When Dave and I weren't assisting with operations, we'd leave the base in our Land Cruiser to check on new leads and make discreet drive-bys of potential cartel locations. Each evening, under the cover of darkness, we debriefed our growing contingent of assets across the city and conducted late-night surveillance of other promising targets, far away from the watchful eyes of cartel spies at the police base. Sometimes, we'd stay overnight at the air force base with army intelligence units rather than return to the Search Bloc so late—the base was home to a military aviation school, so we didn't face the same amount of scrutiny there as we did at the police and military garrisons. Most people just assumed we were American flight instructors.

That may have had something to do with our accessories: no matter the time, Dave and I never left the base without sunglasses and ball caps. We couldn't risk letting the Cali KGB snap crystal-clear photographs of us—the setback the two agents who'd preceded us had suffered.

But our regular reconnaissance missions didn't go unnoticed. Captain Buitrago became even more meddlesome, routinely hanging out in our barracks and inviting us to join him off base for pizza and beer at local Cali establishments. He was always eager to learn of any new intel we'd developed.

While Dave and I didn't trust Buitrago, we knew we had to play along. We had to be careful that he didn't get suspicious that we were suspicious that he was...well, the situation was getting complicated. Sometimes we'd invite him out for a quick coffee to discuss potential operations in an effort to throw him off (always at a place of our choosing). We stuck to the adage of keeping your friends close and your enemies closer. We never revealed anything of substance—only disinformation—but the incessant mind games were sapping us of our mental strength.

One afternoon, Dave and I were in our barracks at the Search Bloc when Buitrago came in and asked Dave if he wanted to go to a massage parlor later that evening. The suggestion immediately invoked flashbacks of Colonel Velásquez frolicking at Campo Amor, followed by equally unwanted images of a half-naked Dave perched on a cheap massage table at some sleazy cartel joint being watched by millions of Colombians on the nightly news. It wasn't a pretty thought, and we knew it was just another attempt by Captain Buitrago and the Cali KGB to try to embarrass and discredit the DEA. Dave didn't take the bait, but we both realized that we'd need to further distance ourselves from Buitrago and the Search Bloc. Neither of us wanted to wind up as the evening's top story, naked or otherwise.

Still, we couldn't distance ourselves from Cali's extensive counterintelligence network. We were routinely followed when we left the base, with most of our departures from the Search Bloc likely prompting a call from Captain Buitrago or another spy to cartel security operatives. Anytime we noticed cartel surveillance on our six, we'd immediately cease operational activity and initiate what's known as a surveillance detection route (SDR), a route planned in advance and designed to subtly expose hostile surveillance.

Thanks to our daily escorted field trips with Captain Buitrago, Dave and I already knew our way around Cali. Our SDRs took us on long, meandering drives through the city during which we'd visit popular attractions and local hangouts or stop for coffee—places far away from our real targets. We collected valuable intelligence about our adversaries, including the makes and models of vehicles and motorcycles, license plates, physical descriptions of the trailing operatives, and taxi numbers. We were using our enemy's own tools against them and established our own counterintelligence database against the cartel's military wing without them ever catching on.

If the Cali KGB had one weakness, it was mobile surveillance. It was, in fact, the only area where we had a distinct advantage, and we could easily recognize when we were being tailed and/or anticipate where cartel operatives would establish "take way" positions.

While we knew the cartel's main objective wasn't to *intentionally* harm us, the thought did sometimes cross our minds. The fact was, they were far more focused on identifying our assets. Dave and I were of less concern to the cartel: they understood that we needed to use Colombian security forces to conduct operations against them, and they had their counter-response to that covered. Informants, however, were another story. Anyone foolish enough to betray the godfathers' trust was a threat and immediately eliminated once identified.

In early December, Dave and I went to meet with Colonel Velásquez and Major Arango during one of our liaison visits to the military base. We made it our habit to stop by once or twice a month. Velásquez advised us of a pending operation against Miguel Rodríguez scheduled to take place at the InterContinental Hotel in downtown Cali. "Do you really think he'll be there?" I asked, not believing for a second that Miguel or any other godfather would dare make such a public appearance.

"I guess we'll find out on Saturday," the colonel said.

Dave and I politely declined to join. It had been just over two months since the Toft ordeal, and we suspected there'd be cameras and/or video recorders present—hardly the ideal environment for us to avoid any unnecessary attention.

The raid itself went as planned with one major issue: neither Miguel nor any other Cali capo was present. The party guests were understandably terrified, and screams echoed throughout the ballroom as soldiers burst in and searched for Miguel in vain.

President Samper and Defense Minister Botero responded quickly, publicly reprimanding Camilo Zúñiga, the newly appointed commander of Colombia's armed forces, for interrupting a private celebration at an upscale hotel—not to mention harassing seemingly innocent Rodríguez Orejuela family members.

Dave and I knew this would be the end for Colonel Velásquez. He was transferred two weeks later, after one year on the ground in Cali. The one man we trusted, the one man who'd made an actual difference in the war against the Cali cartel, was officially gone.

Unilateral Action

As December drew to a close, the Cali police continued their aggressive campaign against the cartel and General Serrano continued to clean house, firing dozens more police officials. In an unexpected twist, Attorney General Valdivieso even suggested reopening the narco-cassette investigation based on new evidence and interviews of individuals and politicians referenced in the tapes. All of a sudden, things seemed to be turning in our favor.

The new year of 1995 brought more hope for the DEA and the Clinton administration. The US now had two dependable allies in Colombia—General Serrano and Attorney General Valdivieso—and expectations to produce results were at an all-time high. So, too, was the pressure.

In early January, in response to General Serrano's request for additional resources, DEA chief Senneca mandated a 24/7/365 DEA presence at the police Search Bloc in Cali. For the better part of the last five months, Dave and I had been living at the police base, recently venturing off base and operating more independently. The permanent DEA presence at the base would further enhance coordination and help ensure an immediate response to any information developed against the Cali leaders. As a result, *all* DEA special agents stationed in Bogotá were assigned to complete weekly tours at the base on a rotational basis.

The arrival of the additional agents at the Search Bloc full-time gave Dave and I more freedom to operate without restriction. We even got approval to secure an apartment in the city, and a trustworthy embassy driver nicknamed "Rambo" was tasked with finding us a fully furnished two-bedroom unit in the Ciudad Jardín section of Cali that we could use as our safe house. It was a beautiful area in the heart of the city's wealthiest neighborhood, and many cartel family members lived there. Despite their presence—or perhaps because of it—Ciudad Jardín was the safest part of the city. And that's exactly why we chose it. The cartel wouldn't dare risk harming any American agents there, or so we hoped.

Dave and I also had new identities to go along with our new home: German agriculturalists who worked at the International Center for Tropical Agriculture (CIAT), a research and developmental organization dedicated to reducing poverty and hunger headquartered in Palmira, almost an hour away. We carried CIAT credentials, ID cards, and Colombian driver's licenses bearing our undercover names and also got a brand-new vehicle to replace our beloved old Land Cruiser: an equally old, armored white Jeep Cherokee. We were thrilled to essentially be on our own but also *extremely* security conscious. We implemented a number of safety measures—arguably *too* many—but considering the situation, there really was no such thing.

Our first safeguard was rudimentary at best. Looking back, the entire setup was about as sophisticated as the security measures in *Home Alone*: we hung Christmas bells from the ceiling behind the front door with stacked empty beer cans below, in the hopes that if anyone tried to enter the apartment while we were sleeping the racket would immediately wake us. It was, clearly, a highly advanced security system, one certain to keep the mighty Cali KGB at bay.

When it came to our Jeep, perhaps that wasn't the most ingenious of choices either. While Dave and I have many strengths, it's safe to say that neither of us would ever be compared to the German field marshal Erwin Rommel, who'd earned a legendary reputation as a brilliant military tactician in the North Africa theater in the early 1940s. Each morning before leaving, we thoroughly inspected the Jeep (parked in the safe house's garage), looking for any type of bomb or other improvised explosive device that may have been placed on or under the vehicle. We then faced the daunting task of actually *starting* the SUV, a job we alternated daily. While one of us would take a deep breath and crank the Jeep's engine, the other would crouch behind a massive concrete support column thirty-five feet away, hands over his ears, just in case a cartel car bomb actually detonated. Hey, there's no point in *both* of us being killed if a bomb exploded, we'd joke. But we only managed nervous laughter at best. It was part of our daily routine, and there was nothing funny about it. At no point did we ever grow complacent about the threat each morning posed.

As we became more inundated with information and requests from investigators and agencies all over the world, Dave and I did our best to follow up on each one, and in doing so, we discovered a disturbing trend: a series of recent high-profile arrests, seizures, and court convictions had stung the cartel over the past year. The godfathers were clearly trying to tie up loose ends, and doing so meant eliminating foreign operatives who posed a potential threat. Backed into a corner, the godfathers were focusing on those who weren't Colombian citizens.

Dave and I planned to target those foreign nationals who had pending extradition requests, along with other high-level foreign operatives, hoping to recruit them as possible sources. We reached out to Operation Cornerstone investigators in Miami and the drug liaison officers (DLOs) assigned to Colombia who represented numerous countries around the world, all struggling with the catastrophic consequences of Cali cocaine flooding their homelands. We also met with our sources regarding any information about foreign cartel operatives.

With Velásquez gone, and even despite the additional DEA presence at the Search Bloc, on most days it really felt like just the two of us. There was a newly heightened sense of danger, and starting the Jeep in the mornings wasn't a joke anymore, if it ever was to begin with. Now it felt more like a recurring nightmare.

CHAPTER 12

Targets of Opportunity

"The journey of a thousand miles begins with one step."
—LAO TZU,
Chinese Philosopher

OVER TIME, THE CALI MAFIA HAD EVOLVED into a massive global conglomerate. But running a worldwide criminal enterprise from Colombia exposed several vulnerabilities: transportation and communication were a major problem, and coordinating international drug shipments and money movements required thousands of calls and faxes each month with operatives around the world. Monitoring key exchanges allowed law enforcement organizations in various countries to arrest top operatives, disrupting and dismantling Cali cartel cocaine and money-laundering cells.

Another main area of concern for the cartel was the extradition or deportation of foreign operatives wanted in the United States and other countries for drug-trafficking crimes. Although the extradition of Colombian nationals to the US had been banned in mid-1991 with the ratification of a new constitution, a bilateral treaty still existed that permitted the extradition of foreign nationals from Colombia to the US and other nations.

Immediately after international drug seizures were made or criminal indictments announced, a host of cartel operators from various countries fled to Colombia to seek refuge. Once there, they obtained false IDs, allowing them to continue to work for the cartel. Dave and I saw these foreign nationals as potential key witnesses with valuable information to share, so we made our own top ten list and began our search. At the very top was a familiar name: Cali accountant and Chilean national Guillermo Pallomari, the highest-ranking non-Colombian in the cartel.

After the raid on his office, along with his subsequent ill-advised statements confirming he worked for the Rodríguez Orejuela brothers (which he later retracted), Pallomari had failed to show for future interviews with prosecutors. He became a material witness in the Proceso 8.000 investigation and, later, a fugitive from Colombian justice. He went into hiding—not just from Colombian authorities but also from Miguel and Gilberto Rodriguez, whom he suspected were now plotting to kill him. For once, his instincts were correct.

Also at the top of our list was Leónidas Rhadamés Trujillo Martínez, the youngest son of the late Dominican dictator Rafael Leónidas Trujillo Molina and a cocaine transportation specialist for Cali in both Panama and Central America. Rhadamés managed a smuggling operation that successfully routed copious amounts of cocaine from Panama to Miami through the port city of Colón, but when US law enforcement interdicted several major shipments, the Rodríguez Orejuelas suspected there was an informant in their ranks and put Rhadamés on the cartel "kill list."

In early February 1995, I was contacted by Royal Canadian Mounted Police (RCMP) Sergeant Varouj Pogharian, who was assigned to the Canadian Embassy in Bogotá. Varouj requested our assistance in locating Sabatino Nicolucci, an international Canadian fugitive with ties to Sicilian Mafia crime boss Vito Rizzuto, head of the Montreal-based Rizzuto crime family. Rizzuto, widely known as "Montreal's Teflon Don," was considered Canada's most notorious mobster. His clan controlled every single aspect of the Montreal underworld: extortion, loan sharking, money laundering, drug trafficking, and all other illegal activities. The family also supplied cocaine to the Hells Angels, the West End Gang, and other assorted criminal organizations in Canada.

Nicolucci began drug trafficking in the early 1970s and started working with Vito Rizzuto in the early 1980s. In 1985 he was arrested regarding the seizure of twelve kilograms of cocaine at the Vancouver International Airport and sentenced to fourteen years in prison, but he served less than half his time and was released on parole in 1991.

Within months, Nicolucci was back in the game, laundering money and coordinating cocaine shipments on behalf of Rizzuto and the Cali cartel. He got caught up in an elaborate money-laundering sting called Operation Compote, a currency exchange house run by undercover RCMP officers to identify and track illicit money transactions and transfers to off-shore accounts. It was the largest undercover operation ever in the history of the RCMP, and in just under three years they traced $31 million that Nicolucci had laundered, much of it the result of cocaine shipments supplied by the Cali cartel.

But before RCMP investigators could take down the massive operation, Nicolucci was kidnapped in Montreal by cartel representatives acting on the orders of the godfathers. As it turned out, the Cali leaders were furious over a $1.7 million drug debt Nicolucci owed them from a previous cocaine load. The Rodríguez brothers also threatened to cut off all future drug shipments to the Rizzuto clan, and cartel thugs ultimately "accompanied" Nicolucci to Colombia, where he was to remain under cartel house arrest until his debt was settled "to the last peso." By this time, Nicolucci had become Canada's most wanted fugitive.

In late February, Dave and I tracked Nicolucci (through telephone toll analysis) to an apartment in the northern part of the city. We were certain it was him, but wary of using any police resources in Cali, we brought in investigators from DAS Interpol in Bogotá. I'd already worked with DAS Interpol on a number of high-profile fugitive extraditions to the US and other countries and always found them to be extremely competent.

Dave and I coordinated with DAS Interpol agents to raid the apartment, and Nicolucci was quickly arrested without incident. He had in his possession a false British passport in the name of Colin Salmon, along with his legitimate Canadian driver's license and social security card, both issued in his true name.

Within days of Nicolucci's arrest, the Canadian Embassy in Bogotá started receiving telephone calls—all of them threats against the staff—and a warning that there would be serious repercussions if Canada continued to pursue his extradition. It was the first time Canada had ever filed a formal extradition request with Colombia, and the RCMP was concerned that the Cali cartel would retaliate, possibly even setting off a car bomb outside the embassy. There was also concern that Nicolucci could escape by bribing prison guards before Colombian courts even finalized the extradition process.

Ultimately, Nicolucci was extradited to Canada the following year to stand trial on an outstanding, unheard-of indictment, including a staggering 437 counts of drug-trafficking and money-laundering offenses. After a lengthy trial, Nicolucci was convicted on 172 counts and sentenced to nineteen years in prison. The back-to-back blows of his arrest and extradition disrupted a major smuggling and distribution route to Canada for the Cali cartel and crippled a key alliance with the Sicilian Mafia and Rizzuto crime family. For us, Nicolucci's arrest meant many things, including overdue proof of progress as well as the honor of receiving the coveted RCMP Moosehead plaque.

Later that February, Dave and I met with Colonel Serna, who told us that he was being replaced as the head of the Search Bloc and promoted to a new position: commander of the Cali Metropolitan Police. We knew he'd always been ambitious, so when he didn't seem all that excited about it, Dave and I couldn't help but wonder why. We later found out that the Colombian prosecutor's office had opened an investigation into possible "irregularities" that had allegedly occurred during a 1994 search operation of a jet aircraft at the Cali international airport suspected to have been transporting $60 million from Mexico to Colombia. Predictably, Deputy Director General Montenegro denied that the transition was anything more than a routine personnel reassignment—so, as usual, we were left to draw our own conclusions.

Serna was replaced by Colonel Misael Murcia Hernández, an experienced officer with a background in special operations who'd worked with the Medellín Search Bloc during the hunt for Escobar. Set to arrive with Murcia was another contingent of commandos from the police Special Operations Group and additional intelligence officials to enhance SIGINT collection and analysis efforts. While our curiosity was piqued by Colonel Murcia's appointment, we were still wary of the Search Bloc: there were just too many operations that appeared to be compromised. But Washington and the DEA were fully committed to working with General Serrano and the national police in the fight against Cali, and establishing a permanent presence at the police base further solidified that partnership.

With no other choice, when it came to the police Search Bloc, it was now ride or die.

In late February, Dave and I spoke to an anonymous source who called the embassy wanting to pass along "important information to DEA agents working in Cali." We met the source later that evening in southern Cali just as the sun was setting.

"I have some information about Cañengo," the asset said, referring to Jorge Eliécer Rodríguez Orejuela, the youngest brother of the Rodríguez Orejuela clan.

Jorge Eliécer was a midlevel trafficker at best, barely on the DEA's radar. He was what we called a "target of opportunity," meaning that if we developed information on him, we would act accordingly, just as we would with any other fugitive. He was wanted in Colombia on drug trafficking and illegal possession of firearm charges and had also been indicted in New York in 1991 for conspiracy to import and distribute 457 kilograms of cocaine.

The asset told us that Jorge Eliécer made periodic visits to a fortune teller for tarot card readings in central Cali to gain insight into his future. "Wait, how can we arrest him if he already knows we're coming?" Dave joked. The source gave us the address of the psychic anyway but rolled his eyes at Dave before we left.

Two days later, Dave and I visited the police base and met with Colonel Serna, who was preparing for his imminent departure to go settle into his new post. He told us that they'd just developed a source who was very close to Jorge Eliécer Rodríguez. Dave and I tried to mask our surprise. "I think we'll have him soon," Serna told us. "Maybe even before I leave."

The more information the colonel shared, the more we realized just how similar it was to everything Dave and I had just learned from *our* new asset. "There's also some SIGINT which corroborates the source," Buitrago added. It was obvious that we were talking to the same asset, which was bewildering. If he *was* the same source, why would he risk conflict by talking with police officials if he was already speaking with us? We continued to spot-check the address he'd given us but didn't pick up on any activity. He wasn't returning our calls anymore, either.

On March 1, the Clinton administration again voiced their dissatisfaction with the Colombian government and President Ernesto Samper, publicly lambasting their apathy toward combating the Cali cartel. As previously threatened, Washington then refused to fully certify Colombia as a compliant or cooperative country with the US in its annual certification review of drug-producing countries. Colombia was now officially deemed "noncompliant," having fallen too short in their promise to work toward reducing drug trafficking and money laundering, addressing public corruption, and openly going on the offensive against Cali. Washington suspended US foreign aid to Colombia, instead recommending that any continued financial aid be provided *only* in matters of national security.

On March 2, Captain Buitrago called and informed Dave and me that Jorge Eliécer was planning to visit his personal soothsayer later that evening. We drove past the location our asset had provided previously, then tried to call him. Nothing. Why would an asset who'd been so eager to talk with us suddenly drop off the face of the earth? "This isn't adding up," Dave said.

When we arrived back at the police base, we were introduced to the new Search Bloc commander, Colonel Murcia. He'd been there only a few hours but was already laser-focused on leading the charge to arrest the youngest Rodríguez Orejuela brother. He invited us to participate in the operation, but we decided to stay behind and monitor any SIGINT traffic in the command center, the asset mystery still bothering us both.

At 7:30 that evening, Jorge Eliécer arrived at the fortune teller's residence trailed by four bodyguards in a Toyota Land Cruiser in true Cali fashion: unarmed and under the radar. Jorge Eliécer appeared nervous and confused as he presented his (false) Colombian *cédula* (his national ID) and driver's license to the police. Clearly, the tarot cards had failed him—he certainly hadn't seen this coming.

Jorge Eliécer was escorted back to the police base and questioned by a Colombian prosecutor, who of course learned nothing. He was later flown to Bogotá, where he was paraded before a horde of reporters and television cameras at CNP headquarters the following day. Naturally a celebration at the Search Bloc followed, as well as another bash at Casa de Nariño in Bogotá. Samper's administration had *finally* produced *some* tangible results against the cartel—and just one day after being heavily criticized by US officials, no less. Both Defense Minister Fernando Botero and President Samper proudly stated that Jorge Eliécer's arrest was a major blow to the Cali cartel and an unmitigated success.

While Dave and I happily joined in the celebration with the police at the base, we remained leery of the Search Bloc. While there was no denying they'd produced the first meaningful arrest of a Cali insider, the operative was by no means an important one, a point that didn't go unnoticed back in DC. "While he's a drug trafficker, we don't consider him a major player in the Cali cartel," said James McGivney, then spokesman for the DEA in Washington.

Dave and I recognized Jorge Eliécer's arrest for what it really was, which was mostly symbolic. While he was nothing more than a midlevel lieutenant, the arrest represented a warning shot across the bow. It was the first time the Rodríguez Orejuela family had been directly affected in over a decade, ever since Gilberto had been arrested in Spain and extradited back to Colombia. It could have been far worse, but the message had been sent that the full force of both the Colombian and US governments was coming, and the godfathers were not beyond their reach.

Dave and I returned to Bogotá for the weekend soon after. We desperately needed a break from the relentless pressure of operating in a high-stress environment—in Cali we could never relax, let alone take a day off. We were always on high alert, never went anywhere alone, and relied only on each other, especially if the shit really hit the fan. We always had to be ready to react to anything thrown at us by the Cali KGB. The stress got to be so overwhelming that it almost felt tangible, as if we were carrying an actual, literal weight on our shoulders.

The following week we were back at it, raiding cartel businesses and properties alongside the Search Bloc in Cali. In early March, we received information from Operation Cornerstone investigators regarding fugitive Julio Cipriano Jo Nazco, a Cuban national who later acquired US citizenship. Jo was a transportation specialist who worked with Rhadamés Trujillo and others coordinating cocaine shipments to the US from Panama and Central America. He'd been implicated in several cocaine seizures, to include 6.7 metric tons hidden in frozen broccoli shipped from Guatemala in April 1992 and 5.2 metric tons found hidden in coffee in Miami in September 1993. After being indicted in the Southern District of Florida, he fled to Colombia, where he continued to facilitate cocaine shipments to the US for the Cali cartel.

At the same time, Operation Cornerstone was making an enormous impact, consistently disrupting Cali cartel operations on a global scale from their base in Miami. Scores of wiretaps on cartel cell heads led to dozens of arrests and significant cocaine seizures. Better still, many of those arrested in the US were willing to talk.

Jo used numerous aliases and possessed several false Panamanian passports, allowing him to move freely throughout Cali. He also oversaw several businesses—all set up to further facilitate cartel operations—and visited them regularly. One day, Dave and I were spot-checking locations when we happened to see Jo standing in front of a lumber company, talking to an employee. He was distinctive looking: part Asian, longish hair, thick moustache, a much heavier body than his cohorts, and sporting large glasses. Since Dave and I were operating alone, we had no authority to unilaterally arrest him, so we contacted our specialized group of DAS Interpol agents, who responded to Cali later that evening.

The next morning we established surveillance on the lumber company, but there was no sign of Jo. That afternoon, as we all sat sweltering and restless in our vehicles watching the entrance of the business, I happened to glance out at the oncoming traffic and, in an incredible stroke of luck, saw Jo drive by in a burgundy-colored Chevrolet. I radioed our DAS Interpol counterparts, who managed to stop him just a few blocks away.

Jo was a cool customer. He presented the agents with a Panamanian passport in the name of Jaime Nonato Toledo Piño, a Panamanian *cedula*, and a Panamanian driver's license and electoral card. He calmly explained that he was a businessman headed to a meeting with clients at the Inter-Continental Hotel in downtown Cali and was impressively convincing as he stuck to his story—until he saw me and Dave. The two of us held up a copy of the Cornerstone indictment, the extradition order, and photographs and fingerprints of Julio Jo, which, of course, were an exact match for Jaime Toledo Piño.

Jo knew the game was over, but he was defiant and refused to speak with us. We transported him back to Bogotá, where formal extradition proceedings were initiated, and from there it was on to a Colombian prison cell, where he spent almost an entire year before being extradited to Miami in 1996.

Finally, things were starting to heat up in Cali. But Dave and I were getting superstitious and treated it like a no-hitter: don't dare mention it, lest you jinx it. We weren't about to let up now. We just hoped our new-found momentum would continue throughout the spring.

CHAPTER 13

Money Talks

"It's always about the money..."

—**KIRSTY EAGAR,**
Author

THE PAST FEW WEEKS HAD SEEN A FLURRY of activity in Cali. We increased pressure on the godfathers and their key lieutenants as much as possible and for months had been engaging in lengthy conversations with CNP Director General Serrano and Deputy Director Montenegro, pushing for the Colombian government to start offering compensation for information leading to the arrest of the major Cali players.

Monetary rewards for the capture of major drug traffickers and terrorists have long been an effective tool utilized by the United States, Colombia, and other nations in the past—it's a method that remains highly effective to this day. The rewards offered for the arrest of Pablo Escobar and other Medellín cartel members had seriously impacted their day-to-day lives, and we wanted to have that same destabilizing effect on the Cali leaders. The offers were broadcast on television and radio and made headlines in the newspapers, making them nearly impossible to miss. But most people weren't willing to put their lives—or the lives of their families—at risk, unless, of course, there was a lofty reward just too significant to resist. And a reward approaching $2 million was a pretty big pot of gold for the average citizen.

If anyone ever thought bureaucracy was bad in the US, trust me, it was far, far worse in Colombia. Even the simplest matters took forever to be resolved, but to his credit, Ambassador Frechette—along with DEA Attachés Senneca and Rinehart—lobbied diligently behind-the-scenes with several high-level Colombian government officials for an approval of the rewards. The lobbying dragged on for months.

Toward the end of March 1995, on the heels of hundreds of raids and the painstaking analysis of thousands of pages of seized documents, the Colombian government was finally able to obtain drug-trafficking charges against all seven of the top Cali leaders. Then they raised the stakes further, offering staggeringly high cash rewards for their arrest. The top amount, the equivalent of about $1.875 million USD (1.500'000.000 Colombian Pesos—COP) was offered for information leading to the arrest of Cali cartel leaders Miguel and Gilberto Rodríguez Orejuela, followed by about $625,000 USD (500'000.000 COP) for the arrests of the cartel's other top men: José "Chepe" Santacruz Londoño, Francisco Hélmer "Pacho" Herrera Buitrago, Victor Julio Patiño Fomeque, Phanor Arizabaleta Arzayús, and Henry Loaiza Ceballos.

The Colombian government then launched a nationwide media blitz and propaganda campaign across TV, radio, and news periodicals—the airways were inundated with advertisements featuring wanted posters of the Cali leaders. But a few of the photos were old or grainy—not ideal, or even accurate, likenesses. Pacho Herrera and Victor Patiño in particular got off easy: their photos were barely recognizable.

A nationwide tip line was also established, giving anyone willing to provide information the chance to do so anonymously. While most of the calls were dead ends, the ensuing psychological pressure on the seven leaders and their family members and associates was as effective as we'd hoped. Tragically, scores of suspected informants who opted for the tip line (lest they be exposed) were killed by the Cali KGB: the phone line had been infiltrated and wiretapped by cartel spies at the phone company, unbeknownst to me and Dave.

The rewards blitz also produced scores of calls to the American Embassy from those wary of calling the government-monitored tip line. Dave and I screened and eliminated most of the calls, but for those that warranted further follow-up, we arranged face-to-face meetings in Cali.

Cali Cartel Rewards and Wanted Posters

We'd always been confident that the cash would generate the quality of assets and leads we hoped for, but it was a struggle to remain patient while sifting through every single one of them.

Flush with new information, the pace at the Search Bloc intensified. Evidence seized during the hundreds of raids conducted by Colonel Velásquez and the military was still coming to light, and the Colombian media continued their exposé on government corruption, often publishing lengthy lists of names and other sensitive material that had been leaked by rival partisans. Santiago Medina, the former treasurer for Samper's presidential campaign, was one of the names raised when talking about who may have accepted cartel drug money. The attorney general's Proceso 8.000 investigation was also thriving, actively exposing and arresting current and former congressmen and other government officials for accepting cartel cash, including former Liberal Party Senator Eduardo Mestre, who was arrested in April.

Colombian politicians were beginning to fall like dominos. The past few months had seen a damn good stretch for us and the Colombian authorities, and our confidence was growing. But behind-the-scenes, there were some Colombian government officials who had no interest in playing along. Their goal was the antithesis of ours: paralyze the DEA's efforts entirely. There was always something shady happening within the Samper administration, and no matter how far we'd come, we still trusted no one—only each other. Samper and his cohorts were always ready to fight anyone who they saw as a threat, and unfortunately for us, the DEA was their favorite target.

CHAPTER 14

Pardo's Letter

"The DEA is not here in Colombia to be a law enforcement agency in an operative sense."

—MYLES R. R. FRECHETTE,
US Ambassador to Colombia

TWO MONTHS HAD PASSED since Jorge Eliécer Rodríguez's arrest, and almost eight since Joe Toft's infamous "Colombia is a narco-democracy" comments, which continued to resonate throughout the country. But it felt like we were headed in the right direction. Dave and I knew that the rewards offered by the Colombian government would pay off soon—literally.

We continued with our Search Bloc liaison, coordinating on a near daily basis with Captain Buitrago and Colonel Murcia. Buitrago was as nosy as ever, asking where Dave and I were staying and endlessly feigning concern for our safety—reminding us of how dangerous Cali was. At one point, in a real stretch, he hung his head and said that he really missed hanging out with us. His acting prowess wasn't exactly on an Academy Award level, but then again, all three of us were acting: we knew he suspected we were out each night, operating unilaterally. But our excuse—preferring to stay at the air force base for the hot showers and far better food—was a valid one. Still, he needed something to report back to the cartel on the DEA's movements.

As the media reveled in the Samper political scandal, some in the government actually suspected (and even falsely attributed) the endless leaks to the DEA and blamed us for Washington denying Colombia full certification, a decision that cost them hundreds of millions of dollars in foreign aid. There were even some who believed that it was the DEA who'd secretly recorded the narco-cassette tapes almost a year ago. It was all ridiculous conjecture, but a surprising number of officials actually chose to believe that the DEA was nothing more than a group of spies desperately trying to subvert Samper's administration.

To defend their theory, they'd continually bring up Toft, whom they'd always blamed for leaking the tapes to the press. The general distrust of the DEA got to be so bad that President Samper once again considered permanently removing all DEA presence from the country.

On May 25, Colombian Foreign Affairs Minister Rodrigo Pardo sent a four-page letter to Ambassador Frechette outlining nine points the government requested in regards to the DEA and their activities in the country. Pardo opened the letter by saying that while he "appreciated" the importance of the DEA's support in the fight against drug trafficking, he was compelled to present his nine points, all of which were designed to severely restrict our ability to operate in the country. It was the very definition of a mixed message—thanks for the help, but here's a list of things that will make any continued help nearly impossible.

Rumors were running rampant throughout Colombia that there were as many as five hundred DEA agents operating in Cali at any given time when, for the most part, there were only two: me and Dave. And regardless, why would Colombia fear the dismantling of the biggest drug cartel in history, the merciless Mafia who posed the greatest security threat to their country *and* to the US? Perhaps they were afraid that the DEA would learn the truth about Cali's support of and financial contributions to so many Liberal Party politicians, including their current president. Or, worse, that we would discover just how deep that corruption went.

The DEA was, and is, the only single-mission US federal agency solely dedicated to drug law enforcement. We had only *one* mission in Colombia: help the government stem the flow of drugs to the US through assisting host-nation counterparts with intelligence, logistical support, and other resources to arrest the Cali leaders and dismantle the cartel. No ulterior motives, no political intrigue. But some Samper administration officials feared the DEA wouldn't just stop with Cali. They worried that we'd continue to follow the evidence—and the drug money—no matter where it led. Which, of course, was directly back to them.

Minister Pardo's letter and its contents regarding the DEA's activity in Colombia was a lot to digest, to put it mildly. The nine parameters (summarized below) weren't surprising—we were used to these kinds of roadblocks—still, it was brazen.

FIRST: The Colombian government must be informed of and approve all DEA actions in the country, and under no circumstances can the DEA act unilaterally.

(Dave and I attributed this to the narco-cassette tape scandal and the related conspiracy theory that the DEA recorded them in an attempt to destabilize the Colombian government. Not only were our activities being monitored by the Cali KGB *and* the Search Bloc, but they were also, now, being heavily scrutinized by the Colombian government.)

SECOND: The DEA should abide by all Colombian laws, respect its national sovereignty, and not intervene in the country's internal affairs, and fully comply with all current treaties, amendments, and agreements.

THIRD: The American Embassy must keep the Ministry of Foreign Affairs informed of the location of any and all offices that the DEA establishes or operates in the country.

FOURTH: All DEA officials must be limited, with no exceptions, to judicial cooperation and sharing of any intelligence relating to drug-trafficking operations between the two nations. All efforts spent toward any collection of relevant information must be done in collaboration with Colombian authorities.

FIFTH: All DEA officials should familiarize themselves with Colombia's policies and laws regarding drug trafficking and money laundering.

SIXTH: Any exchange of sensitive or confidential information should be done in accordance with the standing agreements already in place between the two nations.

SEVENTH: The Ministry of Foreign Affairs is the only entity entitled to authorize the number of DEA officials permitted in Colombia. All authorized DEA officials must be accredited with the Colombian government in accordance with criteria outlined in the Vienna conventions of 1961 and 1963 regarding diplomatic relations. Furthermore, the Colombian government must be informed of the full names and official functions of each DEA officer working in the country prior to authorization.

EIGHTH: DEA agents serve no longer than a four-year tour of duty in Colombia. (This would have reduced the previously established six-year limit by two full years, a consequence of Toft's almost seven-year stretch in the country.)

NINTH: The US ambassador will serve as the one, and only, spokesperson in regards to all DEA and DEA activities in any matters related to the press or media.

Fact was, the US Embassy and the DEA already abided by almost all of those requirements—they were codified in previous agreements and amendments. But the mere suggestion that the DEA would now, or ever, open up their case files or identify confidential assets to government officials was absurd. The letter was a blatant attempt to hinder our investigative efforts into the Cali cartel leaders, period. They were doing anything they could to try to prevent us from obtaining additional evidence that could further implicate senior Colombian government officials in league with the cartel.

The letter particularly infuriated Under Secretary of State for Narcotic Affairs Robert Gelbard as well as Ambassador Frechette, who immediately put out a stern public statement that, in nondiplomatic speak, essentially translated to: It'll be a cold day in hell before the Foreign Ministry ever knows the details of the DEA's movements in Colombia.

While it was no secret that Ambassador Frechette and the DEA didn't always see eye to eye, in this case he had our backs. He remained tough on

Colombia and always held their feet to the fire. He was a shrewd politician who wouldn't stand for being bullied—publicly or otherwise. Privately, however, he expressed his annoyance to DEA chief Tony Senneca. "The DEA is not here in Colombia to be a law enforcement agency in an operative sense," Frechette said. He was making himself very clear: DEA could not conduct any type of unilateral activity in Colombia. DEA could not participate in raids with the police or military, and, lastly, DEA's *only* mission in Colombia was in a support and advisory capacity.

This didn't exactly sit well with me and Dave, but we were hardly in any position to be drafting our own mandates in response.

By now we'd spent close to a year on the ground, and we were finally feeling comfortable operating in Cali. We knew our way around the city and had learned to navigate the treacherous environment and ubiquitous land mines that were omnipresent. But we weren't kidding ourselves. If the ambassador discovered we were staying off base, unilaterally conducting surveillance, debriefing assets, *and* participating in raids, at the end of the day *our* interpretation of the Mansfield Amendment meant nothing. Overseas the ambassador is king, and if we were caught disobeying him, we would most certainly be expelled from his kingdom.

Still, we had to take that chance. We knew that to be truly effective, we had no choice but to operate independently. Also, we'd already put our lives at risk, many times over. Doing the same with our careers, it turned out, was much easier.

A few days after Pardo handcuffed DEA with his letter, Dave and I were summoned to Senneca's office. We were on our way to Cali, but we weren't quite sure what we'd be doing once we got there. Walking down the long, ominous embassy hallway reminded me of my many visits to the principal's office in elementary and middle school. When we walked into the office, the chief was seated at his desk, with Assistant Attaché Rinehart standing next to him. My supervisor, Ruben Prieto, was also there, perched uncomfortably on a leather couch. Dave and I stood stiffly in the middle of the room, ready to receive our punishment like the two naughty schoolboys we were.

All right. Here it comes, I thought. It was a typically cool day in Bogotá and the office windows were wide open, but Dave and I were both sweating.

Rinehart was the first one to put us at ease. "Relax," he said. "You're not in any trouble. We just wanted to catch you guys before you left for Cali. Officially, you know Minister Pardo and the ambassador's position. *Unofficially*, well…you two keep doing what you're doing. Just don't get caught." Rinehart looked at us with a slight grin. We just stood there, speechless.

When we finally looked over to Senneca, he nodded his head once in an affirmative manner. Ruben did the same, but several more times and with a subtle wink. "Copy that," Dave replied, and we grabbed our go bags and raced out of the embassy before anyone could change their minds.

It was a vote of confidence we didn't even know we needed. DEA brass had made it clear that we had their support. It was on us, though, to keep that trust. We couldn't let them down, we couldn't screw up, and we had to be careful—more careful than ever.

In some ways, those nods of affirmation gave us a fresh start. We had a gut feeling that good things were on the horizon, and we weren't wrong.

CHAPTER 15

Checkmate

"Don't kill me! I'm a man of peace!"
—GILBERTO RODRÍGUEZ OREJUELA

IT WAS NEARING THE END of May 1995, and Dave and I were in Cali wrapping up a quick visit, our first since Minister Pardo had presented Ambassador Frechette with his notorious nine-point missive. We'd coordinated several raids with the Search Bloc against Victor Patiño and Henry Loaiza, but both had produced nothing. As we waited for the DEA aircraft at Marco Fidel Suárez Air Base to take us back to Bogotá, my cell phone rang. It was my supervisor, Ruben Prieto.

"A cable just came in from Ecuador," he said. "You two take a look at it as soon as you get back and let me know what you think."

We didn't give Ruben's call much thought—we received at least two hundred teletypes a week from DEA offices all over the world. The number had increased exponentially over the past two months, ever since the monetary rewards for the arrest of the major Cali leaders were first offered.

When we arrived at the embassy, Dave and I went directly to Ruben's office and found him sitting at his desk, smiling. Another DEA colleague, Jiries "Jerry" Salameh (who Dave and I had worked with in Miami), was seated in front of him. Ruben handed us each a copy of the cable and waited as we stood in the cramped office and read it. It was a debriefing of a DEA asset in Ecuador.

According to the report, the asset identified Alberto Madrid Mayor, a.k.a. "Flaco," as the personal assistant for Gilberto Rodríguez Orejuela, a.k.a. "the Chess Player." Flaco reportedly traveled to Gilberto's location each weekday, tasked with the usual assistant responsibilities—answering phones, coordinating meetings, relaying messages, and whatever else Gilberto required. Once his boss was finished working each evening, Flaco returned to his own home.

Flaco was incredibly well trained when it came to surveillance detection and always used circuitous routes and a variety of ingenious methods to ensure he wasn't followed whenever traveling between his residence and Gilberto's ever-changing location. His tradecraft was superior, and it needed to be. He was working for the leader of the most powerful drug cartel in the world.

"Well, what do you think?" Jerry asked us. It was obvious he'd already made up his mind.

"I think it sounds like damn good intel," Dave said.

"Finally, a human source on the ground," I added. "We're never gonna catch these guys through SIGINT."

Up until then, SIGINT was the primary means utilized by Colombian security forces to hunt the godfathers. Though it had been key in locating and killing Escobar, Cali was another animal entirely, and the godfathers had become much savvier when it came to security and communications. Much of the intel reaped from SIGINT was related to lower-tier Cali operatives and so heavily coded it was impossible to decipher. Analysis attempts by the Search Bloc were mostly a guessing game, so it wasn't surprising that not one significant Cali member had been arrested via SIGINT thus far.

DEA, on the other hand, was renowned for their prowess in cultivating sources—something Dave and I prided ourselves on. We longed for the day when we'd recruit a high-level asset from within the cartel, knowing that if we were going to dismantle Cali, it could only be done with help from someone on the inside, someone who could provide us with real-time actionable intelligence.

Although the intel regarding Flaco sounded good, we were skeptical: the godfathers were masters of deception and excelled at providing misinformation. It was commonplace for them to "send in" assets to the

American Embassy armed with phony intelligence, all designed to distract the DEA and waste their time with false leads.

"We should try and corroborate this information about Flaco before we mount some huge operation," I told the group. Ruben concurred. "Make arrangements for the Ecuador asset to travel to Bogotá for a full debriefing," he told Jerry. "In the meantime, Chris and I are going to talk with another source."

The other source Ruben was referring to was code-named "Jordan." Although he had an established reporting record and was considered a reliable asset, none of his information had ever helped launch an enforcement operation against the Cali leaders. His intel was usually vague in nature and served only to help corroborate other information we'd received. Therefore, he was classified solely as an intelligence asset.

Jordan never wanted to meet in Cali, nor would he even think of stepping foot inside the US Embassy—it was a well-known fact that the cartel and other groups used spies to monitor everyone entering and exiting the embassy in an attempt to identify defectors and informants. If any sighting or information he provided compromised his identity, it would result in the immediate execution of him and his family.

I always felt that Jordan was playing both sides: he stayed on the cartel's good side, but if he was ever arrested or indicted in the US, he could use his cooperation with the DEA as a get out of jail free card. But Ruben disagreed and insisted we meet him later that day after he arrived from Cali. When we debriefed him, Jordan identified several close associates and confidants of Gilberto Rodríguez, including Flaco. "He's one of Gilberto's most trusted employees, and he's always with him," Jordan said. Ruben's hunch had been spot-on—it was exactly the corroboration we'd hoped for.

The following day the Ecuador source arrived in Bogotá, accompanied by DEA agent Nelson González. We debriefed him in a local hotel room, where he relayed details about Flaco that were consistent with Jordan's. The Ecuador source described Flaco as being in his mid to late thirties, of medium height, and always dressed in business casual attire. "If you follow Flaco, he *will* lead you to Gilberto," he told us. He even offered to meet with him, giving us a chance to follow Flaco back to where he was staying.

It was a huge break, a long overdue solid lead on a Cali godfather based on information corroborated by not one but two credible assets. But, given the cartel's systematic corruption of nearly every governmental institution in the country, if the operation had any chance of being successful it would have to be done in total secrecy. The Search Bloc was out of the question, and they weren't equipped for this type of operation anyway. The Search Bloc was a heavily armed quick reaction force (QRF), whereas what we needed was a specialized covert surveillance and intelligence unit.

DEA Attaché Senneca met with Ambassador Frechette and the CIA station chief, and they decided to utilize a relatively new police intel group who'd worked previously with the IC. The unit was headed by Lieutenant Colonel Carlos Alberto Barragán Galindo, who had a proven track record of working on sensitive investigations. The unit was properly vetted: each member was handpicked, polygraphed, and had completed extensive training in the US. There was no better option. This team gave us our best chance of arresting Gilberto.

We'd also be working alongside a CIA case officer, Pedro, who would liaison with the team. Ruben and Pedro, however, didn't exactly see eye to eye. Ruben had fought numerous battles with the CIA during his time in Colombia—especially during the hunt for Escobar—and to say he wasn't a huge fan is an understatement.

Since this would be a DEA-led operation, Ruben was concerned about having operational oversight over the unit and how it might affect DEA's managing of resources. Fortunately, Dave and I had worked closely with the IC over the past year, so we knew we'd make it work. We regularly coordinated in Cali with Pedro, Mike, and other case officers and analysts and hoped our personal relationship with Pedro would limit the chances of any melodrama. We couldn't afford to let personality clashes interfere with our mutual goals.

Prior to deploying to Cali, it was decided that Ruben and Jerry would stay with Pedro and the police-vetted unit in hotels—they blended in far better than we did—remaining completely isolated from the Search Bloc to avoid compromise. Jerry was a chameleon, a Palestinian American who spoke excellent Spanish and easily adapted to any environment. His looks—olive skin, jet-black hair, and goatee—gave him the ability to go anywhere in Cali without turning any heads. Ruben, a Mexican American in his late forties, was also a fluent Spanish speaker. With his salt-and-pepper hair and understated appearance, he also avoided any second glances. The two men would also maintain contact with the Ecuador asset during the operation.

For me and Dave, our mission was twofold. By day, we were available to assist with the Flaco surveillance, and by night we'd return to the Search Bloc and stay with the rotating DEA agent under the guise of pursuing a "promising lead" in Yumbo against Pacho Herrera. We were essentially acting as counterintelligence elements within the Search Bloc, once again using the cartel's exact same methods against them.

Yumbo was chosen because of its location (eight miles north of Cali) and for the fact that it was unlikely Gilberto or Miguel Rodríguez would be there. But it was also a known Pacho Herrera stronghold, so should any information get leaked by the Search Bloc, it wouldn't compromise our real objective. Nonetheless, we needed to have our guard up. One mistake, just one Cali KGB spy tracking us undetected when leaving the police base, and the entire operation would be compromised.

On June 3, the Ecuador source arranged to meet Flaco at a restaurant in Cali, which a team consisting of DEA agents, Pedro, Colonel Barragán, and a small group of hand-selected officers covered. Everyone stayed hidden behind their surveillance vehicle's dark tinted windows—just one sighting of a gringo face and the entire operation would go down in flames.

After the meeting wrapped, Flaco got into a red Mazda and headed south. We followed him to an apartment complex close to the polo field in Ciudad Jardín, in the southernmost part of the city. Ciudad Jardín was the Beverly Hills of Cali and the field was less than half a mile from our safe house.

Ciudad Jardín was strikingly beautiful, but it was a very difficult area to operate in. The preferred neighborhood of cartel family members, wealthy businessmen, and Cali elite, the residences looked more like movie sets than actual homes: immaculately manicured, extravagant mansions with Olympic-size pools and gigantic stone walls. Surveying the over-the-top compounds made us feel like we were trapped in an episode of *Miami Vice*, a not uncommon occurrence in those days. There was also a manned police CAI (Immediate Attention Center—essentially a police kiosk) at the main entrance, and anything suspicious warranted an instant call to the Cali Metropolitan Police.

Early on the morning of June 5, our team established surveillance around Flaco's apartment complex, making sure to cover the main exits leading out of Ciudad Jardín. We suspected Flaco's direction of travel would most likely be north, but we had to be prepared for anything.

Surveilling Flaco was a challenge from the start. He was well trained in surveillance detection and employed several countermeasures to determine if he was being followed. To try and avoid us (or anyone else), Flaco drove his Mazda, took taxis and city buses, utilized choke points (a narrow passage that causes congestion), and strolled down alleyways and side streets. Sometimes he'd cross the street, duck into a store, then double back and walk in the opposite direction. He loved disguises and consistently changed his clothes and alternated between different hats and sunglasses.

On the first day, our surveillance team lost Flaco after a few minutes, and the finger pointing began immediately. "What happened? You lost him?" Ruben asked Pedro.

"That was your fault," Pedro shot back.

Our lack of secure communications in coordinating the surveillance forced us to rely on cellular phones as our primary means of tactical communication, which only complicated matters further. But cell phones were the best way to avoid detection by cartel security elements, who regularly monitored radio frequencies as part of their counterintelligence campaign against the DEA and government security forces. Another issue was the lack of experience among the young police-vetted group in covert and mobile surveillance. Flaco was far more skilled in surveillance and detection techniques than they were.

Over the next two days, we didn't fare much better. We did have one upside, however, as his direction of travel every morning never changed—always north toward downtown Cali. This allowed us to set up a series of static surveillance posts along his route in the area we'd previously lost him in, similar to tactics employed in the movie *Zero Dark Thirty*, when stationary surveillance was able to record the movements of Osama bin Laden's courier, Abu Ahmed al Kuwaiti, as he traveled to bin Laden's residence in Abbottabad, Pakistan.

Checkmate

On June 7, we followed Flaco just north of downtown Cali to an area near a Santa Mónica park before losing him. Santa Mónica was another affluent residential area, and we assumed Gilberto was staying somewhere nearby, so fixed surveillance positions were set up the next day at strategic locations along that route. The remaining units set up in and around the park near Avenida 6 Norte. The park was located in a popular downtown commercial area with heavy pedestrian traffic and bustling restaurants, stores, and offices—the perfect area for us to seamlessly blend in while conducting surveillance.

On June 8, we tailed Flaco into the park, the last quarter mile or so on foot. He was on guard as always, ducking in and out of shops and continually looking around to see if he was being followed. His countersurveillance was so intense that Ruben decided to have the team drop farther back rather than risk being spotted. Flaco continued on foot toward a secluded residential section of Santa Mónica before surveillance lost him.

The team was disappointed, but we were close, and we knew it. Flaco's tradecraft had left no doubt in our minds that Gilberto was staying somewhere close by, and in anticipation of an imminent enforcement operation, General Serrano traveled to Cali so he could be present in the event we got lucky and arrested him.

As Ruben and Jerry planned operational details with Colonel Barragán and Pedro, Dave and I continued our efforts at the Search Bloc to conceal the operation. We met with Captain Buitrago and Colonel Murcia and told them that we were making steady progress, close to identifying Pacho's location in Yumbo. Both officials were, of course, thrilled with the disinformation.

On the morning of Friday, June 9, Flaco took his usual route toward Santa Mónica while surveillance units carefully shadowed him. Disguised, he alternated between several different modes of transportation, finishing with a simple walk through the park while constantly looking behind him. A female CNP officer in jogging attire was able to casually follow him as he trekked up a steep stairway, only to lose him at the top of the hill. But the stairway, it turned out, led to Avenida 9a Norte, which bore a quiet, lovely cul-de-sac with five large town houses. There was nothing else on the dead-end street, so we knew that Flaco had to have entered one of the homes.

The problem was figuring out which town house to hit. "Screw it," I said. "Let's hit all five. We find Flaco, we find Gilberto."

Everyone agreed, but at only ten strong there was no way we could launch a viable enforcement operation on five locations—especially when one of them was very likely occupied by Gilberto himself. We had no way of knowing what, or who, was waiting for us inside.

Because a more sizable force was needed, we devised a plan to use the Search Bloc. But given the cartel's undisputed infiltration of the unit, our plan called for the Bloc to be initially deployed against a false target. While Ruben and Colonel Barragán briefed General Serrano on the plan, Dave and I met with Colonel Murcia and Captain Buitrago back at the police base. Since we'd already laid the groundwork with our disinformation about Pacho in Yumbo, we just continued on with that ruse. It would only be when the raid team was a few blocks from Gilberto's suspected location that Barragán would call and redirect the Search Bloc and prosecutor to our true objective.

At 2:15 p.m., sixty heavily armed uniformed troops from the Search Bloc headed north toward Yumbo, where less than half an hour later, they were called and diverted to the actual location. When they pulled up to Avenida 9a Norte a few minutes later, they shut down the street and surrounded the townhomes. Colonel Murcia was predicably livid that he'd been deceived. He'd been hoping to further capitalize on his recent success just three months earlier, when he'd been so roundly praised for the arrest of Gilberto's younger brother, Jorge Eliécer.

After briefing the troops, we divided up into five teams and the raids began simultaneously. A police helicopter circled overhead, making the once peaceful street look and sound eerily similar to the site of a military operation in Afghanistan or Iraq.

When Ruben burst into the middle townhome with his team, he immediately yelled into his radio. "I have eyes on Flaco! He's here!" Ruben immediately requested additional resources, and more troops quickly swarmed the residence, going room to room searching for Gilberto. One bodyguard was detained, along with two domestic employees and Gilberto's shocked paramour, Aura Rocío Restrepo. We knew we were in the right location, but there was no sign of the Chess Player.

Checkmate

The town house was large and would have been considered quite luxurious back in the 1970s with four bedrooms, an office, a library, and marble floors. But the furnishings and decor were outdated and badly in need of an update. It wasn't nearly up to the godfathers' usual lofty standards.

After over an hour of meticulous searching, one member of the Search Bloc began fidgeting with a big-screen projection television on the floor next to a built-in wooden wall unit and closet in the master bedroom. When Ruben saw the officer struggling, he walked over to assist and pushed the TV aside. His heart raced. "Guys! I found something!" he yelled, his voice echoing throughout the town house. He stood and stared at his discovery in awe and disbelief. What he'd found was a *caleta*.

Caletas—hidden rooms and secret spaces designed specifically to hide valuables and, more importantly, valuable people, like Gilberto—were rare, but they had long served as critical hiding places for cartel leaders. They were, in a way, the stuff of legend.

More police ran over to help, eager to see. Inside the closet was a small passageway leading to a hidden room, and everyone held their breath as Ruben and the officer cautiously, silently peered in. No one moved, and the only thing anyone could hear was the faint, muted sound of someone breathing heavily. Little did they know that that someone was Gilberto José Rodríguez Orejuela.

It was not how a godfather wanted to be found. Panting, nervous, afraid, and with money scattered across the floor of the *caleta*, he was clutching a 9mm handgun in each hand and couldn't hide the fear in his eyes. He had no idea what was going to happen next, nor was he used to not being the one in control. But it was obvious that the Chess Player had no moves left. As Colombian special operators leveled their rifles at him, he stared back, frozen. After what seemed like an eternity, he slowly put down his weapons and whispered, *"No me maten! Yo soy un hombre de paz!"* ("Don't kill me! I'm a man of peace!")

For everyone outside of this sleepy cul-de-sac, it was just 3:45 p.m. on a sunny Friday afternoon. For us, it was checkmate.

Gilberto was quickly removed from the *caleta* and escorted to the living room as the town house erupted in cheers of "Viva Colombia!" General Serrano stood by and watched it unfold, beaming. Before long, though, the maelstrom of activity spiraled out of control. What seemed like a

The arrest of Gilberto Rodríguez.

hundred people had crammed into the town house, with officers vying for the best angle from which to take pictures. After suffering through the torrent of blinding flashbulbs, Gilberto was whisked outside, where police officials secured him in the back of an armored vehicle and headed to the air force base, accompanied by a huge police escort. An equally large group then accompanied Gilberto back to Bogotá aboard a police aircraft with General Serrano there to oversee the victory lap, the same self-satisfied smile on his face.

It was no exaggeration, then or now, to call it a historic day. The government of Colombia, along with the US, had *finally* dealt a damning blow against the Cali cartel. A massive press conference was held in Bogotá at CNP headquarters to announce the arrest of one of the most wanted men in the world, though it was far more reminiscent of a circus than a serious news briefing.

Confetti rained down from the top of the five-story building as hundreds of people lined the circular balconies and hallways and cheered while overlooking a makeshift stage. Everyone was angling for a glimpse of Gilberto, who sat somber and silent in the center of the drama. It was an undeniably theatrical, almost poignant scene: Gilberto surrounded by a horde of police officials, humbled and handcuffed, all eyes on him. He wasn't acting, but he knew that when the curtain finally fell, the show would truly be over.

The news of Gilberto's arrest spread rapidly and was instantly picked up by media outlets across the globe:

"This is a great triumph for the Colombian police and the government of Colombia," US Ambassador Myles Frechette declared.

Principal Deputy Assistant Secretary of State for Latin America and the Caribbean Michael Skol added: "We are delighted with the news, because Mr. Rodríguez Orejuela is one of the most important drug-trafficking bosses."

And, finally, President Samper himself: "This is a great victory for the Colombian nation," he said at a packed news conference. "This is the beginning of the end of the Cali cartel, and we will not give up until this scourge is completely eradicated."

That Friday night, we all took a cue from Prince and partied back in Bogotá like it was 1999, though we still had four years to go. We even got a standing ovation from the embassy staff when we walked into the popular bar Mister Ribs. They crowded the room and raised their glasses to us as we took in every second of the evening.

The two DEA assets directly responsible for Gilberto's arrest split the 1.500'000.000 CP reward (over $1.8 million USD), and their identities remained secret. We were proud we'd pushed so hard for the rewards— once again, throwing money at a problem had helped solve it. It was a lesson the cartel knew well, except this time it worked out in our favor, not theirs.

But the government's triumph came with a different kind of cost. Less than twenty-four hours after Gilberto's arrest, a massive bomb ripped through a music festival in Medellín at Parque de San Antonio, killing twenty-nine people and wounding over two hundred. The attack occurred just one block from a police station, and many speculated that it was likely the Cali cartel seeking retribution for the arrest of one of the godfathers— the eldest godfather, no less. Others suggested the bombing had all the

Chris (right) and Jerry Salameh receiving Colombia's Distinguished Service Medal from CNP Director General Rosso Jóse Serrano for the arrest of Gilberto Rodríguez.

earmarks of a leftist subversive group, like the FARC. The police and public braced themselves for yet another onslaught of violence.

In the end, it didn't matter who was responsible: with the celebrations over, the entire country was once again on edge. Partying was replaced by praying, with citizens everywhere begging God to not let their lives go back to the 24/7 fear and panic. The Colombian people were brave, but they were also exhausted. So, just as they'd done during the Escobar era, and just as they'd done for decades, they hoped for the best—but prepared for the worst.

CHAPTER 16

Hunting Don Miguel

*"To hunt successfully, you must know your ground,
your pack, and your quarry."*

—K. J. PARKER [TOM HOLT],
British Novelist

WITH GILBERTO FINALLY IN PRISON, the focus shifted to his brother Miguel, CEO and chairman of the board of Cocaine Inc. The second eldest continued his micromanagement of day-to-day operations of the global enterprise with leaders of Mexican and European crime families, along with cell heads in the United States. He also maintained regular contact with his most trusted operatives and key sources—officials so important and so corrupt they were known only to him.

Back in early June while we were pursuing Gilberto, Dave and I were contacted by a known intermediary and told that an unidentified source wanted to meet with us. The source was headed to Bogotá and wanted to meet with US agents in the northern part of the city before departing.

When we arrived and saw the source, we immediately recognized him as a close associate of Miguel's and trusted officer in the cartel. It was another sign that the rewards were proving too hard to resist, even for those in the inner circle.

The asset was nervous. "I think I know where Don Miguel is staying," he said. "He's gone back to his pool home, near the Versailles neighborhood. But I need a few more days to confirm."

That was fine with us—we were in no hurry. We were still in the middle of our intensive surveillance operation of Flaco.

Dave and I didn't let on, but we knew the house he spoke of. We'd raided that mountainside Versailles mansion with the police Search Bloc once before and come up empty, though all signs had pointed to Miguel being there that day. Our intel was good, so we assumed he'd been tipped off before our arrival.

Three days after Gilberto's arrest, Dave and I were back in Cali hunting Don Miguel when our new asset called from Bogotá. He told us that Miguel was at the Versailles mansion, his presence having been confirmed by a cartel lawyer who'd just been there for a meeting. Jerry and Ruben raced to meet with the source and gather some last-minute details, then flew to Cali to meet up with me and Dave. Pedro and several members of Colonel Barragán's special intel group were also in tow. We wanted to use the exact same team from the Gilberto operation.

We may have been on a roll, but Dave and I knew we still had plenty to learn when it came to keeping up with the leaders of the world's most powerful drug syndicate. We'd only been on their trail for a year, and it had taken all of our time and energy, but we were finally figuring out ways to circumvent the Cali KGB. Still, when it came to the Versailles mansion, we had to admit we needed the help of the Search Bloc's special operators and assault force—only they could handle what the mission required. In the meantime, the rest of our team would surveil the house and wait for the Search Bloc to arrive, just as we had with Gilberto.

The next morning, Dave and I met with Colonel Murcia and Captain Buitrago to coordinate the operation. The two were still fuming over the fact that Colonel Barragán and his team had been involved in the arrest of Gilberto, but for me and Dave, that was old news. We were focused on moving forward.

We briefed the embedded prosecutor and agreed on an early-afternoon raid. Dave was upbeat, but I was leery of using the Search Bloc, keeping me from being fully confident. When Dave asked me what was on my mind, I was honest as always. "Knowing where these guys are, then launching an operation that successfully captures them are two completely different things," I said.

On June 13, we left the Search Bloc in two covered trucks packed with Colombian special forces. The Search Bloc had received a significant upgrade since General Serrano took command, and they'd transformed into a truly formidable action element. When we arrived, everyone's adrenaline was racing. We nearly jumped out of the vehicles before they'd stopped.

The palatial home looked exactly the same as it had last fall, but with a few subtle differences, including an elaborate call-forwarding system with at least twenty-five telephone lines. There were also subtle signs of a recent hasty retreat: there was the lingering, unmistakable odor of cigarette smoke, but the two maids (the only occupants present) didn't smoke. The maids said that the owner was out of town, but the refrigerator was fully stocked with fresh food. There were damp towels on the chairs next to the swimming pool in the courtyard, but neither of the maids seemed the type to be cleaning the house in a bikini.

It was obvious that Miguel had *just* been there—or, worse, still was, hidden away somewhere in another secret compartment or *caleta*. But we trusted Barragán's team, as much as we trusted any unit in Colombia, and they swore to us that no one had arrived or left the house on their watch. We continued to search the mansion for over an hour, to no avail. Then, right as we started to give up hope, we discovered something that jolted us back to life.

While taking one more minute to scour the ground-level master bathroom, Dave gently tugged on a small towel hook on the wall. At this point, most of our adrenaline was gone—along with our expectations. Dave tugged on the hook again and, to our shock, the hook pulled a tile open and away from the wall—just like opening the door of a medicine cabinet.

"What the hell?" Dave said.

"Guys, get in here! We found something!" I yelled.

Jerry brought a chair in from the kitchen so we could step up and peek inside. As soon as we did, the mystery of Miguel's whereabouts was solved.

Behind the wall was a small void, with another door opening directly to the mountains behind the house. Right outside was a path leading to a long drainage tunnel and away from the mansion. It was both a makeshift caleta *and* an escape corridor, and it was, of course, how Miguel had managed to make such an efficient and speedy retreat before we arrived.

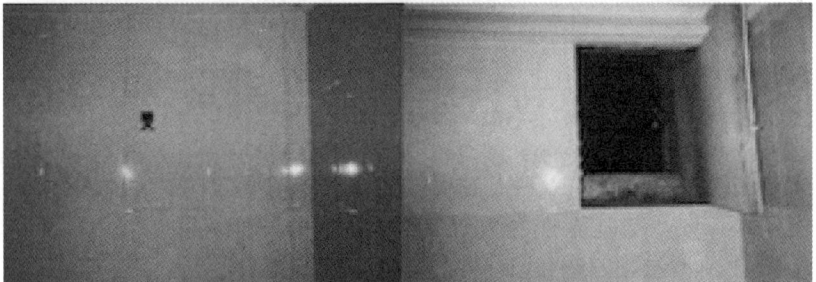

(Top left) *Outside view—Chris* (right) *and Dave* (left) *inside the escape room/Caleta at Versailles Mansion.* (Top right) *Inside view—Escape room/Caleta at Versailles Mansion towel hook.* (Bottom) *Side-by-side view (closed verses open)*

Jerry shook his head in disbelief. "You gotta be kidding me," he said. I took a deep breath and closed my eyes, hoping that when I opened them again, I'd find that this was just a nightmare. It was another punch to the gut, and I didn't know how many more of them I could take.

Eventually we left, knowing we'd missed our best opportunity yet to arrest Don Miguel. Dave and I fumed over the futility of our actions thus far and discussed what we could do differently. We debated using another reactionary force—not that one existed—but more than anything, we expressed our need for an inside man, an asset close enough to the godfathers that they could provide real-time actionable intelligence. One thing was for sure: we needed to change our entire modus operandi, period.

If there was a silver lining to be found in this latest letdown, it was the crash course we got about *caletas*. As we learned, both Gilberto's and the one at the Versailles mansion were rudimentary at best when compared to the ones we heard about from several cooperating Operation Cornerstone defendants. They described elaborate, highly sophisticated hidden rooms, hydraulic vaults, and intricately designed secret spaces the godfathers had constructed in order to hide themselves and/or sensitive materials and documents.

The next day, our asset called to confirm that Miguel had, in fact, been tipped off. He'd left less than an hour before we arrived, and it was obvious that the leak had come from the Search Bloc. The source was disappointed (the leak had cost him a hefty reward, after all), but he still had critical information to offer: Miguel had moved to a town house owned by Salomón Prado Cuero, a.k.a. "Chalo," a wealthy Colombian and trusted financial officer for the cartel. The townhome was located in Ciudad Jardín, which meant we'd be facing the same obstacles as last time.

Apparently, Miguel was using Prado's residence for only a few days, so we needed to act quickly. He was reportedly livid about having to leave the Versailles pool home—out of all his extravagant homes, it was perhaps his favorite. He also resented the fact that his "work" was interrupted—at the time of the raid he was busy trying to legalize his family's economic empire, using trusted couriers to secretly send and receive sensitive documents to government officials.

Property searches revealed two adjacent townhomes owned by Prado in Ciudad Jardín. The residences were located on another small cul-de-sac (this one more crowded than Gilberto's), making fixed surveillance nearly impossible. Once again, the townhomes were incredibly close to our own safe house. We'd definitely picked the right neighborhood.

We conducted a series of discreet drive-bys and saw several people arriving periodically at one of the townhomes clutching briefcases and folders. That was it.

On June 16, the source indicated that Miguel was planning to leave the town house within the next twenty-four hours. As we saturated the main roads nearby, Colonel Barragán requested assistance from the Search Bloc and their assigned prosecutor to raid the property. After a police helicopter arrived forty-five minutes later to provide aerial support, we hit the Prado townhomes in search of Miguel.

In Colombia, it's standard practice for a prosecutor to eschew any use of force when executing a search warrant, instead opting to knock on the front door and wait until someone opens it. Sometimes, that took a couple of minutes—other times as long as it took for the godfather to access his secret compartment. The practice made us crazy, but the fact was, they didn't want to damage expensive properties without compelling evidence a capo was there.

As soon as the team entered the town house, they saw Miguel Rodríguez's fourth wife, Marta Lucía Echeverry, Carlos Millán (a.k.a. "Mario," one of Miguel's drivers), and two maids. The prosecutor wouldn't allow me and Dave to enter the residence initially because, as he told us, he "didn't want such an obvious American presence inside." We stayed outside, hidden behind the dark tinted windows of our vehicle.

It was obvious to the team that they were in the right place, and excitement surged throughout the group. Everyone fanned out and started searching the townhome, which was even more luxurious on the inside, with ornate furnishings, artwork, and a large Jacuzzi.

Shortly thereafter, a few of the Search Bloc troops discovered a call-forwarding device in the kitchen (similar to the one we found at the Versailles home), along with handwritten notes and papers addressed to Don Miguel. They continued knocking on floors and walls, moving furniture and bookcases around, hunting for traps and hidden rooms. In the master bedroom they found clothing perfectly matching Miguel's five-foot eight-inch frame, along with prescription bottles of medicine labeled "MRO." Evidence of Miguel's presence was everywhere, but there was still no sign of the godfather himself.

After deeming the new evidence sufficiently compelling, the prosecutor allowed Dave and me to join the search. We covered every single square inch of the house, but no Miguel. Then, from the other side of the room, I heard Jerry mutter under his breath, *Holy* shit." He was staring at something in his palm. "Take a look at this."

In his hand was a cassette tape marked "llamadas" ("calls"). It was a shocking discovery: an actual recording of incoming calls to the police Search Bloc, including ones made to the US Embassy by some of the rotating DEA agents assigned to the base. At last, we had incontrovertible evidence of what we'd always suspected—the Search Bloc was a sieve and completely, irrefutably infiltrated by the Cali KGB.

After almost two hours of nonstop searching, the prosecutor called it a day, convinced Miguel wasn't there or had left before our arrival. The four DEA agents disagreed, but in Colombia the prosecutor has the final word, period. Frankly, we were lucky he'd even allowed us to enter the townhome in the first place. So, for the second time in a week, we left with our tail between our legs, abandoning an operation thanks to the work of corrupt officials at the Search Bloc. How many times could this happen?

It was the final straw. Dave and I knew we could *never* use the police Search Bloc again, and we'd have to completely overhaul our strategy and tactics. The only silver lining was that the Cali KGB had chalked up the raid to the fact that the DEA was tailing the couriers Miguel was using—so our asset was safe—but he'd also grown tired of risking his life for nothing. What good would $1.8 million do him if he wasn't alive to enjoy it?

We could hardly blame him—we were tired, too. We'd come so close, but here we were, back at square one with no choice but to start the entire operation over. Again.

CHAPTER 17

The Domino Effect

"For every action, there is an equal and opposite reaction."
—SIR ISAAC NEWTON

COLOMBIA'S HISTORIC ARREST OF GILBERTO RODRÍGUEZ was a staggering setback for the cartel. The Cali KGB security network had been seen as invulnerable, and now that image was shattered. Miguel railed against his team, demanding answers. How could this happen? In Gilberto's opinion, it all stemmed from one event: the raid on Pallomari's office almost a year ago. The evidence recovered, along with Pallomari's subsequent ill-advised statements to Colombian prosecutors, paved the way for everything that followed.

Pallomari was the highest-ranking non-Colombian officer in the cartel and officially a fugitive from US justice as a result of his indictment in the Operation Cornerstone case just days before Gilberto's arrest. Far worse for him, he was now a major liability to Cali. With Gilberto behind bars, the last thing the godfathers could risk was letting Pallomari fall into the hands of the DEA. An order for his execution was issued, but again the brothers found themselves having less control than usual. They knew that if Pallomari was arrested before they could get to him, he'd buckle and cooperate with the DEA. The evidence he could provide was more than just damaging—it was ruinous. And if he'd talked in Colombia, imagine what he might spill to American agents if he was arrested and extradited to the US?

It was Gilberto who put out the hit, dictating the order from the confines of his prison cell. Pallomari had made mistakes, to be sure, but he wasn't a total fool. He'd gone into hiding months earlier, burying himself deep underground and cutting all contact with his wife and two children.

Suddenly, the godfathers found themselves struggling to defend themselves on multiple fronts. Miguel summoned his personal security chief, Jorge Salcedo, along with César Yusti, one of the cartel's most efficient assassins, and made his order clear: find Pallomari immediately and eliminate him.

Miguel also tasked the cartel's head of security, Mario del Vasto, with conducting an internal security review to determine exactly how the DEA was able to get to Gilberto. He was also instructed to prepare several safe houses for immediate occupancy and change all security call signs and radio frequencies.

Miguel trusted the two men implicitly. Del Vasto was a highly decorated army officer who'd gained prominence for his years of service fighting the FARC and other left-wing insurgent groups. He was an expert in counterintelligence, counterguerrilla tactics, and force protection. He was also a feared member of Cali's vaunted military wing, the group responsible for all sanctioned cartel assassinations as well as managing the network of spies who infiltrated most of Colombia's security services. It was del Vasto who'd recruited his old army reserve buddy Salcedo into the cartel over six years ago. Their shared history, proficiency, and mutual devotion to their jobs made them a formidable team.

On June 14, del Vasto called for a meeting of cartel security personnel at the corporate headquarters of Club Deportivo América de Cali, the prized soccer team owned by the Rodríguez Orejuela brothers. Salcedo was invited but declined, deeming it unwise to gather in such an open area. Besides, he had more urgent matters to attend to—namely, keeping Miguel safe from the relentless assaults by the Search Bloc and DEA, not to mention helping locate Pallomari.

It was another sweltering afternoon in southern Cali, so del Vasto and the group sought shade near the bleachers on one of América's practice fields. They discussed Gilberto's arrest, reviewed recent intelligence reports and photos of potential locations government security forces planned to raid, and pored over lists of cartel telephone numbers (the ones "authorized" for interception)—information for which they had their many government spies to thank.

Suddenly, an army team—one not connected to the Search Bloc at the 3rd Brigade—burst onto the scene, there to respond to an "anonymous" call reporting the presence of "suspicious, armed men" at the complex. Incredibly, it was the exact same military unit del Vasto had commanded years earlier.

As the small group swept in and started to investigate, del Vasto's team immediately began destroying the confidential reports and photos. Some of the men even attempted to eat the paperwork—anything to get rid of the highly sensitive material—but there was just too much of it. The scene turned chaotic, and the military unit arrested del Vasto and all ten of his security operatives. They were charged with a number of crimes, including espionage, due to their unauthorized possession of highly restricted and confidential information.

Because of del Vasto's arrest, Salcedo found himself on the receiving end of an unexpected promotion, going from the number two man to the cartel's head of security in a matter of minutes. Some in the cartel questioned the situation, as did Dave and I. Just how was it that a small military unit—a unit not responsible for counternarcotics operations—became involved in del Vasto's arrest in the first place? Any enforcement actions taken against the cartel were always carried out only by either the police or the army Search Bloc. It wasn't adding up.

Over the past year, Dave and I had relied on three general truths: (1) There's no such thing as a coincidence, (2) everything happens for a reason, and (3) nothing is ever exactly what it seems. All three were in play with this latest development. We knew something was off.

June 1995 was shaping up to be the most productive month yet since Colombia's pursuit of the Cali cartel "officially" began shortly after Escobar's death in December 1993. Gilberto's arrest had created a domino effect, and it was amazing to think that the discovery of one small *caleta* had snowballed into the potential unraveling of Cali's entire infrastructure.

Five days after the arrest of del Vasto and his men, Henry Loaiza (a.k.a. "El Alacrán" or "the Scorpion") surrendered to government officials at a military installation in Bogotá. Loaiza, largely seen as the cartel's minister of war, was also considered the number seven man in the Cali Mafia ranks. By the time he turned himself in he had a $625,000 reward on his head.

Long wanted in Colombia on terrorism charges, Loaiza was accused of being involved with right-wing paramilitary groups along with a number of complicit Colombian police and military elements. The motley crew was accused of the gruesome torture and eventual murder of 107 people (with over 200 more people also killed between 1988 and 1994) in the town of Trujillo, during which many of the bodies were dismembered and tossed into the Cauca River, where they floated downstream and were seen by the town's residents. It was an especially cruel (and effective) gesture, designed to ensure that any left-wing guerrilla supporters in the area understood what they were up against. Loaiza was also a suspect in the June 10 bombing in Medellín that killed 29 people and wounded over 200.

Five days after Loaiza's surrender, the cartel's number five man, Victor Patiño, also surrendered to Colombian authorities in Bogotá. Patiño, a former police officer, was known as the "King of Buenaventura" due to his control over the western port city from which the cartel shipped thousands of tons of cocaine. Both Patiño and Loaiza told authorities that they'd surrendered because of the extreme pressure Colombian security forces had exerted on them and their families. Coupled with the huge rewards out on both their heads, they gave in.

While the surrenders were significant, many in Washington expressed concern over the potential terms. Both men were vicious criminals with little to no regrets, but their choice to turn themselves in, by law, allowed for leniency. Drug traffickers who voluntarily surrendered were eligible for significant benefits: up to a one-third sentence reduction for the sheer act of surrendering, and up to another third off their sentence for cooperating with government officials.

Those who chose to surrender routinely enlisted an army of savvy attorneys who negotiated sweetheart deals with the government. The deals often enabled them to keep the majority of their vast fortunes and serve minimal sentences in comfortable, unsecure prisons. Typically, they'd serve five or six years, maybe less, then be released and allowed to return back to their old lives—and money.

This injustice was not lost on the US government, and they continually pressured Colombian officials to reinstitute the extradition of drug kingpins. Extradition was the *one* thing drug traffickers feared more than anything—including death—and the fight against it was one of the impetuses behind the war Escobar and the Extraditables had waged against their government. When Escobar's was quoted as saying "better a tomb in Colombia than a jail cell in the United States," he was saying it in earnest.

Along with the relentless heat, June had ushered in a heightened level of pressure. But things were shifting in a more hopeful direction, due in large part to the sustained enforcement activity throughout the Valle del Cauca and the advertised, hefty bounties in play. The domino effect had produced some impressive results: three of the top seven cartel leaders were now behind bars, and the Cali KGB had suffered the devastating loss of eleven security operatives. But Dave and I were still restless: three godfathers remained at large, and we couldn't assume they'd just follow the leads of their two former colleagues and give themselves up. Besides, we could barely stomach the thought of them negotiating deals allowing them to keep their vast fortunes, run their empires from their cushy prison cells, and avoid accountability entirely. If we wanted the three remaining dominoes to fall, we had to make it happen ourselves.

CHAPTER 18

Down Goes Chepe

"Not everything is as it seems, and not everything that seems is."
—JOSÉ SARAMAGO,
Nobel Prize–Winning Novelist

CHEPE SANTACRUZ HAD BEEN LIKE A MEMBER of the Rodríguez Orejuela family for many years. A loyal friend since their preteens, he'd come a long way from his days of stealing cars and kidnapping for ransom. His ascent was swift, going from a small-time Colombian hood to veritable legend in the New York underworld. He was feared for his brutal and unpredictable nature and revered because of his drive and business savvy. He was the number three man in the Cali cartel and, like his three fellow godfathers, had billions of dollars to show for it.

Each of the Cali leaders managed their own fortunes, and each had their own ideas about how to do so. While one might err on the side of simplicity, another would prefer more complicated arrangements, requiring professional financial advisors and economists. Preferences aside, the three fundamental stages of money laundering remained the same: *placement*, getting illicit proceeds into the financial system; *layering*, moving the money constantly to disguise its true origin; and *integration*, investing the clean money back into the legitimate economy.

With so much dirty cash to supervise, each man had to first conceal the origins of the money, then find a way to reintegrate it back into the system.

Chepe's European money-laundering operation was a textbook example of how to do that and do it well.

In 1985, prior to Panamanian authorities fully dissolving the First InterAmericas Bank, millions of Cali drug dollars needed to be moved. Chepe's financial sensei, Edgar Alberto García Montilla, along with José Franklin Jurado Rodríguez, a Harvard-educated Colombian economist who helped establish the Cali Stock Exchange, were tasked with establishing new European money-laundering gateways to "clean and legitimize" the money.

In the mid to late 1980s, Panama was seen as a money-laundering haven and considered a country of primary concern by the US government. To disguise the transfer of money from the high-risk jurisdiction, millions of dollars in cash were converted into money orders. Those orders were then wire transferred to European financial institutions—over 135 accounts in seventy banks in at least nine different countries. Cali's initial deposits ranged from $50,000 to over $1,000,000, with many of the accounts opened in the name of Santacruz's various mistresses and in-laws. Jurado maintained power of attorney over the accounts and continually transferred and shifted relatively low amounts of money between them to avoid suspicion.

Jurado also established a network of shell companies throughout Europe and began funding the new front companies by transferring money from the previously established accounts. He was then able to wire transfer money from shell company to shell company—not only in Europe, but also to myriad Santacruz accounts back in Colombia as well as in the United States. Once transferred to Colombia, the money was thoroughly laundered and Santacruz was able to integrate that fresh, "clean" money—tens of millions of dollars—back into the economy by investing it in commercial real estate and other residential properties. Chepe had chosen his gurus wisely.

But their scheme crashed and burned in June 1990 after the arrest of both Jurado and García in Luxembourg. The two men had been successfully wiretapped by law enforcement officials, and both were convicted and sentenced by a Luxembourg court in April 1992 to between four and five years each. Two years later, Jurado and García were extradited to Brooklyn, New York, on drug-trafficking and money-laundering charges, all of which were linked back to Chepe's prolific New York cocaine operation. In April 1996, Jurado and García both pled guilty and were sentenced to seven and a half years and ten years in prison, respectively. All told, $46 million of Santacruz's personal stash was seized and recovered in nine different European countries as well as Panama.

Chepe was the least gentlemanly of the Gentlemen of Cali, particularly when it came to his appearance. Standing almost six feet tall, he was burly, gruff, and looked more like a professional wrestler than a Mafia don. He usually dressed in overalls or jeans, forgoing the elegant suits and ties the other godfathers preferred. Despite his craggy appearance, Chepe was charming and affable (although unsophisticated) and loved to party, make friends, and tease them relentlessly—including Miguel. He coined the nickname "Limón" for Miguel, saying he always had a sour expression on his face as if he'd just sucked on a lime. No one else in the cartel would *dare* think of mocking Miguel like that—or at all.

But Chepe had a dark side. He could become extremely violent and lash out in a matter of seconds and, once provoked, would go out of his way to antagonize the poor soul who'd made the mistake of wronging him.

Early on, Chepe started buying real estate en masse: luxury homes, apartments, ranches, anything he saw that he liked. The more ostentatious, the better. He had no problem pissing people off—in fact, he relished it. If he had to choose a motto, it would be "screw you."

In 1979, Chepe was denied membership into Cali's most prestigious club, the Club Colombia, where he wanted to have his daughter's quinceañera. However, his reputation as a drug trafficker associated with the Cali cartel preceded him. When he heard about the refusal, Chepe was so incensed that he obtained the architectural plans of the club's complex and had an exact replica of it built in the Cañasgordas neighborhood in southern Cali—the most expensive part of the city, no less. His replica turned into a sprawling facility on fourteen acres of prime real estate and mirrored the swanky social club in every single way, right down to the massive pool with one small, distinguishing detail: he had his initials (JSL) painted in black on the porcelain pool floor, one final little fuck you for good measure.

Chepe had many grievances, but the constant thorn in his side was the fact that the US continued to meddle in Colombia's affairs. He was so enraged by what he considered to be their unwelcome intrusion that he decided to openly mock what he referred to as the "imperialistic American government" by starting construction on *another* even loftier replica: his very own White House, which Chepe coined "La Casa Blanca." At more than thirty thousand square feet, he wanted to show his contempt for the US in as public a way as possible, potential repercussions be damned. Frankly, Dave and I would have loved to have seen Chepe's completed reproduction, but he never got the chance to finish it. Still, we never tired of driving by the partially constructed Casa Blanca.

In 1992, Chepe was implicated in the murder of Manuel de Dios Unanue, a Cuban American journalist and former editor in chief of *El Diario La Prensa*, New York's largest Spanish-language newspaper. De Dios was lauded for his excellent reporting on corruption and crime and had published the acclaimed book *The Secrets of the Medellín Cartel*. He'd also written a series of articles about José Santacruz and the Cali cartel's drug-trafficking and money-laundering operations in the city. The articles made an enemy of Chepe, who contracted a team of assassins to kill de Dios.

On March 11, 1992, a Colombian gunman shot de Dios twice in the head inside Mesón Asturias, a Spanish restaurant in Jackson Heights, Queens, marking the very first time a journalist was killed on American soil by Colombian drug traffickers. Three people were ultimately convicted for their participation in de Dios's murder.

In September 1992, Chepe's sister, Cristina Santacruz, was kidnapped by the VI front of the FARC, who demanded $12 million for her release. Chepe being Chepe, he flatly refused, vowing never to pay one single penny for his sister's release. Instead, he chose to kidnap Amparo Torres Victoria, the sister of Pablo Catatumbo, an important FARC leader who was in charge of peace negotiations with the Colombian government. After nearly three months of negotiations, both sides agreed to a hostage exchange. Finally, in January 1993, Cristina Santacruz and Amparo Torres were both released, with no ransoms ever being paid on either side.

Dave and I always thought that if any of the Cali godfathers chose to go out in a blaze of glory, it would be Chepe. His larger-than-life persona and impetuous nature made him the obvious choice for the type to go down and go down hard.

Down Goes Chepe

In late June, Dave and I spoke to an asset in Cali who claimed Chepe was in Bogotá with his attorneys, negotiating a potential surrender with Colombian government officials. While we thought it sounded more like cartel disinformation than anything else, we decided to pursue it nonetheless.

Dave and I had already launched scores of operations in an attempt to arrest Chepe over the past year, but he'd always managed to evade detection, remaining as highly elusive as he had been in New York. He reportedly owned over two thousand properties throughout Colombia, including lakefront mansions in Lago Calima, ranches in both Cali and Medellín, and countless apartments scattered across the Valle del Cauca. He was adept at playing the invisible man, a phantom who could be anywhere at any time, including Bogotá.

While Dave headed off to the capital to follow up on the Chepe lead, I stayed in Cali with Mike to focus on our next major undertaking, a covert surveillance operation with a Colombian Navy–vetted intel team. Based out of Buenaventura, the team was brand new and was further supported by a special operations group—the equivalent of US Navy SEALs.

When Dave discussed the recent Chepe intel with Generals Serrano and Montenegro, neither was surprised—they, too, had information that Chepe was in Bogotá. In mid-June, Chepe reached out to a journalist to help mediate his surrender to Colombian authorities. Although nothing ever materialized, General Serrano said the police continued to spot-check several locations Chepe was suspected of frequenting.

Dave had a gut feeling that this was all some kind of premeditated plan, that Chepe would waltz into police headquarters one day out of the blue, bellowing, "Here I am!" But that wasn't Chepe's style. Then again, as we'd learned so many times before, not everything is as it seems.

On the evening of the Fourth of July, 1995, Dave attended a large embassy function at the ambassador's residence in Bogotá to celebrate America's independence. Sometime around 8:00 p.m., he got a call from one of his police contacts: Chepe had just been arrested at Carbón de Palo, our favorite steak house in northern Bogotá. Dave was shocked: Carbón de Palo? That wasn't some private, little-known speakeasy; it was a hugely popular and crowded restaurant. Why would Chepe risk it?

Things began to make sense when we heard that General Serrano had instructed plainclothes police officials to check out high-end clubs and restaurants in Bogotá's northern neighborhoods, knowing that Chepe indulged only in the very best steak, whiskey, and wine. When one of the officers walked into Carbón de Palo and surveyed the room, he spotted the godfather at a table with three other men in the back of the restaurant.

The officer rushed to call General Serrano, who, coincidently, lived just a few blocks away. The general hastily dispatched his small personal security detail to assist—time was of the essence, and they were the closest available force.

Once assembled, the officers cautiously approached Santacruz's table. Voice trembling, one of the men nervously told the Cali don that he wouldn't be able to finish his perfectly grilled steak. "Um, also," he said, "you're under arrest."

Then Chepe did something no one expected: he complied. After he was ushered out of the restaurant and into a waiting car, a convoy of police vehicles drove wildly through the city streets, rushing to transport their prized prisoner to CNP headquarters.

It was a scenario so implausible it left us bewildered: just like that, the number three man in the Cali cartel had gone down without a fight, without even so much as one word of protest. It was literally the *last* thing Dave and I would ever have expected from Chepe.

Back at the ambassador's residence, Dave hung up, raced out of the party, and called me en route to police headquarters. "Are you sitting down? The police just nabbed Chepe in Bogotá!" he said. "I'm on my way to see him now."

"You're kidding me," I replied. "Two down, two to go!"

Once in custody, Chepe was thrust in front of a mob of reporters and photographers, put on display, and showcased like an Area 51 alien just as Gilberto had been before him. Both the US *and* Colombia celebrated the July 4 holiday, but for the latter it now took on greater significance: the arrest of another godfather. The police and General Serrano were on a roll, and President Samper and Defense Minister Botero were both quick to laud their efforts and applaud the government's recent successes to dismantle the cartel.

The Chepe Chasers, that hodgepodge group of investigators in New York who'd worked so tirelessly trying to arrest "Victor Crespo," also celebrated. Of course, many of them were disappointed that they weren't the ones slapping the cuffs on the godfather. After all, Chepe's trail of destruction was hardly limited to his native country: this was the man who'd eluded justice in the Big Apple for years, the man who'd left nothing but death and despair in his wake.

His legacy in New York was a devastating one. It was Chepe who'd flooded the city with cocaine since the early 1970s, and the lives he destroyed—and took—were countless. He took pleasure in conspiring to kill anyone who dared challenge or threaten him, just as he did with journalist Manuel de Dios Unanue. Chepe Santacruz had been the Chasers' unicorn, their equivalent of the 1967 Shelby GT500, or "Eleanor," in the Nicolas Cage film *Gone in 60 Seconds*. Now Chepe himself was gone—at least for the moment.

After Chepe's arrest, rumors circulated that he'd already negotiated a deal with Colombian authorities to surrender in the coming days. But by flagrantly socializing and dining in such a public atmosphere beforehand, he'd greatly embarrassed the government. So, the gossip mill speculated, Colombian officials reneged on their agreement and turned on Chepe, arresting him during what he thought would be one of his final meals as a free man.

Dave and I still don't know the truth behind the arrest or the days leading up to it. But to this day, we both find it highly unlikely that the man who'd evaded the DEA and New York investigators for a decade, the Colombian authorities for *another* decade, and whose elusiveness had haunted us every single day for the past year would suddenly, improbably, put on a show in such a popular restaurant. The situation managed to violate all three of my unwritten truths.

Regardless, Chepe was finally where he belonged: behind bars. But for how long? When he was younger, his friends called him "the Student." But Chepe was never one to actually learn a lesson—unless it was the hard way. Could he be expected to adjust to life in prison, where he'd have zero autonomy?

Meanwhile, more dominoes continued to fall. On July 7, Cali's chief facilitator and front man Julián Murcillo Posada was arrested in Bogotá by the national police on drug-trafficking and illicit-enrichment charges. Murcillo was a key member of Cali's political division and one of the primary liaisons between the godfathers and Colombian politicians. He was also a key piece in solving the Proceso 8.000 puzzle and the millions of cartel dollars that had flowed into the Samper campaign.

General Serrano didn't mince words when he summed up the events of the past few weeks: "I believe that with the capture of Gilberto, with the surrender of Henry Loaiza, Patiño Fómeque, the capture of Chepe Santacruz, and the capture last night of Julián Murcillo Posada, indisputably, there's very little left of the Cali cartel."

The day after Murcillo's arrest, Phanor Arizabaleta, the oldest of the main Cali traffickers and number six horseman of the cartel, surrendered in Bogotá to DAS officials. He was wanted on a number of charges, including drug trafficking, money laundering, murder, kidnapping, and extortion. Phanor claimed that he chose to surrender in large part because Chepe had suggested it—a statement that perhaps gave more credence to the theory that Chepe had indeed prearranged a surrender, though we could never prove it.

The events of the past month were overwhelming. No fewer than *five* of the seven most wanted drug traffickers in the world had either been arrested or had surrendered to Colombian authorities. And of those five, two were actual Cali founding members: Gilberto Rodríguez and José Santacruz. These were men who had spent years—decades, even— running a cartel that operated with near impunity, living out their lives of decadence and destruction without the slightest hint of reproach or recrimination. Now the lives they once knew were rapidly disintegrating before our very eyes.

But Cali wasn't done yet. Pacho Herrera was still at large, and Dave and I remained laser-focused on Don Miguel. The calculating and coldhearted man they called El Señor was the crown jewel, the ultimate prize, and the head of the serpent. And as long as Miguel remained a free man, the cartel still had a pulse.

CHAPTER 19

Field of Dreams

"I want to see two Americans I can easily identify
as being from the US Embassy."

—JORGE SALCEDO

IN AUGUST OF 1991, an enormous cargo shipment arrived at the Port of Miami, sent by a company called Tranca C.A. The cargo was made up of concrete fence posts and had shipped from the town of La Fria in western Venezuela to its Miami subsidiary, Tranca Inc. Nothing about it seemed suspicious— it was merely the latest of thirteen shipments Tranca Inc. had received from its parent company since August 1989. But on closer inspection, US Customs and DEA agents discovered that around two thousand of the posts had been hollowed out and packed with cocaine. In all, almost twelve tons of cocaine were found—the second-largest cocaine seizure in history, next to the Sylmar, California, seizure in September 1989. Both cargos, of course, were tied to the Cali cartel.

By mid-1995, Operation Cornerstone had resulted in the arrest of over seventy-five Cali operatives and the seizure of almost one hundred thousand pounds of cocaine. Just days before Gilberto Rodríguez's arrest, fifty-nine additional defendants were named in a second, superseding Racketeer Influenced and Corrupt Organizations Act (RICO) indictment against members of the cartel. The indicted ranged from the four godfathers themselves to the still-MIA accountant, Guillermo Pallomari, along

155

with other key operatives, facilitators, and lawyers. According to Kendall Coffey, the US attorney for the Southern District of Florida, Operation Cornerstone was "the single most significant prosecution in history against the Cali cartel."

After Gilberto's arrest in June, I contacted Operation Cornerstone lead case agents Lou Weiss (DEA) and Ed "Eddie" Kacerosky (Customs Service) in Miami. I knew there were several high-level cooperating defendants and sources that could provide significant intel regarding Miguel Rodríguez and asked if they would interview each and compile a list, including Miguel's key associates, the people he met regularly, and the locations he hid out in or frequented most often. I hoped that the information would enable us to tail a trusted Mafia member straight to El Señor's latest lair, just as we'd done with Gilberto.

A few weeks later, a map of Santiago de Cali and a two-part, seven-page list of handwritten notes arrived at the embassy, courtesy of Kacerosky. The notes were impressively comprehensive and included various names, locations, phone numbers, and map coordinates. Number one on Kacerosky's list of names: Ruben Dario "Jesus" Zapata, a.k.a. "Mateo." He was, as Kacerosky noted in bold, "Miguel's most frequently used chauffer." Surveilling him would almost certainly lead to something actionable.

After reading Kacerosky's report on Mateo, I felt like I already knew him. The physical description was perfect: "Approx. 5'5" tall, 160 lbs., with straight, black hair and a black moustache. He's in his 30's, light-skinned, and likes to wear sunglasses." Kacerosky also listed a pager number, a description of the cars he drove, and the address of a business he owned. The business, Kacerosky advised, was where we'd most likely find him.

But the real kicker was Kacerosky's final entry: "According to approx. six sources, Mateo crosses paths with Miguel three or four times a day." Dave and I were sold—we had our next target, and we were going to follow him directly to Miguel.

After the Prado raid, Dave and I pretty much severed all ties with the Search Bloc—save for the occasional liaison visit to the base—and accepted the fact that they'd never find Miguel, Pacho, or any major Cali operatives on their own—they were just too corrupt. We decided to work instead with a newly established Colombian Navy–vetted intel and commando team based in Buenaventura, almost eighty miles away. We'd been referred to them via our friend Mike, so we both felt confident about the new partnership. It was unlikely that the cartel was aware of this unit since they'd never been assigned to work in Cali or charged with hunting down any of the godfathers—at least, that's what we hoped. If true, it would give us another big advantage. We'd also abandoned our safe house in Ciudad Jardín for a new one procured by the navy unit just a few miles north of the old one.

As it turned out, the navy intel team was exactly what we needed: small, and made up of both intelligence officers and special operators. We still needed some sort of reactionary force to descend on Miguel's location (once we found it), but we had a plan for that, too.

After Chepe's arrest, Dave joined me back in Cali, where we prepared for the surveillance operation on Mateo set for the following morning. Though this area was the polar opposite of the last—set in a rough part of town—the location was just as difficult to surveil. To ensure that no one stood out in *this* neighborhood we had to dress down, not up. We had one of the navy officers set up camp across the street disguised as a homeless person, while another rented a vendor cart not far away, selling gum, cigarettes, and water. The two blended in perfectly.

The first day, we spied Mateo almost immediately and tailed him as he ran errands and visited local attractions throughout the city with an unidentified woman. His stops were so frequent and so diverse that at one point it felt like we'd tailed him everywhere in Cali *except* Miguel's secret location. After seven straight days of sitting in a car for twelve-plus hours and following Mateo all over the city and back again, we knew something was off. Reluctantly, Dave and I decided to put the lead on hold and revisit Kacerosky's list. What started out as our best lead to locate Miguel had turned out to be nothing more than a total wild-goose chase.

Turning our attention to lead number two, we pondered the idea of following Guillermo Villa Alzate, the former Colombian prosecutor assigned to the Inspector General's Office and current trusted attorney for Miguel Rodríguez. But the threat of another fruitless surveillance was unbearable. There had to be a better plan of attack.

I went back to the dossier, where Kacerosky's number three name, Cali cartel security operative Jorge Salcedo Cabrera, piqued my interest. An entry next to his name read, "After you get this list and kick it around down there, call me on Salcedo. I think there's a chance in concert with a buddy of his here we grabbed that we telephonically can convince Salcedo to help you locate Miguel. Call me on this before doing anything. Obviously, Salcedo's buddy will push this in the hope of receiving a sentence reduction."

This was promising. Dave and I knew that if Salcedo decided to cooperate, he'd be the perfect person to provide us with the real-time actionable information we'd so desperately needed.

In the early-morning hours of Wednesday, July 12, I called Kacerosky in Miami to get his thoughts on Salcedo possibly helping us go after Miguel. Salcedo's "buddy," as Kacerosky called him, was Joel Rosenthal, a former assistant US attorney and one of three former federal prosecutors indicted in Operation Cornerstone. After leaving government service, Rosenthal was accused of protecting the financial interests of the Cali cartel, among other things. During one of Rosenthal's trips to Cali, he struck up a friendship with Salcedo, who often served as a translator for the other, non-Spanish-speaking American lawyers. Eventually, Rosenthal pled guilty to a lesser charge of money laundering and was cooperating with the Cornerstone team in the hopes of having his sentence reduced.

Kacerosky told us that Rosenthal had received cryptic messages from Salcedo before, suggesting that "they might be able to help each other." He'd also left a Colombia-based pager number for Rosenthal to contact if interested. Given Salcedo's position, it was difficult to imagine who, aside from the godfathers themselves, could be more of a help. He could potentially be the single biggest threat to his bosses. Then again, he could also be the single biggest threat to us.

Later that Wednesday, Kacerosky and Rosenthal paged Salcedo, who returned the call from one of the public telephone banks in southern Cali. During the call, Salcedo, Rosenthal, and Kacerosky discussed Rosenthal's legal problems and the chance that Salcedo might step in to assist. Then they got to the real ask: Would he be interested in helping the US government locate and arrest Miguel Rodríguez? To their surprise, he was. Salcedo agreed to pass any actionable leads on Miguel's whereabouts to Kacerosky in Miami, who'd relay the information to me and Dave back on the ground in Cali.

After the conversation, Kacerosky was ecstatic. But when he called me to relay the good news and fill me in on the plan, I couldn't pretend to be as enthusiastic. Logistically, the plan was far from ideal, I told him: in the time it would take for Salcedo to pass information to Kacerosky in Miami—in addition to the time it would take for Kacerosky to get that information to me and Dave in Colombia—several hours could pass (and even more if we happened to be in Bogotá), robbing us of the critical prep time needed to coordinate any raid against El Señor. It was too complicated and time-consuming to be remotely feasible.

"The *only* way this will work is for me and Dave to have direct access to Salcedo. We need to talk to him in person—on the ground, in Cali," I told him. "There's no other way this will work." There was a pause, then Kacerosky said, "Let me call him back and see what he says."

While Dave and I waited for Kacerosky's return call, we discussed the odds of us getting our way (not good). We braced ourselves for the likelihood that Salcedo would tell Kacerosky that the idea was way too dangerous, and he wasn't going to risk his life by doing something as reckless as meeting two American DEA agents in Cali. And, honestly, we probably would have said the same. We also doubted that Kacerosky would relinquish control over such a valuable asset, a high-level Cali insider who'd miraculously just agreed to help us go after the biggest prize in law enforcement—a prize who also happened to be his boss. We weren't even sure Kacerosky would call Salcedo in the first place.

It wasn't that we distrusted Kacerosky. Dave and I knew him from our time in Miami—albeit not very well—and we'd worked on a few smaller cases together. But this was a unique situation, and the stakes were high. As the primary case agent for Operation Cornerstone, Kacerosky had built a reputation inside the Customs Service as an exceptional investigator, a bulldog whose iron-willed attitude had rubbed many within the DEA the wrong way. I'd always maintained a good relationship with him, but still, the odds that Kacerosky was simply going to "pass off" the potentially most valuable asset in his career—let alone to a rival organization—were pretty damn low.

About ten minutes later, my cell phone rang—it was Kacerosky. I put the call on speaker so that Dave could hear.

There was a short pause, and then we heard: "He said yes."

Dave and I looked at each other in shock. While most people might think it's common practice for law enforcement agencies to share information on investigations of mutual interest, it's far from the norm. This was a rare exception, brought about by the mutual respect shared between rival investigators who also considered themselves friends, coupled with the fact that Kacerosky wanted to do what was best for the investigation, regardless of who got the credit. Dave and I were sincerely grateful we'd gotten this chance to go after Miguel.

Before we hung up, Kacerosky provided us with the phone number to a location where Salcedo would be waiting for our call. Salcedo knew better than anyone how advanced the cartel's ability to intercept any telephone line in the country was, so in order to circumvent the Cali KGB, he chose a local beauty salon of a family friend, a place he *knew* his security and intelligence cohorts wouldn't be listening.

I called sometime around 9:00 a.m. and put the phone on speaker. Affecting my best Caleño accent, I said in Spanish, "May I speak with Jorge, please?"

"*Un segundo,*" an older gentleman responded. The next voice we heard from the other end of the telephone was subdued, even soft.

I continued on in Spanish, "I'm a friend of Eddie's. I think we should talk." Salcedo agreed, responding to me in perfect English.

"We're in Cali now," I said, speaking quickly and stressing the urgency before Salcedo could change his mind. "The sooner we can meet, the better."

He proposed we meet at three o'clock that afternoon at CIAT, the international research and developmental center located in the city of Palmira, seventeen miles east of Cali. I was horrified. "CIAT? There's no way!" Dave was waving his hands frantically in front of me, mouthing the word "NO!" over and over.

CIAT was a good hour away from our current location and essentially a no-man's-land, smack dab in the middle of nowhere. It was surrounded by miles and miles of sugarcane fields, making it the perfect spot for the Cali KGB to set up an ambush or trap for two unsuspecting American agents. We knew fairly little about Salcedo's background at that point, but what little we did know was more than enough to make us nervous.

In fact, at first glance, Salcedo's history didn't exactly paint the picture of a righteous man. We knew he'd been recruited by the cartel to help kill Pablo Escobar at Hacienda Nápoles and that he was an experienced counterintelligence operative. We also knew of his efforts to procure the five-hundred-pound bombs in El Salvador to drop on Escobar at La Catedral. We did recognize, however, that good men and women sometimes got caught up in bad circumstances. Regardless, it didn't exactly seem like the wisest idea to meet the main counterintelligence officer for the Cali cartel in a remote sugarcane field. The mere suggestion of it set off a series of alarm bells.

I countered by telling Salcedo that we needed to meet somewhere closer to the city, somewhere that provided us with a little more cover and protection. But Salcedo was adamant. "Impossible," he said. "If we're seen together, believe me, it won't end well for *either* of us."

My anxiety doubled and Dave looked at me, aghast. As I was still reeling from the image of the two of us being buried in a sugarcane field, Salcedo piled on, adding two additional conditions for the proposed meeting.

First, I'd have to come alone.

"No way is that happening," I said. "We *never* go anywhere in Cali by ourselves. I have to bring my partner."

Salcedo took a minute to think, then agreed to let Dave join me. But he wasn't budging when it came to his second requirement. "Okay about your partner, but no Colombians, under any circumstances," he said. "I want to see two Americans I can easily identify as being from the US Embassy. If I see anyone who even *looks* Colombian, I'm gone." He made it very clear that there was no room for further discussion. If we didn't comply, the deal was off.

I agreed, but didn't feel good about it. "Believe me, Jorge, you won't be disappointed when you see us," I said, grateful for the first time ever that we couldn't look more American than if we were wearing an actual American flag over our shoulders.

Salcedo told us he'd be at CIAT at 3:00 p.m. sharp, driving a gray Toyota Land Cruiser. He instructed us to park off one of the small gravel roads and that he'd find us. When he hung up, I looked over at Dave. "I cannot believe you just agreed to that," he said. "We have zero control of that location." I knew he was right.

As we drove back to our safe house, we discussed all the worst-case scenarios. Was it a trap, or an ambush? Was the cartel trying to provide disinformation to distract us? The more we speculated, the more nightmarish the possibilities became. Would we be kidnapped? Tortured? Killed? We had no idea what to expect but tried to ease our nerves by preparing for every conceivable scenario—inasmuch as that was even possible.

One thing Dave and I did know was that if we arrived before the cartel had a chance to deploy any surveillance assets, we'd be able to recognize a potential trap ahead of time. So we decided to get there several hours early to establish a defensive position—if one was even available—and reviewed communication plans and alternate rendezvous sites in case we got separated.

"Shit, we still need to call the embassy," Dave said, almost as an afterthought. "We have to get special approval before we can meet this guy. He's a *Tier 1* counterintelligence officer for the cartel, for God's sake."

"Look, the ambassador, the DEA, no one's going to authorize it," I said. "And that's why we're not even gonna ask."

It was risky, but Dave knew I was right. No one—not now, not ever—would approve a plan for the two of us to meet with such a high-level cartel intelligence operative, let alone in the middle of a remote sugarcane field an hour outside the city with no backup. It violated countless rules, not least the ambassador's most critical directive to never leave the police or military base without an escort. But Dave was hesitant.

"Think about it this way. If we meet Salcedo and he's serious and on board, then it's worth the risk." By that point I'd almost convinced myself.

Ultimately Dave gave in, and once back at the safe house we set about gathering up our gear. With no idea what to expect, we took everything we could: M4 carbines, extra magazines, our DEA-issued Glock 17 pistols with extra mags, backup weapons, radios, binoculars—anything that could fit into our go bags.

I could sense Dave was still concerned. "We should at least tell Mike where we're going…just in case," he said.

"Just in case what? Just in case they need to know where to look for the bodies?" I replied, only half joking.

"Yeah. Something like that," Dave said. Suddenly, the reality of what we were about to do hit us both. He was right—we did need to tell somebody where we were going, because the fact was that we may not be coming back. We went and grabbed Mike to take him out onto the apartment balcony where we'd have some privacy.

"Mike, listen: we're meeting a cartel intel officer out by CIAT later today," Dave said. "Can you cover us?"

"CIAT?" Mike blurted out. "Are you guys fucking crazy? I'm not going out there. And you'll never get approval for the meet anyway!" When Dave told him that the plan was already in motion and that we wouldn't be asking for permission—from anyone—Mike was appalled.

"A counterintelligence officer for the cartel? There's *zero* fucking chance of me going out there, and neither should you," Mike said. He began to plead with us. "Seriously, please rethink this. You guys are crazy."

But our minds were made up. Before leaving, we briefed Mike but didn't identify Salcedo, just in case. Mike agreed to establishing a communications plan so he could monitor our status and send in the calvary if we didn't respond as scheduled.

On the long drive to CIAT, Dave and I again reviewed our plan. We'd never been this far from the relative safety of our clandestine little refuge, nor had we ever met with such a high-ranking cartel officer. The more we talked, the more we both started to silently second-guess our decision.

As we drove down the deserted highway toward the city of Palmira, sugarcane fields were visible in all directions for miles. Eventually we turned onto a gravel road, headed toward CIAT, and saw that it was even more remote than we'd thought. The true epitome of the middle of nowhere.

Now almost noon, we parked near a dirt bank not far from where we pulled in—the only relatively high ground in the area. Then we grabbed our gear bags and rifles and trudged through the sugarcane field toward the nearby hill from where we'd be able to scope out the entire area. Dave identified potential escape-and-evasion routes and areas where we could hold up and defend ourselves—if it came to that.

It was brutally hot, and as we continued to scan the area for cartel security or hostile actors, we got more and more drenched in sweat. We still had three full hours until our meeting, but our anxiety was somewhat assuaged by the fact that we were in a good position: if anyone approached the area, we had the perfect vantage point to detect them for miles in any direction.

Sugar cane fields near CIAT in Palmira, Colombia, the site of secret meetings with Salcedo to plan the arrest of Cali godfather Miguel Rodríguez.

After about an hour, Dave looked over to me and said, "We shouldn't be out here." I kept silent. If I spoke, I knew I'd only end up agreeing. By then, I was almost as worried that we might pass out from heat stroke.

Finally, at exactly 3:00 p.m., a vehicle turned off the main highway onto the gravel road and headed toward us. It left a plume of dust in its wake as it drove, stopping at every intersecting road, presumably to give the driver time to look for our car. Looking through our binoculars, Dave ID'd the vehicle as a silver Toyota Land Cruiser with what looked to be one occupant inside. "Yeah, only one that we can see, anyway," I shot back.

I grabbed my bag and headed down to our car, parked next to the massive sugarcane. While I established a defensive position near the rear of the vehicle, Dave continued to watch and provide updates via radio as Salcedo's car made his way toward us.

Eventually, Salcedo spotted our car and turned toward it. He passed, made a U-turn, and parked on the opposite side of the road some seventy-five to a hundred feet away. By this time, Dave had worked his way down to join me at the rear of our car. We cautiously emerged from our concealed position in the sugarcane—using the rear of our car as cover—our M4s leveled on Salcedo in the driver's seat.

We were on high alert. If anything bad was gonna happen, this would be the time.

Salcedo exited his SUV and walked slowly in our direction. As he got closer, I saw something in his hand and yelled out, "That's close enough! Hands in the air!"

"I'm unarmed!" Salcedo yelled back.

I continued to aim my M4 at his chest, signaling for Dave to go check the SUV. My heart was pounding.

"It's clear, no other occupants," Dave said, then approached Salcedo from behind and did a full search. "He's clean."

So, he was alone, and he was unarmed. I started to breathe a bit more normally.

As Dave escorted Salcedo over to our vehicle he turned to him, smiling. "So, Jorge, are we American enough looking for you?" The three of us laughed, and just for one quick moment the tension was broken.

Dave directed Salcedo to the front passenger seat and settled into the back seat directly behind him, Glock out and in the ready position. I sat next to Salcedo, at the wheel.

Salcedo passed me what he'd been holding in his hand.

I looked down to see what I held in my palm: it was a Colombian national identification card. Our adrenaline rush shifted, and our anxiety turned into elation. "Now we're getting somewhere," I said to myself.

Our dream scenario had come true. We were officially meeting with Jorge Salcedo Cabrera.

CHAPTER 20

A Gold Mine

"If you want to find gold,
you've got to love the process of digging."

—ALAN MENKEN,
Composer and Pianist

ALTHOUGH WE WERE RELIEVED Salcedo had come unarmed and alone, Dave and I remained wary of a potential trap. Any number of disastrous scenarios could still unfold: corrupt police officials could drive up, arrest, and discredit us, or cartel assassins could arrive instead and make us *wish* we'd been arrested. We both kept looking over our shoulders, waiting for the other shoe to drop.

As for what Salcedo was thinking, we could read his face: it was obvious. He was relieved that we were, as promised, *very* American, but he was also clearly concerned about something else: our youth. For the record, we were seventeen years younger than Salcedo. And while Salcedo was far from old, he was a seasoned pro—the head of security and counterintelligence operations for the Cali KGB—and we were two kids, foreigners, barely out of our twenties, on a mission to bring down the most powerful man in all of Colombia. Also known as his boss.

Foolishly, we assumed he knew nothing about us or our backgrounds. When we started to introduce ourselves, he beat us to the punch. "Chris Feistl and Dave Mitchell," he said.

Of course he knew who we were. Thanks to the Search Bloc and the government spies on the cartel payroll—the ones under *his* command—he probably knew everything about us, right down to what we'd had for breakfast that morning. It was a deeply unnerving feeling.

"Thank you for meeting me. I wasn't sure you'd show," Salcedo said, with the same gentle voice I'd first heard over the phone. "You guys have balls, I'll give you that."

He wasn't at all what we'd expected. In fact, he was the exact opposite, especially given his title and history: he had that soft, dulcet voice, a humble demeanor, and even walked with a cautious gate as if trying not to make an impression at all. Everything about him was subtle, even his clothes: a long-sleeved, nondescript button-down shirt and slacks. We couldn't help but notice that he was a dead ringer for someone far less unassuming: Sean Connery as Russian submarine commander Marko Ramius in *The Hunt for Red October*. I was looking at Salcedo, but in my head all I could hear was "Right full rudder. Reverse starboard engine!"

With his 9mm pistol still firmly in hand, Dave asked Salcedo why he was out here in the middle of a sugarcane field secretly meeting with two American DEA agents. Salcedo said that this was a one-time meeting only, and it wouldn't last long. He was on standby in case Miguel needed him, so he had to return to Cali. But he had come because he wanted to help us find El Señor...which, he stressed, wouldn't be easy. "The cartel has an intelligence network like nothing you've ever seen," he told us, with a faint hint of pride. He also said he'd been promoted to head of security for the cartel, a consequence of the arrest of former security chief Mario del Vasto one month ago.

We were confused. We were sitting with the new head of security for the Cali cartel...and he was willing to *help us* find Miguel? Didn't he know where he was already? When we asked just that, we got a surprising answer. "I'm not sure, to be honest," he said. Since Gilberto's arrest, security around Miguel had significantly increased, and he never left the confines of his secret sanctuary. That didn't make sense, and Dave and I flipped back into skeptic mode.

We were on the brink of joining forces with the man literally in charge of cartel security, but he had no idea about his boss's exact location? And, crazier still, he had no interest in the reward for Miguel's capture? The reward, it's worth noting, was the equivalent of $1.875 million US dollars. No, he insisted, he didn't want any money from the Colombian government. But he did have one demand.

"Before we go any further, and no matter what happens, I want only one thing: safe passage for me and my family to the US," Salcedo said. He'd just pulled the pin on the grenade, but now things were starting to make sense.

"That'll take a lot," I told him.

"And I have a lot to offer," he said. "But I need to know that I can trust you. I need to be *sure* that you can handle this."

Dave managed to get one word out—"Look"—before Salcedo cut him off.

"Do I have your word?"

There was a brief silence, and I glanced back at Dave, who was nodding his head. I paused for a moment, then said, "If you can really do what you *say* you can, then we give you our word: we'll get you and your family out safely."

"Then it's settled. My life is in your hands," Salcedo said.

Suddenly, Dave and I had a very heavy weight on our shoulders, and we knew it. If the operation failed or Salcedo's involvement became known, he and his family would most certainly be killed. It wasn't easy for us to maintain the appearance of confidence. Salcedo's expression, meanwhile, gave almost nothing away. He looked vaguely defeated, like a man without much hope left. Like a man who knew that we were probably his last and *only* hope.

Dave asked if Salcedo at least knew the area where Miguel was hiding, and he did: after he'd been forced to move from a town house owned by Salomón Prado because of a raid by the Search Bloc a month ago, Salcedo explained, he'd been moved to the Santa Rita section of the city, close to the Cali Zoo. Then he told us something that made our blood boil. They'd been alerted to the raid by corrupt officials within the Search Bloc, and Miguel *had* been there when it was raided.

Dave and I looked at each other, the same "What the fuck?" expression on our faces. We'd coordinated that raid with Colonel Barragán's team and thoroughly searched the premises. We remembered every detail, especially when it came to the hunt for the *caleta* we knew was there. And it had been. The *caleta* had been brilliantly hidden beneath the Jacuzzi—the same extravagant Jacuzzi Dave and I distinctly remembered admiring.

When Salcedo brought up the separate failed operation to arrest Miguel at the Versailles mansion, Dave and I braced ourselves for what we knew he'd say next: Miguel had also been there before that raid but had been tipped off by the Search Bloc and left before we arrived.

Salcedo's confirmation about not one but *both* Search Bloc betrayals was bad enough, but it got worse once we learned that it had been Salcedo himself who went back to the Prado townhome, removed Miguel from under the Jacuzzi, smuggled him out through the garage, and drove him to another safe house. We were fuming. When we told him that we'd been on both raids *and* worked with the Search Bloc to coordinate them, he simply responded, "I know."

For a second, I thought Dave might lose it. Even though none of this was even remotely shocking, we were newly enraged. We tried to talk Salcedo into revealing his Search Bloc contacts, but he refused. We hadn't earned his trust yet, he said, and besides, he'd heard Miguel and Gilberto mention corrupt DEA and US Embassy officials who were reportedly on the cartel payroll, too. Once again, we were caught off guard and scoffed at the accusation. "That's total bullshit," Dave said.

We cautioned Salcedo that to receive full credit for his cooperation, he needed to be 100 percent truthful and forthcoming with us, always. He knew we had good sources, and we told him that we'd find Miguel—just as we'd found Gilberto—with or without his help. But Salcedo respectfully disagreed, chalking up Gilberto's arrest to dumb luck and even dumber security lapses by del Vasto's crew. Even though we'd made it to the places Miguel was hiding, he said, the Cali KGB *always* knew in advance when we were coming. Plus, he reminded us of how brilliantly constructed some of the *caletas* were. He had us there. Cali architects weren't just uniquely talented, they were architectural geniuses.

The more we talked, the more comfortable Salcedo became, and we could see that he'd begun to second-guess everything he'd been so confident about prior to our meeting. Each time he brought up a specific cartel operative, we fired back with our own insider details to prove our bona fides. Eventually, he realized that we weren't just two young, inept American DEA agents after all and accepted the fact that we actually had a pretty good handle on the cartel and their activities. We were both testing and vetting Salcedo, and he was doing the same with us. So far, both sides were passing.

Salcedo next mentioned Guillermo Pallomari and Miguel's plan to have him killed, saying that the godfathers were extremely concerned that after his recent indictment in the Operation Cornerstone case, Pallomari would be arrested and extradited to the US, thanks to his Chilean citizenship. He urged us to focus on finding him as quickly as possible and stressed that he alone was the key to keeping the godfathers in jail and destroying Cali's financial empire. "He knows everything about their finances, including the cartel's $6 million contribution to Ernesto Samper's presidential campaign," Salcedo said. He even suggested that if we approached Pallomari, there was a good chance he'd cooperate.

Dave and I were already chomping at the bit to find Pallomari, but Salcedo and the cartel were still in the dark—he was somewhere in the city, they assumed, but they didn't know any more than we did. Wherever he was, he was in serious danger. César Yusti—arguably the cartel's most lethal assassin—was fast closing in on his location, and Yusti was relentless. "It's only a matter of time," Salcedo said.

We all agreed that we'd pursue Miguel first but immediately switch gears if Pallomari's location was discovered. Miguel had ordered Salcedo to assist Yusti, so we knew he'd be the first one to share any new developments. Looking back, it was at that moment that Dave and I began to fully understand the incredible amount of pressure Salcedo was under.

Our talk turned back to Miguel, and Salcedo came through with even more information, including precise details about the godfather's lifestyle, preferences, and obsessive behavior. Miguel *only* used Mazda 626 sedans and Panasonic telephones. He preferred locations that backed up to a steep hill or mountain with just one way in and one way out, as those locations couldn't accommodate a rear route of approach by vehicle, and traversing them on foot was extremely difficult. Miguel always said that Colombian security forces were too lazy to trek all the way down a mountain (we couldn't help but laugh at that), and with only one way in and out, perimeter security would be able to easily detect their arrival, giving him ample time to escape or hide in a hidden compartment. That, coupled with the countless cartel spies within the Search Blocs, made Miguel confident that he would never be caught.

Miguel's daily routine rarely changed: he woke up late, spent the bulk of the day coordinating cocaine and money-laundering operations with US cell heads and Mexican cartel leaders, then stayed up until the wee hours of the morning talking with European and Russian crime families as well as Italian Mafia bosses. He relied on a sophisticated twenty-five-line telephone call-forwarding and switching system to communicate—one that could automatically transfer and route calls to Miguel no matter where he was—making them impossible to trace and his location impossible to determine. Miguel also suffered from several ailments, including hypoglycemia, so he had to eat certain types of foods—fresh fruits, vegetables, etc.—at specific times of the day and night to help regulate his blood sugar. These dependencies made him more predictable. We knew they'd be key in helping us locate his current safe house.

After the close calls at the Prado and Versailles locations, only a select few knew Miguel's exact whereabouts, and despite being his head of security, Salcedo wasn't one of them. But Salcedo *did* know where Miguel wanted cartel perimeter security to be stationed: near a service station and a small bridge along Avenida 4, which itself was adjacent to another road (Avenida 3) with only one way in and out. Salcedo pointed out that based on where security was positioned, there were only a dozen or so locations in the Santa Rita area that fit Miguel's specific requirements for a residence, so by surveilling the area at night and taking note of which lights went off last, we'd have the best chance of identifying Miguel's hideout. He also described a dense wooded area in the mountains a half mile away from which we could conduct nighttime surveillance and watch to see which lights would go out last. The one final light on, he added, would be the beacon to lead us to El Señor. It was a brilliant suggestion.

Salcedo also shared several things to look out for during our searches: Miguel's trademark Panasonic phones, the call-forwarding station, Mazda 626s in the garage, at least two domestic employees on hand, a bounty of fresh fruits and vegetables in the refrigerator, and, of course, one of the two personal assistants who now stayed with him at all times: Jorge "Fercho" Castillo and Jesus "Mateo" Zapata. Miguel preferred to alternate between the two, and Fercho was the one currently on duty. Mateo, Salcedo speci-fied, was on vacation.

I looked at Dave and rolled my eyes—of course, Murphy's Law yet again. Right up until *yesterday* we'd been following Mateo all over the city, only to discover now that while we'd been wasting our time, he'd been enjoying his time off.

What a gold mine Salcedo had turned out to be. In the course of only two hours, he'd given us more inside information about the cartel than Dave and I had dug up in a year.

While we were surprised by the quality and scope of it all, we still had no idea what was motivating him to betray the godfathers' confidence. Dave asked him again to explain. He was putting his entire existence on the line: Why?

There was a long pause, then Salcedo finally spoke. He was an engineer by trade and had been a captain in the Colombian Army reserves, he said. In early 1989, he was recruited into the cartel with one goal: to help kill Pablo Escobar. This presented a moral conflict for him: he never imag-ined he would work with criminals—let alone some of the most powerful in the world—but at the same time, he viewed the opportunity as an honor. Escobar had gone from being a man of the people to a monster, a narco-terrorist, and enemy of the state. So he'd weighed his options. If he accepted, he could justify the decision by believing that he was doing Colombia a great service. But accepting would also mean allying with the Cali cartel—and would that alliance be breakable? Eventually, he realized that any internal debate was pointless because he never had a choice to begin with. The simple act of meeting with the godfathers had taken away his ability to choose. The minute they'd shared their plan with him there was no way out, and certainly no way he could say no.

Reluctantly, Salcedo resigned himself to his fate and accepted their offer, but only after being given their word that when Escobar was dead and buried, his tenure with the cartel would come to an end.

But when Escobar *was* killed and the bloody conflict finally over, that promise proved to be empty. When Salcedo respectfully attempted to tender his resignation directly to Miguel, it was flatly refused. He under-stood why: he knew too much. And any escape, he knew, would only result in one of two things: arrest or death.

We realized he was holding back tears as he recalled first trying to leave. "I'm not like them. I'm not a drug trafficker. I'm not a murderer. The only thing harder than getting *inside* the cartel is trying to find a way to get out. And that's why I'm here with you." He bowed his head. "My life and the lives of my family are now in your hands," he repeated.

Hearing his story put everything into a new light. This was a family man who'd gotten himself into a nightmare from which he couldn't escape, and from this point on, his and his family's lives would hang in the balance of every move we made. "Don't worry, we won't let you down," I said. "I promise you. And unlike Miguel, I keep my promises."

Salcedo nodded his head and looked down at his watch. It was nearly 6:00 p.m.—what was supposed to have been a quick meeting had lasted almost three hours, the three most important hours we'd spent in Colombia thus far. We'd formed an unlikely alliance and needed each other to accomplish our respective missions, something we couldn't do without trusting one another. Of course, that was easier said than done.

As Salcedo readied to leave, he wished us luck on our surveillance operation that night and offered to meet again early the next morning to discuss the results. What we'd thought would be a quick, one-time encounter was now something much more.

He began to open the passenger door but paused for a moment, and we braced ourselves for a change of mind. Instead, he leaned back in and shared a few parting bombshells. He said the godfathers knew about the "secret CIA spy plane" that had been sent to Cali to assist Colombian security forces on their hunt: the Schweizer RG-8 Condor. They also knew where it was kept: in a restricted-access hangar at the air force base. He described the single-engine aircraft perfectly, down to the last detail: it resembled a glider with a wingspan of over seventy feet, and it flew very high, very slow, and very quiet. It was equipped with a forward-looking infrared (FLIR) imaging system, high-resolution cameras, and advanced electronics.

"Who told you that?" Dave said sarcastically, half-heartedly implying that it was mere conjecture.

"I've seen it. I've touched it. I've *studied* it," Salcedo said. "If you want, I'll even get you a photograph of it." (Which, for the record, he did.)

Salcedo also said that he had many friends in the Colombian Air Force, most notably a major who allowed him unfettered access to the base, and informed him when police, military, or DEA and CIA aircraft were arriving.

But he saved the biggest and best nuggets for last.

Our jaws dropped when he told us what we had long suspected but never confirmed: our primary liaison contact at the police Search Bloc, Captain Efrén Buitrago (whom Salcedo referred to as "the Vulture"), was one of the cartel's most prized and most corrupt assets. Along with a corporal referred to only as "the Shadow" (because he was always with Buitrago when Salcedo met him), Buitrago consistently reported back to del Vasto and, more recently, to Salcedo himself about our activities at the base, as well as the other DEA agents now assigned there. He added that there were others, too—corrupt officials whose identities were so sensitive that they were known only to Miguel.

Even though we'd had our suspicions for ages, the confirmation about Buitrago left us reeling. Dave, for one, was beside himself. He'd always disliked the captain, and now I had to worry that he might lose his temper and put his hands around Buitrago's neck the next time we saw him. He'd been lying to our faces for months, and enjoying it the entire time.

Salcedo also warned us that several phone lines at the Search Bloc were wiretapped, including the direct line into the DEA barracks. He cautioned us to never trust *anyone* in Cali and confirmed the fact that Miguel would never, ever be captured by using either of the Search Bloc's resources. Any QRF or arresting troops would have to come from Bogotá, over two hundred miles away.

For obvious reasons, Dave and I devised a plan to communicate with Salcedo as securely as possible. We obtained burner cell phones and used them only to communicate with each other and agreed to pass phone numbers and coded messages via my SkyPager (the only paging service in Colombia not yet infiltrated by the cartel, Salcedo told us). We chose an interchangeable name, "Carmen," to use for one another when sending digital or text messages via pager and devised a simple but effective method to use when passing phone numbers: subtract one number from each number displayed. So, if Salcedo sent me 773-2865, we'd subtract one digit from each number to reveal the true number: 662-1754. It was just one small additional layer of security, but we needed to use every trick in the book.

Lastly, we needed an alias for Salcedo. We couldn't use his real name or reveal his true identity to anyone—that was the single most critical thing. Just one verbal misstep overheard by cartel spies or intercepted over an open phone line monitored by the Cali KGB meant his certain death. We looked him over one last time, and suddenly *The Hunt for Red October* came to my mind again. "Right full rudder. Reverse starboard engine!" From that point on, we would be dealing with a man named Sean.

CHAPTER 21

Lights Out

"Luck is what happens when preparation meets opportunity."

—SENECA THE YOUNGER,
Roman Philosopher and Statesman

SIR SEAN CONNERY—a.k.a. the man formerly known as Salcedo—left our meeting near CIAT just as the sun was starting to set behind the peaks of the Farallones de Cali mountains. The heat that had tortured us for hours was beginning to fade, and Dave and I sat silent in the car, both of us lost in our own worlds as we tried to take it all in. The day had been one of the most stressful of our careers, but now we felt almost peaceful.

Our environment, which not too long ago had appeared to be a minefield of lurking *sicarios* and imminent disaster, was now nothing more than a common sugarcane field swaying gently back and forth with the breeze. It was Dave who broke the silence with his trademark humor: "We're lucky this wasn't our onion field," he said, referring to the 1963 murder of a California police officer so disturbing it was made into the 1979 thriller *The Onion Field*.

"Thank God for that," I replied.

We were upbeat—we'd just spent three hours with the man who could very well deliver the fatal blow to the Cali cartel. Still, an unsettling feeling remained. "Let's get out of here," I said to Dave. His *Onion Field* comment had sent chills down my spine.

Lights Out

During our long trek back to the safe house, Dave and I did our best to review everything that had happened. Salcedo was more valuable an asset than we had hoped, and our biggest fear now was just keeping him alive. From this day on, he'd be operating as a double agent, vacillating between two identities: one, a protector of Miguel Rodríguez, and two, a covert ally of the men he was pretending to protect his boss *from*—namely, the DEA and Colombian security forces (in other words, us). It was a fine line, but he'd promised to help us bring down the world's most wanted drug baron, and we'd promised to protect him and his family. We wouldn't rest until they made it safely into witness protection back in the United States.

When we arrived back at the safe house, Mike was visibly relieved. We made sure to downplay the gravitas of our meeting so as not to raise expectations, and we certainly didn't reveal who we met with. Besides, Mike was an intelligence officer, not DEA. Still, we knew everyone was going to want in on this, which we dreaded. The last thing we wanted was an endless barrage of calls back and forth between Colombia and DC, all marveling at the fact that we'd found the key to the city, the human Rosetta Stone of Cali and Chosen One who would hand us Miguel on a silver platter. No doubt they'd make every effort to take over (and control) every aspect of the operation from afar, and we weren't about to let that happen. And we certainly didn't want to answer any questions about Salcedo/Sean's actual position in the cartel, or who had authorized a meeting with a cartel counterintelligence officer (reminder: no one), or God forbid, where we'd met and with what security (none). This entire mission revolved around keeping secrets, and now we had more than a few of our own.

Dave and I were spent. It had been weeks since either of us had had a decent sleep, and we were looking at another late night, so Dave's old standby "eat and sleep when you can" approach sounded like our next best move. We grabbed a quick bite at the safe house, then headed to the back bedroom for a short siesta on our set of ancient bunk beds.

A few hours after dark, we headed out to the spot Salcedo had recommended as the best vantage point from which to conduct surveillance and hone in on the area we suspected Miguel was hiding out. We were fairly confident that we wouldn't encounter any cartel scouts in the mountains—we were well outside the perimeter security and the entrance to the Santa Rita neighborhood—but we were prepared for whatever, or whoever, might come our way.

After carefully navigating down a narrow, overgrown path with the help of flashlights, we arrived at a partial clearing. Using our binoculars, we could see a good portion of the targeted area. For the next three or four hours we rarely blinked, just watched and waited as lights extinguished one by one in several of the apartment buildings as people turned in for the evening. By midnight only a dozen or so lights remained on.

As the night turned into early morning, we watched as the number of lit windows became fewer and fewer until only two were left, both in the same white apartment building. We counted the number of floors starting from the ground up, but it was difficult to be sure we had it right. It was just too dark, and we were too far away.

Sitting in the dark, bug-infested hills, we couldn't help but picture Don Miguel in his office, leisurely chatting with his coterie of Italian Mafia figures and Russian organized crime bosses while we kept watch outside. Just as Dave was perilously close to entering his "sleep when you can" mode, the last two lights finally went dark: the first around 4:00 a.m. and the second less than a half hour later. I gave Dave a quick elbow to the ribs, jolting him back to life. "Do we think it's one of those?" he asked. "I'm not sure," I said, "but I have a pretty good feeling about it."

By dawn, our backs were stiff, and we were both still weary when we met Salcedo at a large construction site just north of downtown, the future site for the Chipichape shopping mall. We were running on caffeine and sugar—more specifically, black coffee and *pasteles de Gloria*, addictive guava pastries we never tired of. Salcedo, who'd also been up in the hills watching the area from a different location and vantage point, concurred with our initial observations. We planned to return later that evening to verify the lighting pattern, but first we had to positively identify the building where the last lights went out.

Salcedo agreed to assist by pulling cartel perimeter security at the Avenida 3 entrance at noon for what he called a "routine fifteen-minute security briefing" so we'd have just enough time to make *one* quick pass through the neighborhood to get the name of the building. He sketched out a rough map of the area, describing the Avenida 3 road as an upside-down U. He doubted that a single car driving through the neighborhood during the day without stopping would raise any red flags, not least because security personnel would be away from their post and meeting with their boss. Regardless, it was our only option—we couldn't risk Salcedo being seen anywhere near the neighborhood.

The cartel's first and primary defense always revolved around its abundance of corrupt government officials, coupled with the hundreds of wiretaps the Cali KGB conducted through Carlos Espinosa, their main contact at the Emcali telephone company. Just one quick text or call to Miguel or Salcedo by corrupt officials alerting them to imminent hostile government action would give the godfathers ample time to plan accordingly.

In addition, the cartel stationed countless lookouts and taxi drivers alongside strategic choke points near police and military installations. These well-paid sentinels were on duty 24/7 and immediately alerted Salcedo each time transport trucks carrying troops departed the base. Perimeter security established just outside Miguel's safe house served as the final line of defense and, depending on the situation, would warn him either to flee or hide in place.

At exactly twelve noon on Thursday, July 13, Dave and I concluded an SDR to identify any cartel surveillance that might have been tailing us. We drove down Avenida 4 along the Cali River, approached the turn off to Avenida 3 and the Santa Rita entrance, and, seeing that it was all clear, entered the neighborhood. We had just fifteen minutes to complete our task.

We drove alongside the river and eventually spotted the building where the last two lights had extinguished the night before. I slowed down just enough to read the name on the building. "Colinas de Santa Rita!" I said, and Dave scribbled it down in his notepad. We continued on with our loop and exited on the opposite side of the river with just a few minutes to spare.

After we arrived back at the safe house, we called Sandy Smith, our trusted intelligence analyst at the embassy in Bogotá, via secure telephone. Sandy was a wizard when it came to research, so we asked if she could work her magic to obtain ownership information on apartments in the Colinas de Santa Rita building. Our hope was that we'd come up with a name that linked back to a known cartel *testaferro* or front man.

A few hours later, Sandy called with an update: two of the apartments, 402 and 801, were linked to a notorious Cali *sicario* named Guillermo León Restrepo Gaviria, known as "Memo" or "Memo Lara." One of Cali's most ruthless assassins, Memo Lara had been implicated in the grisly 1992 murder of journalist Manuel de Dios in New York. Chepe had contracted Memo to coordinate the hit after de Dios wrote several articles exposing Cali's illegal activities in the city.

After Sandy's update, we couldn't wait for night to fall so we could return to our clandestine lair high in the hills and resume our surveillance activities. The lighting pattern we'd tracked the first night seemed to correspond to apartments on the fourth and eighth floors, but we had to be absolutely positive before taking any further action. That meant more watching and waiting, so we grabbed our go bags and headed back out for another long night of leg cramps and mosquitos.

It's not that we weren't used to being uncomfortable. Our many weeks and months of sleeplessness and surveillance had turned into a full year, and the wear and tear was starting to show. The exhaustion, combined with the stress of operating in such a hostile environment, had wreaked havoc not just on our minds but on our bodies as well. Dave and I had both lost weight—over twenty pounds each—and our eyes were sunken and rimmed with dark circles. Our circadian rhythm was in complete disarray, and we were always dragging no matter the time of day or night.

That evening, we made our way back to our hillside post for our second round of surveillance. As expected, we tracked lighting patterns nearly identical to the night before. At midnight, the same lights that had been on twenty-four hours ago soon dissipated, and by 1:00 a.m., the only windows that remained lit were on the fourth and eighth floors of our target building. The eighth-floor light was the first to extinguish, leaving just the fourth-floor light, which stayed on for the next few hours. Finally, at almost 4:30 a.m. (the exact same time as the night before), the final light went dark. Dave smiled, killed his one hundredth mosquito of the night, and said, "I think we found him."

After another sleepless night, we drove to our favorite downtown bakery for our usual one-two punch of java and guava pastries. We were almost certain that we'd found Miguel's new hideout but needed to confer with Salcedo before doing anything else. No matter how tired we got, the first thing on our minds was always that his life hung in the balance, not ours.

At sunrise, we set off to meet with Salcedo at the same construction site we'd met before. While these early-morning meetings were brutal for me and Dave, they were ideal for Salcedo. Miguel was still fast asleep and rarely required the services of his security chief until later in the day.

While we waited for Salcedo, I decided to have a little fun with him. I wrote down 402 and 801 on two separate pieces of paper and put one in my left hand and the other in my right. When he arrived, Dave told him that we'd *positively* identified Miguel's location. Salcedo smiled and said, "Really?" I told him to pick a hand, holding my two clenched fists out in front of me. He gently tapped the top of my left hand, which I opened to reveal the paper that read 402. Then I opened the right, flashing the number 801.

Salcedo was impressed. He gave a nod of approval and smiled. "It's the fourth floor."

About thirty minutes after that light had gone out, Salcedo told us, he'd called Miguel's number. After the call was transferred through the call-forwarding station, a light came back on in the same fourth-floor apartment--presumably Fercho turning it on to be able to see enough to walk over and pick up the call—confirming Salcedo's suspicion.

All of us were in agreement that we'd officially found Miguel's new safe house. It all added up: the lights, the link to Memo Lara, and finally, Salcedo's little late-night hang-up ruse. The next order of business would be to devise our plan, then we'd launch the operation against our prized target. There were three of us working together now, and we weren't going to stop until we took down the man known as El Señor.

CHAPTER 22

Cease and Desist

"I think he's a dead man walking.
And it's all our fault."
—CHRIS FEISTL

The Raid

THE SUN HAD BEGUN TO RISE by the time Dave and I were nearing the end of our strategy session with Salcedo. We'd just agreed to launch a predawn raid the next day, July 15, at 5:00 a.m., right after Miguel would have gone to sleep. Thanks to Salcedo, we knew that we couldn't rely on the Search Bloc as our primary strike team, nor could we breathe a word of it to Captain Buitrago or his secretive sidekick, the Shadow. And we certainly couldn't out anyone: if the DEA took action and removed any cartel spies, it would immediately point back to Salcedo. Only after we'd secured the immediate area could we contact the Search Bloc and their embedded prosecutor for assistance.

We proposed using the same group of officers from Colonel Barragán's unit who'd successfully arrested Gilberto, coupled with a contingent of anti-narcotics (ANTIN) special operators from Bogotá. The combined forces would travel overland from Bogotá with Ruben, Jerry, and Pedro: the exact same team we'd used in previous raids. The most important thing was to avoid detection from cartel spies at the Search Bloc.

Cease and Desist

When Ruben briefed General Serrano on our plan to arrest Miguel, he immediately authorized the operation, not bothering to ask about the location of the proposed raid. General Serrano and Colonel Barragán were the only Colombians who knew the target, but we kept Salcedo's identity as a double agent secret. For additional operational security (OPSEC), the remainder of the team was advised that they would be raiding a cocaine laboratory near the city of Buga, roughly an hour north of Cali.

The task force was set to depart Bogotá in a convoy and arrive at a rest area outside Cali by 3:00 a.m., where they'd be briefed by me and Dave before continuing with the operation. But we still had one issue: How could the forces pass by cartel perimeter security without alerting the detail manned by Salcedo's most trusted assistant, Enrique Sanchez? Established cartel protocol dictated that whenever any police, military, or other suspicious vehicle crossed the barrier, security operatives would radio Miguel's assistant (presently Fercho), then Miguel would be immediately removed from the location or escorted to the safe house's *caleta*.

Salcedo suggested we try to secure delivery trucks, as those would blend in perfectly with the early-morning traffic and not set off any alarms with perimeter security. But with the operation fewer than eighteen hours away, that was easier said than done.

Dave and I set about scouring downtown Cali for any delivery trucks big enough to conceal the entire raiding party. We didn't have much luck, so we decided to return to the safe house to try and muster a few hours of sleep. When we arrived, we learned that Mike had just gotten wind of the planned operation, and he wanted in.

Mike had been an enormous help to us thus far. He'd provided us significant logistical support, a safe house, a highly trained Colombian Navy team, and several vehicles, among other things. There was no downside, so we added him to the team.

Midnight came and went, and after searching what seemed like the entire eastern part of downtown Cali, we finally located two chicken trucks, both helmed by drivers willing to make a deal with us. One driver agreed to a deal for the Colombian equivalent of $1,000 for four hours—no questions asked—but we had to have the truck back to him by 5:30 a.m. That was easy—we planned to be at the Santa Rita apartments by then. The problem was that the *other* driver agreed to the same price but refused to leave his truck under any circumstances. He had zero interest in knowing what we needed it for, but whatever it was, he and his truck were a package deal. With the clock ticking, we agreed and took off for the meeting location about thirty minutes away.

The overland reinforcements arrived at 3:00 a.m., and Dave and I briefed them, repeating the cover story that the target was a cocaine laboratory outside the city. It soon became obvious, however, that everyone was more focused on the elephant(s) in the room, namely the two chicken trucks there for no apparent reason. We explained that the trucks—minus any chickens—would covertly house the raiding party, allowing them to evade suspicion and arrive safely at the location.

Still confused, the heavily armed group began to climb aboard the trucks, and the complaints were immediate. Everyone was grumbling about the putrid smell and the unsanitary conditions, a chorus of squawking so persistent that, volume-wise, they probably could have given the chickens a run for their money. Dave and I did our best not to laugh, as we'd be riding in the clean, cool, blissfully chicken-free cabs up front. Meanwhile, the truck driver stood and watched the entire comedy unfold. No doubt he was second-guessing his demand to tag along.

At 4:15 a.m., I took off with the reluctant driver in the first truck, while Dave manned the second. As planned, we took a circuitous route through the Cali streets to throw off any spies or taxi drivers who might have picked up on the vehicles. When we got close to the zero barrier, I told Dave to slow down, then wait thirty seconds after I passed through cartel perimeter security. At 5:00 a.m., I spotted the security detail just off the side of the road. From what I could tell, the detail consisted of two taxis, several motorcycles, and a handful of operatives drinking coffee and smoking cigarettes.

So far, so good. Dave's truck passed without interference, and we continued on toward our destination a mile or so ahead.

The minute we arrived at the Colinas de Santa Rita building, the operation started unraveling. I glanced at my pager and saw a message sent earlier that morning by "Carmen," the interchangeable code name we'd agreed on with Salcedo. Cancel the party; it's not a surprise anymore, it read. My heart sank.

Suddenly we were paralyzed, asking ourselves how the raid could possibly have been compromised after all the additional precautions we'd taken. The only people who knew were me, Dave, and, of course, Salcedo. Not even General Serrano knew the exact location. How could the cartel have known? Then Dave and I remembered something Salcedo said during our first meeting, something we'd dismissed without a second thought: Miguel reportedly had American contacts inside the embassy. We weren't buying it then, but now we were rethinking things.

While we were processing Salcedo's news, ANTIN forces had surrounded the perimeter of Colinas de Santa Rita, quickly securing the fourth and eighth floors of the building to prevent anyone from leaving. The remaining officers flooded the street and cordoned off the area with yellow tape while the Search Bloc was called to provide further support.

Just before dawn, the prosecutor and the Colonel Murcia-led Search Bloc arrived along with Captain Buitrago. To make matters worse, the prosecutor forgot to bring the necessary search warrant paperwork, and had to go to the downtown regional office to get it. That would take at least an hour. We'd now lost both our tactical advantage *and* the element of surprise.

"You've *got* to be kidding me," Dave said, throwing his hands in the air.

As Dave and I stood fuming, Colonel Murcia approached and asked us why the Search Bloc hadn't been made aware of our raid, a question we couldn't exactly answer, so we told him to speak directly to General Serrano. Dave became nearly apoplectic when he laid eyes on Buitrago but managed to control his temper—barely.

In all the time that had passed, Miguel could have crawled all the way to Bogotá, as far as we were concerned. The best we could hope for was that he hadn't fled and was still inside the apartment, tucked away in a cramped *caleta*. That image gave us the motivation we needed to persevere.

The *Caleta*

At 7:00 a.m., the prosecutor finally returned with the proper paperwork and authorized entry into the building. I immediately went to the garage in the hopes of finding a Mazda, while Dave and the rest of the forces headed straight for apartment 402.

The first thing I spied in the garage was a white Mazda 626, license BBW-712, parked in space 402. Maybe things were turning around, I thought. I raced back out and headed upstairs, where I found Dave in the kitchen. We started looking for any of Salcedo's telltale signs and found them everywhere: first, the twenty-five-line telephone call-forwarding station, followed by the Panasonic phones. The refrigerator was stocked with Miguel's requisite fresh fruits and vegetables, and when we entered the living room, we found two people sitting side by side on the couch: a distressed, disheveled-looking man and an equally distressed female domestic employee dressed in her work attire. I asked the man his name.

"Jorge Castillo," he responded.

I turned to Dave and whispered, "Fercho. We're in the right place—Miguel's here. Or at least he was." Dave and I grilled Fercho about Miguel's whereabouts, but he gave us nothing, and the maid followed suit. No one was talking.

The group continued to search the four-bedroom, four-and-a-half-bathroom apartment. It was a surprisingly modest place by Miguel's usual standards—no bigger than 2,500 square feet, and not nearly as extravagant as most of the mansions we'd raided over the past year. A quick sweep of the place revealed nothing.

As Colonel Barragán's team continued hunting for any incriminating evidence or documents, about a dozen members of the Search Bloc—resigned to the fact that Miguel wasn't there—sat lazily on a bed in a back bedroom, engrossed in a soccer match. Dave walked in at the exact same moment a goal was scored and the room erupted into a chorus of cheers. It's a wonder his head didn't explode.

An hour or so later we heard a familiar voice and turned to see General Serrano, who'd just arrived from Bogotá. Apparently, he'd flown in on a CNP aircraft helmed by his personal police pilot, obviously in the hopes of escorting Miguel back to Bogotá in grand fashion, parading him in front of the hordes of photographers clamoring to take Miguel's photo just as they'd done with his brother, Gilberto. The troops who'd been so preoccupied with the soccer match just seconds before now jumped up en masse, scurrying about and pretending to search the bedroom. General Serrano shared a bit of small talk with them but didn't stay long and departed a short time later to return to Bogotá.

While the general consensus was one of apathy, Dave and I were convinced we had the right place. All the signs (and our instincts) told us that Miguel was still there, or had just left. Along with Colonel Barragán's team, we pored over every inch of the walls, searching for any place that might make for a good *caleta*.

At one point Jerry joined another team led by Captain Buitrago and headed over to apartment 801, which they searched to no avail. They also interviewed the shaken occupants, who said they'd only recently moved in and knew nothing about Miguel. Everything appeared to check out— no red flags, no obvious lies.

Back in 402, Dave and I shifted our focus to an office with a built-in library and a large, red wooden desk that sat in the middle of the room. Atop the bookcase were several candles (all still lit) and a small piece of paper with the letters "M.R.O." handwritten in blue ink—another indication that this was the godfather's lair. The rest of the search was uneventful, until we caught a glimpse of another piece of paper on the desk with a combination of numbers and a few words in Spanish. We took a closer look: *BBA-658, Toyota, azul, el carro que lleva los monos* (BBA-658, blue Toyota, the car that carries the gringos). Holy shit. It was the license plate from our Toyota Land Cruiser we kept at the Search Bloc. We were the gringos.

As soon as the other team wrapped up their search, they returned and told us that not one shred of evidence suggested Miguel had ever even been in 801. But what about the lights? They'd definitely gone on and off nearly in unison, there was no disputing that. What were the chances that it was just coincidence that 801 was associated with a Cali assassin?

By 10:00 a.m., we'd made no progress, and the group was restless. Dave and I decided to page Salcedo and sent him a message saying the house was vacant. He responded immediately: Call Carmen. His message came with a phone number, so we did the prearranged math codework, subtracted one digit from the numbers, and dialed.

Salcedo answered on the first ring. He told us that Miguel *had* been warned General Serrano was coming to Cali sometime after midnight and demanded he double perimeter security and monitor both the police and army Search Bloc. "You have a leak," Salcedo said. "Impossible!" Dave countered.

We were at a loss. *No one* had operational details about the raid except me and Dave, and our OPSEC was solid. But someone had spoken to Miguel, and we needed to find out who. We thought of Captain Buitrago—who was still lurking around—but ruled him out. He didn't have a clue about the pending Santa Rita raid.

Salcedo explained that the minute the second chicken truck passed security, established protocols went into effect, and the cartel phone tree lit up. The truck was traveling at a slightly higher speed than it should have and caught the attention of heightened security, who immediately radioed Fercho to tell him to secure Miguel. He also said that he knew for sure that Miguel *had* been there…but he didn't know if he still was. Salcedo was anxious and had to rush to a security meeting with Miguel's son, William Rodríguez Abadía, and other security personnel but promised to call back as soon as he could.

Dave and I were losing hope. Our plan had been shot to hell, and now we had a mystery leak on our hands. Along with the remaining few police officers still willing to help, we went back to our hunt. It was all we could do.

Salcedo called a few hours later and asked if there was a large red desk in the apartment office. There was, we told him, but we'd already searched it and found nothing, save for the chilling note with the details of our old vehicle. Salcedo lowered his voice. "There's a hidden compartment in the desk, and in it you'll find Miguel's *most* sensitive documents. Get to those and you'll buy yourself more time to search. I'll call again later."

Dave and I signaled to Jerry, and the three of us went back into the office. We scoured every inch looking for any discreet latches or buttons, bewildered as to where a secret space in the desk could possibly even exist. Captain Buitrago kept an eye on us the entire time, making it crystal clear that he was watching our every move. But for one minute he was briefly out of sight, and Jerry seized the moment. Picking up the entire back of the desk, he pushed it forward with all his might. The desk made a colossal *thud* as it smashed against the marble tile floor and instantly splintered apart. Colonel Murcia, Captain Buitrago, and several others raced in to see what the hell was going on. Buitrago spoke first, asking, "What did you find?" We didn't say anything, not that there was anything to say. We hadn't found anything—yet.

We crouched down and examined the wreckage. The first thing I spotted was an open, broken compartment in the back of the desk, revealing three thin leather briefcases. Jerry and Dave grabbed them and took them out to the dining room table.

The police officials gathered around us, anxious to see what we'd found. Colonel Barragán took some of the documents and began to examine them more closely as Dave, Jerry, and I struggled to peer over his shoulder. Almost immediately Colonel Barragán's face drained of all color, while Dave's expression turned into one of shock. Barragán stuffed the papers back into the briefcases and said, "I have to get these back to General Serrano in Bogotá. Colonel Murcia, you're in charge."

As we stood speechless, Barragán turned and walked out of the room, briefcases in hand. Dave and I huddled up with Jerry and Ruben. We couldn't believe what we'd just seen: a photocopied check made payable to Santiago Medina (President Samper's campaign treasurer) for 40 million pesos ($50,000), scores of copies of other checks and payoff records to hundreds, if not thousands, of high-ranking officials, documents on what appeared to be official Colombian government letterhead, and more. We only got a quick look, but that was all we needed. We'd just hit another jackpot, and prayed we'd be able to get our hands on *all* of the copies.

After Colonel Barragán left, the scene went downhill. The discovery of the documents had briefly pumped new life into the raid team, but they soon lost interest. For the second time, the group sat back down on the plush couches and chairs and resumed their soccer talk.

Along with four agents and Barragán's small handful of officers, we continued to look for the *caleta*. At one point, Colonel Murcia grew so frustrated that he briefly walked out of the apartment, leaving the team leaderless and without direction. Still, we persisted.

At some point in the late afternoon—by then we'd lost track of time—my pager sounded and brought us back to life. It was Salcedo: He's there! He's in a *caleta*! Whatever you do, don't leave!

We summoned Ruben and Jerry and the four of us split up, going from room to room for what seemed like the hundredth time. We'd covered every single square inch of the apartment, and our knuckles were now red and sore from the endless tapping on walls, floors, and closets.

Dave and I decided to head outside where we could talk more freely and paged Salcedo from a Pizza Hut along the Cali River. He called back from a pay phone at a nearby restaurant which, incredibly, turned out to be only a few hundred yards away. He assured us that the hidden compartment *was* there—in one of the bathrooms, to be more specific—but he didn't know which one. Once again, he promised to call back as soon as he gathered more intel during his meeting with William. We were grateful for the flurry of activity on Salcedo's end—it allowed him to dash in and out and talk privately without raising any red flags.

Once back in the apartment, we put all our focus on every inch of each bathroom...*nothing*. It was now almost 5:00 p.m., and we'd been in the apartment for nearly ten hours, but we weren't walking out of that apartment unless El Señor was walking out with us.

The prosecutor, however, was done. "We need to wrap this up and wrap it up soon," he announced to the group. Jerry and Ruben headed out to take measurements of the bathrooms in the apartments above and below 402 to see if there were any discrepancies that made the ones in 402 unique, while Dave and I stayed behind, the walls of the bathrooms beginning to close in on us. We paged Salcedo again. Nothing.

Eventually the prosecutor reached his limit. "In ten minutes, we're out of here!" he said, before stepping outside to smoke a cigarette. We cringed.

Half delirious, we decided that if we only had one shot left, we should key in on the half bath across from the office, the only one we felt hadn't been thoroughly scoured. I crouched down on the floor, trying to avoid the scattered puddles of urine. Then I opened the sink's cabinet and it hit the toilet. *That's strange.* Was it just shoddy workmanship, or something else? With only minutes to spare and just as we both started to genuinely panic, I spotted a thin, barely visible tube concealed behind the cabinet, seamlessly blended into the wall. Dave took some quick measurements of the bathroom, and realized that it was smaller than the two apartments directly above and below. This was it. This *had* to be the *caleta*.

I yelled for Jerry to bring the tools, and Captain Buitrago and others rushed in to see what was happening. When Buitrago asked us what we'd found, we ignored him.

Jerry burst in, black bag in one hand and a sledgehammer in the other. He took out a drill, attached a twelve-inch bit, and drilled into the wall until the bit broke. He quickly changed bits as we held our breath. Captain Buitrago turned to Dave and grabbed his arm. "How did you find that? Who's your source?" Silence. Jerry drilled again, and the second drill bit broke, too.

Buitrago, enraged, turned to Dave again. "Who's your source? Tell me! Who's your source?"

Jerry kept his focus. He put in the third bit, plunged the drill forward, and hit a sudden and clear lack of resistance. "It's through!" Jerry cried. "There's a void back here!"

"We got him!" I said. Captain Buitrago raced out of the washroom, ashen, as Ruben grabbed the sledgehammer and began to furiously bash away at the back wall. The tile started to break, and we knew that with just a few more swings the DEA would have their prize. In just a matter of seconds, we all thought, the Cali godfather himself would finally be in handcuffs.

The Collapse

Even amidst the cacophony of hammering and smashing, we could distinctly hear Captain Buitrago complaining on the balcony to the prosecutor that American agents were in the bathroom causing serious damage to the walls. Damn right we were. The last thing on our minds was the cost of future renovation.

At that moment, a well-dressed man in a suit and tie marched into the washroom, a small black case in his hand. He surveyed the scene and told us, in his most authoritative tone, "You are to cease and desist immediately. You are conducting a unilateral operation and damaging property in violation of Colombian law. The warrant said nothing about damaging property."

"What?" Dave and I said in unison. Dave's expression darkened. "Is this a joke?" he asked. "We just found the one thing we've spent literally *hours* searching for. We all know that Miguel Rodríguez is right behind this wall! Also, who are *you*?"

To our dismay, he told us: he was, in fact, the chief prosecutor and head of the regional attorney general's office in Cali.

Somehow, we managed to regain our composure just long enough to show him the holes from the drill and the void behind the wall, explaining again how Miguel was just mere inches away, listening to us talk about him.

He was unmoved. "You have no authority here," he said. "And I'm going to need each of your diplomatic *carnets*. Now."

Our fucking *identification*? "Wait a minute," I pleaded. "Please, listen to me. Do you not understand that the actual head of the Cali cartel is directly behind that wall? Just give us one more minute!"

That didn't go over well. "*You* listen. I'm the one in charge in this room. Not you, not Colonel Murcia. *Me*." He turned his back to us. "Colonel Murcia, bring the American agents into the dining room."

Colonel Murcia and Captain Buitrago walked the four of us into the living room like we were being marched down death row. It was a walk I had envisioned a hundred times before, except in my mind instead of *us* being marched it was Buitrago, with me and Dave escorting him directly to jail for aiding and abetting the Cali cartel.

I thought back to Foreign Affairs Minister Rodrigo Pardo's nine points on limiting DEA activity in Colombia. Well, kudos to Pardo, I thought, because it damn sure seemed to be working out pretty well for them today.

"Sit down and give me your *carnets*," the regional prosecutor demanded, then walked to the front door, locked it, and tucked the keys into his pocket. For the very first time, Dave and I felt truly uncomfortable—nervous, even. The prosecutor whipped out a portable typewriter from his black case, sat down, and started typing. Checking the front door, I found that it was indeed locked—a deeply disconcerting discovery.

"Your *carnets*," the prosecutor repeated. We handed them over.

"Are we under arrest?" I asked.

"No," the prosecutor replied.

"Then we're leaving," I countered.

"You can't leave," the prosecutor shot back.

"Then we *are* under arrest," I said. "And we have the right to call our embassy." The regional prosecutor knew he couldn't object, so Ruben grabbed his cell phone from the table, contacted Assistant Attaché Rinehart, and told him what was happening.

As the prosecutor pounded away at his ancient typewriter, I asked if we could please move around and stretch a little bit. Squinting his eyes at us over the typewriter, he nodded an affirmative. I turned to Dave and together we walked casually back to the office, where what remained of the desk wreckage was still scattered across the floor. I realized we had another urgent problem: still in our possession were photos of the building, hand-drawn maps, our phones, even our pagers—we couldn't risk them falling into the hands of the prosecutor should we be searched or removed from the building. But the regional prosecutor was on a mission, and we had no idea what was going to happen to us.

We called over to Mike, who was outside in the hallway. He rushed over to face us from the other side of the office window, and, as covertly as possible, we pulled back the window's metal grates and slipped him our pagers, our cell phones, the photos—anything that could link us to Salcedo. We were pretty sure we were about to face severe repercussions in Bogotá after this debacle, but he was still our number one priority.

When we returned to the living room the regional prosecutor was still working away, clearly enjoying giving us the silent treatment as he typed his formal complaint, his *denuncia*. It was now 6:30 p.m., and we'd been detained for over an hour.

It was a challenge to focus, but our thoughts kept returning to Salcedo. He had *some* cover, sure—he'd never been to the apartment before, he had no prior knowledge about the secret compartment in the desk or even the *caleta* in the bathroom. But could the cartel figure out he was the leak some other way? Or would they just skip the conjecture and clean house, executing anyone they deemed a suspect?

The regional prosecutor typed his last few words and pulled the paper from the typewriter. "I need each of you to sign here," he said.

"Actually, we're not required to sign *anything*," I said.

"Well, then…you're free to go," the regional boss said sarcastically, shrugging his shoulders—a begrudging admission that what I'd just said was true. "Colonel Murcia, escort the Americans out of the building." The prosecutor glared at Dave as he handed him a copy of the complaint.

A large crowd was still gathered outside the Colinas de Santa Rita building, crammed in behind the yellow tape the police had put up to cordon off the area earlier that morning. By now the entire country knew that a major government operation had been undertaken to arrest Miguel Rodríguez, and an army of reporters and media trucks was impatiently waiting for any news. As Colonel Murcia walked us down the steps to the garage in order to avoid the frenzy out front, I asked him to station guards outside both the apartment and the building.

"Colonel, I promise you: he's in there, behind that wall. He has to come out sooner or later and when he does, you can grab him. Whatever you do, *please*, just don't leave!" Murcia nodded. He promised he would stay.

Bracing ourselves for the hysteria, we ran out of the garage and into a waiting SUV, the hordes of Colombian press ready to pounce. We sped out of the neighborhood with them in hot pursuit, running behind the vehicle snapping photos and screaming. Inside the SUV, Dave and I were too stunned to speak. A *friend* (or friends) connected to the cartel had intervened, and the operation was officially a failure—*another* failure. Worse, Dave and I now had to make the call we both dreaded. We pulled over to the same Pizza Hut pay phone we'd been to hours before and called Salcedo.

"*Hola!*" he said, in a tone that made it clear he was expecting good news. Telling him that we were, in fact, leaving—had already left—was brutal. "What?! You can't leave! He's there!" Salcedo was horrified. I told him everything: we knew he was there—we'd even found the compartment in the bathroom—but the prosecutor had shut down the raid anyway.

"Then you have to go back. How could you leave? This will make your whole career!" There was a pause as he struggled to compose himself. "If you leave, I'm a dead man!"

Salcedo was justifiably desperate. He tried everything in his arsenal to get us to go back, and I told him how the four of us had actually been *arrested* and escorted out of the building—there was no going back. I told him we'd at least been able to get the police to stand guard outside the apartment and building—but I knew that meant nothing. It was over.

"I'm sorry…we both are," I told him. "We let you down. That was the last thing we wanted to do." There was silence on the other end of the phone.

We offered to come collect Salcedo and his family to take them to Bogotá under DEA protection, but he refused. We all knew the danger he now faced, but he thought he could, somehow, weather the storm. Dave grabbed the phone from me and begged him to reconsider. We were determined to keep our word and get him and his family to the US safely, but he wouldn't allow it. We were helpless.

"I'll be okay," Salcedo said, trying to reassure us. "I know you did your best." There was a short pause, then he hung up.

Devastated, we headed to the Cali airport to wait for the DEA aircraft to arrive from Bogotá. It was now almost 9:00 p.m., and we were both furious with ourselves for not finding the *caleta* sooner. What if our actions that night—or lack thereof—cost Salcedo his life, or his *family's* lives? It was a horrible thought, but we couldn't stop thinking about it.

As we sat in a state of disbelief, Salcedo called back with an update: the cartel was putting a plan in motion to extract Miguel from the *caleta*. Dave called Colonel Murcia and told him that no matter what, he had to ensure that the uniformed police presence didn't abandon their posts outside apartment 402 and the Santa Rita building under any circumstances.

It was after midnight when we flew back to the capital city, and Ruben and Jerry passed out in the back of the plane almost immediately. They were almost as exhausted as Dave and I were, but they weren't carrying the same heavy, emotional burden. They, too, had been inches away from arresting the world's most-wanted drug kingpin and had failed, just as we had. But not at the possible cost of other people's lives.

Trying his best to drum up even the smallest bit of hope, Dave turned to me and said, "Hey, maybe it's not over. Maybe we'll get another shot." I closed my eyes and shook my head, and after a minute Dave spoke up again. "What do you think will happen to Sean?"

I bowed my head back down close to my chest, eyes still closed. "I think he's a dead man walking," I said. "And it's all our fault."

CHAPTER 23

You Wanna Do What?

"Desperate times call for desperate measures."
—HIPPOCRATES,
Greek Physician and Philosopher

THE FLIGHT BACK TO BOGOTÁ took less than an hour, but to me and Dave it felt like an eternity. There was no chance of us getting any sleep—our mutual panic over Salcedo's fate was too all-consuming.

This was the low point of our careers, and we knew it. And it wasn't because we'd failed to capture Miguel—of course, that was a big part of it—but it was because someone had put their life in our hands, and we'd let that someone down. We had no idea what might be happening to Salcedo, but the images that raced through our minds were ghastly.

Later that Sunday morning as I tried to catch a few hours of sleep, my DEA cell phone rang. It was *the* boss, Tony Senneca. *Oh shit,* I thought. *This can't be good.* The entire Cali team, along with Attachés Senneca and Rinehart, had been summoned to Ambassador Frechette's residence to discuss our detention, arrest, failure—*whatever* we were calling it—to arrest Miguel.

Over fourteen hours had passed since we'd last had contact with Salcedo. News reports began to air on Colombian television about the operation to arrest Miguel, and as usual, the DEA was front and center. At one point an actual copy of the official complaint filed against us by the Cali prosecutor appeared on the screen, flashing the names of the four

196

DEA agents who conducted "a unilateral and illegal action" for everyone to see.

I picked up Dave on the way to the ambassador's residence, and we quickly reviewed our talking points. Dave literally lived across the street from the ambassador, so we only had a few minutes to get our story straight. When we arrived, we were all escorted into the mansion's library. The residence was stunning, as elegant and refined as the Explorers Club in New York City. Hundreds of books lined the mahogany bookshelves of the massive library, giving the space a distinguished if also somewhat austere feel. Dave, Jerry, Ruben, Senneca, Rinehart, and I sat on two couches facing each other, and once again I felt like a mischievous kid sitting in the principal's office. We all knew what was coming. "Well, *this* isn't gonna be fun," I said to Senneca.

"Just let me do the talking," he replied.

The ambassador was rarely in a good mood, especially when it came to dealing with the DEA. It wasn't that he didn't respect our work (we believed he did, for the most part), but the truth was that the DEA always managed to wreak some kind of havoc for the mission in Colombia that, inevitably, caused a headache for the State Department—going back to the days of Escobar and Joe Toft. Chaos came naturally to the DEA, but in our minds that actually meant that we were doing our job. That didn't always go over well with career diplomats in foreign countries. Technically speaking, Dave and I *had* violated every directive set forth by the ambassador when it came to Cali. Deep down, we knew we deserved whatever was headed our way.

Frechette was an astute and redoubtable ambassador. He always held the Colombian government's feet to the fire and never hesitated to tell them what was on his mind, even when it was something they didn't want to hear. They didn't necessarily fear him, but they certainly respected him. Frechette was the right ambassador at just the right time: no one else was better suited to deal with President Ernesto Samper and his administration. In DEA speak: when it came to the Colombian government, he didn't take any shit.

When the ambassador walked into the room, all of us stood. He was wearing his usual attire—white shirt, suspenders, slightly loosened tie—along with his usual scowl. As he walked past, he glared at us from just over the rim of his glasses. He carried a stack of papers in one hand, and before we could even begin to speculate what they might be, the tirade began.

"Sit down," he commanded.

"Here we go," I said to myself.

"Was I not clear in my directive that you were to assist the Search Bloc *only* in a support and advisory capacity?" the ambassador bellowed, his face growing flushed. "So, tell me: Why were you even *on* the raid, and what exactly where you doing drilling holes and smashing the bathroom wall with a sledgehammer, of all things?"

"Mr. Ambassador..."

Frechette shut Senneca down without even looking at him.

"Shut up. I want to hear from one of *them*," the ambassador said, staring directly at me and Dave.

I started off, and immediately my talking points turned into a kind of incoherent rambling. "Well, Mr. Ambassador, the police lost interest in the raid early on—they sat down and turned on the TV, they were watching a soccer match, and, I mean, as for later on, well, that was because we were acting on credible information that we'd just received from our asset that Miguel was hiding in a secret compartment in the bathroom..."

The ambassador wasn't impressed. "I see. And in acting on that 'credible information,' you managed to get yourselves arrested!" He flung a copy of the prosecutor's formal complaint onto the coffee table along with a copy of that day's *El Pais* newspaper, which featured a grainy photograph of four DEA agents exiting the garage of the Santa Rita apartment building on its front page.

"Let me make this perfectly clear. If *anything* like this happens again, you'll all be on the first flight back to Miami. Understood?"

"Yes, sir," the six of us said, in unison.

"You're damn lucky the police found what they did, or you wouldn't even be sitting here right now," Frechette continued. Then his tone slightly changed. "As it turns out, it looks like your source was right."

The ambassador's shift caught us by surprise. We sat riveted as he told us what happened after our hasty retreat—he'd gotten the story from General Serrano himself when they'd spoken earlier that morning.

Several hours after we'd left the scene, the general ordered police to return to the apartment sometime after midnight. When the group reconvened in apartment 402, they found the bathroom wall broken apart, along with heaps of evidence scattered inside the exposed *caleta* and on the floor: bloody clothing, an oxygen tank and mask, and more. Frechette handed us several photographs of the bathroom showing the smashed-in wall and some of the evidence. Dave and I had already worked ourselves into a frenzy imagining Miguel triumphantly emerging from the *caleta*—now we were looking at the real thing. "Son of a bitch," Dave mumbled.

Frechette told us more about the explosive cache of documents we'd recovered from the hidden compartment inside the desk, and the sheer amount of information was overwhelming. A preliminary review of the documents by CNP officials revealed a list of almost 2,800 (2,800!) names that included military personnel, police, members of Congress, mayors, state governors, judges, journalists, and countless other corrupt officials working in the highest levels of government. There was also the photocopy of the $50,000 check made payable to President Samper's former campaign treasurer Santiago Medina and (supposedly) a hand-written letter sent from Defense Minister Fernando Botero to the Rodríguez Orejuela brothers, personally thanking them for the money the Cali cartel had contributed to candidate Samper's presidential campaign.

The documents would surely dominate the news once leaked, which was only a matter of time—nothing stayed secret in Colombia for long. But how many of those documents would US officials get their hands on? A few? Most? *All* of them, even the most sensitive ones?

The ambassador gave us a minute or two to digest everything, then asked if we had any updates on our asset.

"No, sir, nothing. Chris and I just want to know if he's still alive," Dave said. "We're hoping to head back to Cali in the next few days." It was a crafty response. Dave knew not to push it, opting instead to try and subtly determine our fate.

There was a long silence before the ambassador put us out of our misery.

"Very well, then. Just remember the rules," Frechette said. "No unilateral action under *any* circumstances. Understood?"

"Yes, sir," we said, again in unison.

Frechette nodded. "Remember: let the Colombians take the lead. This is their country."

Walking out of the ambassador's residence that afternoon, Dave and I knew that it was a miracle we were remaining in Colombia, and an even bigger miracle that we'd be doing so with no additional consequences. The discovery of the smashed-in wall was nothing short of a revelation, and the one-two punch of the hidden compartment and bevy of documents was no doubt the *only* reason our assignments weren't curtailed. But our good fortune didn't equal a good mood. Not knowing what may have happened to Salcedo and his family was torture. We'd left him several more messages and gotten no response in return.

Three full days had now passed since we'd last heard from Salcedo. With each passing hour, we felt more helpless. The burden was ours alone—if Dave and I didn't take any action, no one would.

That Tuesday evening, I called Dave and asked him to meet me at a bar in Bogotá's Zona Rosa. I didn't dare say what I had in mind over the phone.

Dave, thinking I had good news to share, knew otherwise when he saw my face. He spoke first.

"I think Sean's dead," he said. "I think he's dead, and as for his family..." He stopped, looked down, and shook his head slowly from side to side.

"Hopefully, he's just laying low," I said, unconvincingly. We assumed that anyone who'd spoken to Miguel in the last week or two was a suspect, but we had no idea how many people that could be. Dave, despite fearing the worst, was adamant we do something. He wanted to return to Cali and not leave until we found him—or at least found out what happened to him.

"We gave him our word," Dave said. "We can't just leave him and his family there to be—"

I cut him off before he could finish. I didn't need to hear the end of that sentence.

"I have an idea," I said. "But I don't think you're gonna like it."

"What is it?" Dave asked, pulling his chair in closer.

"I want to meet with Buitrago and then, you know... make him talk," I said awkwardly.

"You wanna do what? Are you insane?" Dave understood where I was going with this, but he still couldn't believe it. "You wanna 'make' a *captain in the Colombian National Police* talk?!"

"He's a corrupt piece of shit!" I yelled, smashing my fist onto the bar so hard our beer bottles shook. I almost never lost my cool, so Dave was stunned. "If anything happened to Salcedo, he's the one who'd know," I said. "Whatever it takes, remember?"

Dave knew I wasn't backing down. "Of course I remember. I just hope you know what you're doing."

"That makes two of us," I said. The truth was I had no idea.

Dave was reluctant, and rightfully so. Any action taken against a CNP official would lead to the most severe of repercussions, and here we were, only a few days after our ass-kicking in the ambassador's office, openly debating not if, but how, we could violate his directive about unilateral action once again. We wouldn't just be breaking our word, we'd be breaking the law—more like shattering it, actually. If ever there was a point of no return, this was it. We'd be lucky if the only ramification was being declared persona non grata and removed from the country, but the more likely outcome would be our swift termination from the DEA, possible prosecution, and the complete collapse of our careers. Still, we figured we owed Salcedo that much.

It was easy to imagine what people would say: Why do you care? Why risk your livelihoods on an informant, let alone a criminal informant for one of the most brutal drug cartels of our time? Valid points. But, in our minds, irrelevant ones.

Neither Dave nor I were foolish enough to think Salcedo hadn't made serious mistakes—but he'd chosen to risk his life in order to save his family and atone for those mistakes. Also, again, we'd given him our word. People choose to live their life by their own standards, but in the law enforcement game, at the end of the day, all you have is your word. Your word is your bond, your integrity, and your reputation. We had an obligation.

Dave and I left the bar that night with a tentative plan in place: prepare to travel to Cali on July 20, in just two days' time.

The next morning, we called Captain Buitrago and said we needed to meet with him when we arrived and that it was urgent, relying on the ruse that we'd received new intel from our source about Miguel's whereabouts. We suggested a meeting spot near the Cali airport.

Buitrago was weak. We knew it wouldn't take much to get him to talk—at least that's what we told ourselves. Hell, he'd probably give everything up if we just asked him nicely. Failing that, a good old-fashioned threat to expose his corrupt activities to General Serrano and Colombian prosecutors should be enough of a motivating factor. We weren't sure how it was going to play out or how far we'd have to go, but we had to see it through.

July 20 was Colombian Independence Day, a national holiday commemorating the day in 1810 when residents of Bogotá staged an uprising against Spanish rule, marking the beginning of the independence movement. Before departing for Cali later that afternoon, Dave and I stopped by the apartment of an Alcohol, Tobacco, and Firearms (ATF) agent and good friend named Bill, who was hosting a celebratory barbeque.

As we were busy devouring burgers and mingling with other guests, my SkyPager vibrated. My heart was racing as I looked down at the screen: *Call Carmen!* I yelled for Dave, and together we ran to the balcony and deciphered the number in the message. I can't even begin to describe the relief we both felt—to this day, I've never seen Dave so ecstatic. Not only was our asset alive, but we could cross "Confront Captain Buitrago and probably lose our jobs" off our to-do list, which made both of us breathe a hell of a lot easier.

When we spoke, Salcedo told us that the cartel was actively searching for the spy—and that his name *was* on the short list of possible suspects. But he assured us he was okay—at least for the time being—and he was just trying to act as normally as possible, keeping his family in place and sticking to their usual routines. Keeping him alive was the fact that Miguel refused to believe that Salcedo, his loyal, trusted head of security, could possibly be the traitor—and Miguel's opinion was the only one that mattered. But there were others who felt differently, namely Miguel's eldest son, William, and Genaro Ángel, the man responsible for Cali's ingenious cocaine concealment methods and co-designer of more than a few of the cartel's *caletas*. Ángel was a cagey and unpredictable operative, and also extremely close to Miguel.

There was one other man who was suspicious of Salcedo, someone who posed even more of a threat than William or Ángel: Humberto Valencia, the former army Search Bloc sergeant who'd served under Colonel Velásquez. Valencia had recently been fired for failing a polygraph test administered by the military, who'd been investigating ongoing compromises and corruption in the specialized unit. Since he was already on the cartel's payroll due to his moonlighting gig as an asset, he became just another former military official joining the ranks of the Cali KGB in a full-time capacity. He was intelligent, experienced, and intimidating, and also one of the growing number of operatives Salcedo had to keep a close eye on.

Salcedo also told us that Miguel had been moved again, with only a *very* select few aware of his exact whereabouts. Once again Salcedo was not among them, and all he could offer us was the general area, nothing more. He needed more time to narrow down potential targets and eliminate others.

This time, the cartel wasn't taking any chances with Miguel's safety. Ángel had been put in charge of the "first ring" or inner security at Miguel's new location (at William's behest) while Salcedo was charged with overseeing the second ring—or outer perimeter—security. The new assignment hampered Salcedo's ability to identify possible locations, since he couldn't risk being seen anywhere close to the area where Ángel's inner security ring and men were stationed.

Over the next several days, Dave and I had only sporadic contact with Sean. We were impatient to get answers to the many questions we had about what had happened that surreal Saturday night—there were so many things we still didn't know. But with cartel spies lurking around every corner, we had to be more vigilant than ever, especially when talking on the telephone or meeting with Salcedo. Dave and I only used our burner phones and alternating public telephones when we spoke with him. The full story came to us slowly and incrementally, but over time Salcedo began to fill in the missing pieces of exactly what had happened in the wake of the Santa Rita raid. It was a puzzle that was growing more complicated every single day.

CHAPTER 24

The Boys Are Back in Town

"The life of spies is to know, not be known."
—GEORGE HERBERT,
English Poet and Orator

JORGE SALCEDO WOULD NEVER GET USED TO living a double life. Exhausted from the stress of alternating between his role as loyal chief of security for the head of the Cali Mafia and his new, equally dangerous gig as double agent for the DEA, he was walking a very fine line. Recommending additional security precautions and improvements to Miguel was demanding enough, and at the same time he was doing the exact opposite, trying to identify weak spots and ways to infiltrate the cartel's defenses. He was also busy trying to gather more intel on Miguel's exact location. Amidst all that, he was still able to describe to me and Dave the details of what had transpired following the failed raid one week ago.

After our untimely eviction, the scene in apartment 402 got even more dramatic. William called another emergency security meeting to discuss Miguel's extraction from the apartment—a meeting Salcedo wasn't initially invited to. At that point, Salcedo was well aware of the fact that he was considered one of—if not the—prime suspects. As he sat pondering his next move, he received a page from Fercho. When Salcedo called back, he was shocked to discover that it was actually El Señor himself who wanted to speak with him.

Salcedo listened as Miguel, frantic, explained what was going on: sometime after we'd left, Fercho had carefully smashed open the rest of the *caleta* in the bathroom and removed Miguel from the tiny compartment. Being a prisoner in a cramped space with barely enough room to turn around in for over eighteen hours had left Miguel a mess: he was breathing heavily, his nose was bleeding, and his clothes were disheveled and sweaty. He was also still trapped inside the apartment, with police from the Search Bloc standing vigilant outside the building. Miguel wouldn't be going anywhere without someone's help, and it was Salcedo's help he wanted.

Miguel's call gave Salcedo the only reason he needed to attend the meeting. During a discussion about possible extraction plans, Salcedo learned of a new safe house in a "white building" that was being readied for Miguel in the Normandía or Juanambú area, not far from the compromised Santa Rita apartment. It wasn't much to go on, but it was a start.

Meanwhile, Miguel was desperate. In addition to Salcedo, he also called Captain Buitrago for assistance in extracting him from the apartment. Buitrago, who was already familiar with the Santa Rita complex, was able to easily gain entry into the building, covertly remove Miguel from the apartment and into the garage, then smuggle him out in the trunk of his car—all while police officials were, in theory, supposedly standing guard outside.

While William, Ángel, and Sergeant Valencia remained wary of Salcedo, Miguel remained obstinate, refusing to believe that he had anything to do with the raid. He knew Salcedo had never been to the apartment, nor did he have any clue about the *caleta* or its location. In an ironic twist, Miguel assigned Salcedo the task of personally hunting down the guilty party, essentially asking Salcedo to investigate himself. Miguel next ordered Salcedo to debrief Fercho in order to find out everything he saw and heard, in the hope that it would help determine how the DEA ultimately got to him.

To Salcedo's relief, Fercho's description of what had occurred inside apartment 402 that day provided some welcome cover. Fercho said that American DEA agents had been periodically communicating with a woman they called Carmen, and it was obvious that *she* was the informant. Captain Buitrago corroborated Fercho's account of this mystery woman—he'd also overheard some of the conversations with Carmen/

Sean/Salcedo and drawn what he thought were the obvious conclusions. While Salcedo did as much as he could to play up this new lead, he couldn't rule out the possibility that Carmen could be a code name or alias—and maybe not even a woman. But suspicion had shifted ever so slightly away from Salcedo, buying him some much-needed time.

Fercho also offered up another nugget of information that solved a mystery that had been driving Dave and me crazy for the past week: how Miguel knew that we were coming in the first place. The source was General Serrano's personal pilot, Juan Carlos, a commissioned officer and friend of the Rodríguez Orejuela family whose flight school they'd footed the bill for years ago. We hadn't seen that one coming, but at least we knew for sure that it wasn't anyone from the American Embassy.

The explanation made perfect sense. Anytime the general planned a trip, he contacted Juan Carlos to ready the aircraft and be on standby. After receiving the general's late-night travel notification, Juan Carlos called Miguel to warn him—the cartel knew that if General Serrano was coming to Cali, it was because a major police operation was underway and the general would be hoping for a prime-time photo op. Security then was doubled around the godfathers, and spies at the Search Bloc were notified to report on any planned enforcement activity. From that point on, everyone was on high alert.

One of the many things Dave and I learned about Salcedo over the course of our conversations was that he was extremely deliberate—he never, ever took action without thoroughly thinking it through. If anyone had earned the nickname "the Chess Player," it was Salcedo, not Gilberto. Though we never proved it, Dave and I always suspected that it was Salcedo pulling the strings behind then security chief del Vasto's arrest at the América de Cali soccer field back in June. When Dave and I asked him about it, he denied any involvement, and we didn't press the issue.

But we also didn't buy his denial, so we weren't surprised when we heard that Sergeant Valencia—who also now posed a danger to Salcedo—was arrested by military intelligence officers outside his home on corruption-related charges. This time we didn't need to ask, but we did anyway. It *was* Salcedo. He was eliminating potential threats and creating more suspects at the same time.

On July 24, Salcedo told us about two potential buildings where Miguel could possibly be staying. He didn't have the names or addresses and couldn't risk attempting to find out—he couldn't afford to be seen anywhere near the area. He said he was sending photographs and a hand-drawn map of the two target buildings via Avianca Airlines courier service—they'd be in our hands in Bogotá the following day.

The package arrived the next afternoon. It contained photographs of two buildings marked 3 and 4, along with a sketch of the Normandía area with two buildings also labeled 3 and 4. Later that evening, Salcedo called and gave me the names and addresses of the two target locations, courtesy of a friend: Hacienda Buenos Aires, Calle 5 Oeste, Number 5A-50 and Edificio Alicante, Calle 2 Oeste, Number 5-06 (the buildings numbered 3 and 4, respectively).

A few days later, Salcedo offered up more critical information, including specific locations of perimeter security and cartel sentries along the Cali River and a fixed position from which Dave and I could surveil the two buildings under the cover of darkness. On August 1, we discovered that a tenth-floor apartment in Hacienda Buenos Aires was linked to Claudia Escobar (no relation), Miguel Rodríguez's paramour. This was the last chess piece we needed to finally get back in the game, and Dave, Jerry Salameh, and I made plans to travel back to Cali.

Image of two possible Miguel Rodríguez safe houses, taken from the surveillance post at the Statue of Sebastián de Belalcázar in the Parque del Acueducto: number three, Hacienda Buenos Aires, and number four, Edificio Alicante.

Later that afternoon, the boys were back in town for what we hoped would be one more shot at Don Miguel. We opted to fly into the air force base in our DEA airplane, something we did whenever possible (provided we obtained the required clearances in advance), because it made it far easier to bring along all our tactical gear and weaponry and spared us the hassle of dealing with airport security.

After landing, Jerry headed off to the navy safe house to stow our gear, while Dave and I prepared for a quick meeting with Salcedo. The Cali KGB remained on high alert, and we had to assume that Salcedo was being continually watched by cartel operatives. We needed to be more careful and hypervigilant than ever before.

The three of us convened at Parque del Acueducto, a picturesque hillside park adjacent to the iconic statue of Sebastián de Belalcázar, the Spanish conquistador credited with founding Santiago de Cali in 1536. I passed Salcedo an envelope containing a new burner cell phone and pager. "Make sure you get rid of the old ones," I said.

Salcedo nodded his head in the direction of two apartment buildings directly in front of us. "Those are the ones," he said. "Miguel has to be in one of them." Both buildings were white, roughly a thousand yards away, and differed slightly in height: one was about ten stories high and the other about twenty.

Salcedo then raised his hand and pointed north. "In the clearing on top of that mountain is an old flood-control channel," he said. "It should mask your approach to the edge of the mountainside. From there, you'll have to deal with a descent down the mountain that won't be easy, especially at night, but you should be able to circumvent perimeter security and arrive at the target undetected."

Dave and I nodded. We figured it wasn't going to be a simple mission—none of them had been.

"Meet me back out near CIAT after dusk tonight," he said, "and we'll review everything in more detail."

The entire encounter took less than two minutes, but true to form, Salcedo had given us everything we needed to know.

We looked over to the two towers, giving ourselves a minute to take them in. The bright white exteriors gave them a bland, innocuous look, but we knew that the activity unfolding inside and around them was

The statue of Sebastián de Belalcázar (surveillance location). In the background is Hacienda Buenos Aires, the arrest location of Miguel Rodríguez.

anything but mundane. They were extremely well protected, for one—not just by the surrounding mountainous terrain and the expected sizable cartel security detail, but also by the Cerro de Las Tres Cruces (the Hill of the Three Crosses) and the large, iconic eighty-five-foot statue of Cristo Rey (Christ the King), with his outstretched arms and regal gaze. The view was undeniably cinematic, with the surroundings giving the area a pious, almost saintly feel. Perhaps El Señor was looking for some kind of divine intervention, hoping that his choice of locale would lend him an air of righteousness and reverence, one more level of protection. But Dave and I knew that when it came down to it, Miguel spent most of his time thinking about money and power, not sainthood. He wasn't about to die for anyone's sins, not even his own.

CHAPTER 25

Coming Out Party

*"Never underestimate the effectiveness
of a straight cash bribe."*

—CLAUD COCKBURN,
British Journalist

Sugarcane field, Palmira, Colombia, August 1, 1995

DAVE AND I ARRIVED at the sugarcane fields at dusk. We were only about
a mile north from our initial meeting with Salcedo three weeks earlier, and
as we reconned the area we couldn't help feeling a strong sense of déjà vu.
We'd encountered more traffic than expected on the main throughway, so
we drove farther down a gravel roadway and deeper into the cane fields as
an extra precaution.

When Salcedo joined us, he came bearing gifts: more photographs of
the two target buildings, photos of the clearing and flood-control channel
from the top of the mountain, and a new hand-drawn map of the surrounding Normandía area. Dave and I had borrowed another vehicle from Mike,
and the three of us were huddled inside, examining Salcedo's bounty and
discussing possible strategies and approaches to the targets. If we'd been
forced to hazard a guess at Miguel's location, we would've picked Claudia
Escobar's apartment on the tenth floor of Hacienda Buenos Aires, but the
association itself wasn't enough—we needed much more. There was still

210

too much uncertainty—we didn't know the interior layout of the building or how many apartments there were per floor. And this time there could be zero room for doubt, because this time would be our last. If we failed, there would be no second—rather, third—chance to launch an operation against El Señor with Salcedo's help.

The best option to arrive at the buildings undetected appeared to be via the flood-control channel, then by descending the mountainside—it was essentially the only option if we wanted to effectively bypass cartel security. But attempting to navigate steep mountainous terrain in pitch-black conditions was both risky and dangerous. And even if we managed to pull it off, it would still take us forty-five minutes to get to the target location from the time we arrived at the insertion point and accessed the flood-control channel—and that's if everything went according to plan.

The only other option was via Avenida 4 along the Cali River, then along a series of quiet one-way surface streets through the serene neighborhood. We could never pass by two or three separate perimeter security points in a military convoy without alerting cartel sentries, especially in the early-morning hours. Our arrival had to be perfectly stealth, so flawless that Miguel wouldn't have time to even *think* about accessing the *caleta*. If we blew it and he hid himself away, chances were we'd never find him.

We weren't long into our planning session when the familiar flashing lights from several police vehicles sped past on the main road, followed closely by two taxis. Instinctively we froze. "That's our cue," I said. "Time to go."

Just then, a police van stopped in the middle of the intersection a few hundred yards away. I immediately grabbed the photos, maps, and other papers and stuffed them under the driver's seat of the car.

There was no way we could let those be found. It went without saying that two Americans hidden away in a remote cane field (and in possession of enhanced photographs of buildings in Cali) wouldn't exactly go over very well with Colombian authorities—just ask Major del Vasto. The very nature of the photographs would set off alarms, but far more importantly, we couldn't risk compromising the safety of our asset.

Knowing it wouldn't take long before the police spotted our vehicles, the three of us got out of the car to gain a better tactical advantage and have more time to react if needed. As predicted, the police van turned and raced toward us. From our semiconcealed position behind the two vehicles, Dave and I tossed our weapons, identification, phones, and everything else we had on us deep into the sugarcane fields. Even the subtlest of signs that we might be DEA agents would put Salcedo's life in danger. "Remember, you guys work at CIAT," he said. "If we get arrested, I'm a dead man. Do whatever you need to, but we can't get taken!" It was the first time we'd ever heard him sound panicked.

By this time, two young Colombian police officers—one lieutenant and one sergeant—were upon us. Leveling their Uzi submachine guns directly at our chests, they ordered us to raise our hands and asked for identification. Dave and I were worried—to say the least—but Salcedo was terrified. We faced possible nightmarish repercussions (again), but they paled in comparison to Salcedo's. I had echoes of Ambassador Frechette's booming voice reciting his "never, ever leave the base without an escort, and *no* unilateral action" speech racing through my mind, but Salcedo's entire life was running through his.

While the sergeant was busy patting us down for weapons, the lieutenant again asked for identification and demanded to know exactly what we were doing in the area. Dave and I calmly relayed our cover story: we were agricultural scientists and employees of CIAT and were researching means of alternative crop development—along with whatever other bullshit poured out of our mouths. We apologized and said we didn't have our CIAT credentials with us (as they were now deep inside the sugarcane fields along with all our other IDs). We were just out here meeting a friend after work and would be heading back to Cali soon.

They weren't buying it. Thankfully, Salcedo had some false identification with him, which he handed over to the lieutenant.

Since Dave and I had no identification and couldn't offer up a better reason than "meeting a friend" in the middle of nowhere, the lieutenant said he would have to file a report and take the three of us to the police station in Palmira for further questioning. "Shit," Salcedo mumbled under his breath. "We can't let that happen."

The lieutenant asked us yet again why we were there, adding that a taxi driver had just been robbed at gunpoint and had his car stolen not far from where we stood.

"Really? All the way out *here*?" I said.

Apparently, Murphy's Law was still toying with us. What were the chances of a robbery and carjacking happening miles away from Cali, in the middle of sugarcane fields, at the *exact* time we were there plotting the arrest of the leader of the Cali cartel? In our world, apparently, they were pretty good.

By this point, the lieutenant's patience had grown thin. Visibly annoyed, he said he wanted to search our vehicles before taking us to the station. *You've got to be fucking kidding me*, I thought. If they found what I'd stashed under the front seat, any attempts to explain would be pointless.

"Okay, hold on," I said, stalling so Dave and I could contemplate our options—if we even had any. "Wait, don't you have the keys?" I asked him. He knew exactly where they were—burning a hole in my right pocket—but he played along perfectly.

"We may need to take these guys down," I whispered to Dave as he continued his fake search. "We can't go anywhere with them."

Dave and I were both pretty confident when it came to our hand-to-hand combat skills, so we knew that a solid plan B would be to disarm and subdue the two officers, buying us just enough time to get the hell out of there with Salcedo in tow. Under *no* circumstances were we going to the police station—if that's even where they were really taking us. It wasn't an option. Besides, we weren't convinced the taxi story was even true—for all we knew, the officers were corrupt and on the cartel payroll. Suddenly, I couldn't get Kiki Camarena's brutal abduction and murder in Guadalajara out of my mind.

As I was speaking with the lieutenant, Dave capitalized on the brief distraction and quickly shifted to plan C. He figured that the new approach would give us a far better shot at success than some half-assed spontaneous showdown, and he was right. He discreetly slipped Salcedo a wad of Colombian pesos (which we always carried in case of any unforeseen operational expenses, like the two chicken trucks we'd rented for the Santa Rita raid). Salcedo took the cash and presented it to the officers. "Here, please just take this and leave us alone," he said. "You're embarrassing my friends for no good reason."

"We've done nothing wrong," I chimed in.

But the young lieutenant was sharper than I'd given him credit for. "If you haven't done anything wrong, then why are you offering me money?"

Damn. That was a valid question, and I struggled to find a decent comeback. The lieutenant and sergeant stepped aside to talk for a minute, buying us a bit more time. Finally, they broke their huddle, stepped back over, and again demanded to search our vehicles. *Leave it to us to find the only two honest cops in all of Cali*, I thought.

The sergeant walked me over to our car while the lieutenant escorted Dave and Salcedo to his. I guided the sergeant toward the passenger's side door first, knowing that the stack of photos, maps—everything—lay hidden beneath the driver's seat.

"See? There's nothing there," I said, holding open the door for him to lean in and see. I grimaced when I saw him lean farther in to inspect the front and rear areas and glove box and, finally, remove and verify the vehicle's registration to ensure it wasn't stolen. After searching the trunk, he seemed satisfied that at the very least we weren't armed robbers or taxi thieves. But we weren't out of the cane fields quite yet. They still had no idea why we were out there, and we hadn't exactly given them any good answers.

The sergeant escorted me back toward Salcedo's vehicle just as he was closing the trunk. "I told you, my friend, we've done nothing wrong," Salcedo said. The lieutenant just stared at the three of us, unconvinced.

Then, out of nowhere, Salcedo dropped a bomb. A big one.

"Okay, look." He let out a dramatic sigh. "I didn't want to have to say this, and it's kind of embarrassing, but … we're gay."

If pins actually dropped in sugarcane fields, trust me, you could have heard one at that moment. The lieutenant's jaw dropped, while Dave and I somehow managed to keep our composure—perhaps the best under-cover work of our careers thus far. It was the last thing any of us expected to hear, and it was brilliant. Salcedo, still feigning humiliation at Academy Award–winning levels, humbly offered up the cash once again.

"Please, just leave us be? We're not bothering anyone," Salcedo said softly, keeping his hand extended with the pile of pesos in his palm. "We don't have anywhere else to go."

The lieutenant and the sergeant looked at each other, then back at us, perplexed. It was a safe bet that this was *not* a situation they'd gone over in their job training. Meanwhile, Dave and I were bracing ourselves for plan B. I was hoping Dave's army airborne training hadn't gotten rusty.

Coming Out Party

The lieutenant looked me over again, shook his head, then waved over the sergeant to talk just out of earshot. After a minute or so, the sergeant returned and took the money from Salcedo. We were free to leave.

We waited until the police were completely out of sight, then trekked into the sugarcane field to find our identification, phones, and weapons. We all needed a minute to compose ourselves.

Finally, Salcedo broke the silence. "That was *too close*," he said. His hands were still trembling.

"How the hell did you even come up with that?" Dave asked.

"Well, I knew the police would believe it, mostly because of Chris's long hair," he said, and glanced at me, smiling. "Didn't you notice that they looked at you the longest?" He and Dave laughed.

"Whatever," I fired back, rolling my eyes. "I'm *so* glad I could be of assistance." And the embassy was worried I wouldn't blend in!

From that point on, Salcedo was always comfortable with me and Dave and never doubted that we would do everything in our power to keep him and his family safe—no matter what. I wondered what he'd think if he knew how far we'd been willing to go with Captain Buitrago only two weeks ago.

In the end, our late-night romantic rendezvous cost us the equivalent of about $300 (roughly $2,100 USD today). Later, when we submitted our "Claim for Reimbursement" report and supporting documentation to clear the advanced operational funds, our superiors thought it was a prank—Dave's DEA Form 6 (Report of Investigation) was literally entitled: "Payment of Bribe to CNP Official on August 1, 1995."

But if we ever thought that the incident in the sugarcane field was as surreal and stressful as things could get, we were wrong. Shortly afterward, Salcedo began to receive a nonstop stream of security and intelligence updates, and things began to unfold at a furious pace, most of them entirely out of our control. Dave and I were struggling to keep our heads above water. If the encounter with the police that night had taught us any lesson at all, it was that anything could happen. And no matter what, we had to be ready.

CHAPTER 26

Our Big Break

"Fortune sides with him who dares."
—VIRGIL, Roman Poet

WE'D BARELY RECOVERED FROM THE DEBACLE in the sugarcane field when Dave and I met up with Jerry at the statue of Sebastián de Belalcázar for our late-night unilateral surveillance. The statue itself was one of Cali's most iconic landmarks, and the area had always been a popular hangout where people gathered to watch the sunset, gaze at the burning sugarcane fields in the distance, and take in the vibrant views of the city. It was also an ideal spot to gather with friends, as it was filled with a variety of street entertainers, local artists, and enterprising vendors peddling their confections from small food and beverage carts every evening.

More importantly, the elevated park provided us with the perfect—and I do mean perfect—vantage point from which to conduct unobstructed surveillance of the two ivory towers. Because of the location of the buildings and the fixed positions of cartel security along key choke points, it was virtually impossible to surveil the apartments from a closer point. The buildings were directly in front of us only a half mile away, there was just one way in and one way out, and both were situated near the base of the mountain. Everything fit: now all we had to do was pinpoint Miguel Rodríguez's exact location.

Absolutely no one in the Colombian government had any idea what Dave and I were doing. Even within the confines of the DEA, it was essentially confidential—no more than three or four people knew. There was no way we could alert anyone to the fact that we had new intel on Miguel's possible location—even Mike and his navy team at the safe house didn't know, and we were staying under the same roof. They weren't entirely ignorant—they knew enough to know that we were operational; they just weren't privy to any of the details. We'd become like ghosts to them, showing our faces for only a few hours of sleep or a quick meal, constantly coming and going at all hours of the day and night.

We were practically ghosts to the other seventy-five or so people reveling in the nightly festivities at the dimly lit park, too—no one paid us much attention. We wore our usual ball caps and settled back in one of the darker corners with our cold beers, pretending to watch the burning sugarcane through our binoculars when, in reality, we were covertly monitoring the lights in the two target buildings. While we were fixated primarily on what we suspected was the tenth floor of Hacienda Buenos Aires—Claudia Escobar's floor—we waited until all the lights in both buildings were extinguished for the night before leaving.

We'd only been in position for an hour when Salcedo paged me. He wanted us to meet with him at the Unicentro mall—a strange request, as we were all still reeling from our close call earlier that night. When Dave and I arrived, we saw right away that Salcedo was distraught. He was dressed in all black and had parked in the darkest section of the parking lot. Despite his obvious nerves he got down to business, explaining to us that in our haste to get the hell out of the cane field, he'd forgotten to relay critical information he'd overheard from security personnel earlier that day: Fercho, El Señor's loyal assistant, was still in hiding. Miguel was worried that the police were actively looking for him after the discovery of the damaged *caleta*, so he'd swapped him out for his other trusted right-hand man, Jesus Zapata (Mateo), and the two were now together. Miguel had also rotated his domestic employees, bringing in two Afro-Colombian females from Buenaventura. Learning about the staff changes was key—it would help us confirm we were at the right location once we raided the apartment.

We were on our way back to the statue when Salcedo called again and asked us to circle back. It was fast approaching midnight, and now we were on edge, too. We pulled into the parking lot fifteen minutes later and Salcedo appeared, looking even more frazzled than he had before. By now, there was no denying that the trauma from the encounter in the cane field, coupled with the constant stress of his role as a double agent, was manifesting itself not just internally for him but externally as well. The once unflappable security chief was showing obvious signs of anxiety, which, given his current position, was a huge red flag. For the first time, Dave and I were concerned that other Cali operatives would take notice, if they hadn't already. If Salcedo couldn't pull himself together, it wouldn't be long before suspicion turned into certainty. And if that happened, we all knew how it would end.

Salcedo told us that Yusti had just called him with an update: the threat to Guillermo Pallomari was now extreme. While Salcedo had been slow-walking Miguel's order to locate him, Yusti had been making steady progress after Jaime Gil Osorio, Pallomari's Colombian attorney, was "persuaded" to assist in the hunt. Gil reluctantly revealed to Yusti the southern Cali neighborhood Pallomari was taking refuge in, which happened to be less than a mile from where we were currently meeting. Yusti bragged to Salcedo that he was certain he'd uncover Pallomari's exact location within the next few days—then it was just a matter of finishing the job. It was what Yusti did best: find, attack, and kill.

The cartel also had a separate team of assassins following Pallomari's wife, Patricia. They were camped outside her business in downtown Cali, patiently waiting and hoping she'd let down her guard and lead them directly to her husband.

Salcedo understood that the information Pallomari possessed regarding the Cali syndicate wasn't just vast, it was invaluable. He knew exactly how the cartel operated, and there was no way he could hide out forever. What Pallomari needed was protection, something he could get only if he managed to land safely in the hands of American agents.

Dave and I hadn't had much luck in our own efforts to locate Pallomari. There were only two of us, and we were consumed with the search for Miguel. Salcedo urged us to reach out to Pallomari's wife at her business, Universal Link. If we could warn her about just how serious the threat against her husband was, and she could relay that information to him, there was a chance that Guillermo might decide to cooperate.

But approaching Patricia at her business was extremely risky. With assassins watching her every move, there was no way Dave and I could set foot in the building without being exposed, which would trigger an immediate upgrade to Miguel's already formidable protection setup. Perimeter security would be doubled or even tripled, or they'd move him to a different location entirely. Worse, the meeting could also be construed as a sign that Pallomari was *already* cooperating with the DEA, putting Patricia and her two children (not to mention me and Dave) in even greater peril. We had a lot to think about.

When we finally returned to the park, only one light remained lit in the two target buildings: Hacienda Buenos Aires. We counted the floors from the top of the building down to the illuminated apartment, then again from the ground floor up. Still unsure of the exact layout, our best guess was that the light emanated from the tenth or eleventh floor. It finally extinguished for the night just before 2:00 a.m.

Our regimen of early-morning and late-night meetings with Salcedo continued. Dave and I needed to gather as much intel as we could as quickly as possible: time was fast becoming our enemy. Attorney General Valdivieso and his Proceso 8.000 investigation were gaining momentum, and the walls of the proverbial dam were cracking. We feared a massive tidal wave was headed our way.

Shortly after the Santa Rita raid, some of the documents we'd recovered from Miguel's desk began to leak. Santiago Medina, Samper's treasurer during the presidential campaign, made a voluntary statement to Colombian prosecutors confirming that the check for $50,000 from Miguel Rodríguez had, indeed, been accepted by campaign staff. Nine days later, Medina was arrested for illicit enrichment—a.k.a. receiving money from the cartel. It was Medina's arrest that officially started the tsunami.

Opting to cooperate with the Attorney General's Office, Medina made more statements, going so far as to *directly* accuse President Samper and former campaign manager (now defense minister) Fernando Botero of having knowledge that drug monies from the Cali cartel had entered the campaign. In fact, Medina said, they'd *both* ordered him to accept the cash. In a televised address to the nation, President Samper again denied having any knowledge of cartel money ever being received and called for a full investigation.

AFTER ESCOBAR

On August 1, 1995, the Colombian prosecutor's office requested that the Supreme Court initiate a preliminary investigation into Defense Minister Botero based on Medina's explosive statements. The following day Botero resigned, and what was left of President Samper's administration was on the verge of collapse.

Back in Cali the snowballing political drama only added to Miguel's anxiety. He demanded constant updates on the Pallomari hit and ramped up the pressure on Salcedo and Yusti. Eliminating the accountant was Miguel's highest priority. Pallomari could corroborate everything Santiago Medina said, and until he was put to rest—literally—he was a ticking time bomb.

Our meetings with Salcedo were now averaging two or three a day in between our nighttime surveillance activities, and each meeting brought more information. Miguel had heard from some of his corrupt sources that one of the ways the DEA had identified the Santa Rita apartment was by watching the lights of each apartment and noting which ones turned off last, so he'd begun to extinguish all lights in his residence prior to 2:00 a.m., which coincided with our previous night of surveillance.

Over the next two nights, our unilateral surveillance eliminated Edificio Alicante and all other apartments in Hacienda Bueno Aires, except for what we suspected was the tenth floor. As anticipated, on both evenings that was where the last light was turned off.

Of all people, it was a local real estate agent who gave us additional critical information we needed. Through undercover inquiries, we'd confirmed with the agent—who'd listed an apartment for rent in Hacienda Buenos Aires—that the building had nineteen stories and, most notably, had only one large luxury residence per floor.

On our third night of surveillance, Jerry, Dave, and I were huddled at our hillside post next to the statue of Belalcázar. It was just before 1:00 a.m. on August 4 and our target was dark, save for one dim light emanating from the tenth floor—which we now knew was just one enormous apartment. As Dave and I keyed in and looked more closely, I spotted some activity.

"Holy shit, a light just came on," I said, zooming in on the apartment window. "Looks like it could be the kitchen. There's movement!"

"What? I can't make anything out!" Dave said, shaking his binoculars and trying in vain to see what I was seeing. If I hadn't been so laser focused, I would have jumped at the chance to have a laugh at his expense, because his "binoculars," I knew, were actually "Official Russian KGB binoculars" he'd ordered through a spy catalog *just for this very moment*. But at the time, I could only manage a chuckle, as I was busy trying to hold my own binoculars steady—my sleek, perfectly functioning, 100 percent official DEA-issued binoculars.

"Hold on. It looks like…Oh my God." I held my breath.

"What? What is it?" Jerry asked. He was the only one without field glasses, and it was killing him not to see.

"It looks like…like two black maids cooking or washing dishes," I said, stunned. These had to be the two replacement maids.

"Are you sure? I can't see *shit*," Dave said. He lowered his prized spyglasses and glared at them, disgusted that his five-star-rated equipment had proven to be about as valuable as a cereal box prize (which, essentially, is what they were). Something told me he wasn't gonna be getting his money back, either.

'Yes! I'm sure!" I said, as I continued to surveil the maids. "That has to be them. That's gotta be the place." The three of us sat there in silence, letting the significance of the discovery—and what it meant—settle in. It was the very definition of a big break.

"Okay, guys, I think we can put our plan in motion," I said.

About an hour later, the entire apartment went dark. We assumed that Miguel had needed a late-night snack to control his hypoglycemia, hence the staff working in the kitchen. As we were preparing to leave, I innocently asked Dave if I could see his "special" spy binoculars. The second he passed them over to me, I wound up like a power pitcher in the bottom of the ninth and tossed them as far as I could down the side of the hill and into the abyss.

"Hey!" Dave exclaimed. "My KGB binoculars!" His genuine disappointment made the situation ten times funnier. "Sorry, bro, but it's where they belong," I said as Jerry doubled over with laughter.

"I guess you're right," Dave said, resigned to the fact that his "super-secret spy specs" were gone forever. I'm not sure if he's ever fully recovered.

We were now on a serious high, but there was still a ton of work we needed to do before we could launch any kind of operation to try and arrest Miguel. The three of us headed back to the navy safe house to try and get some sleep. We knew that the next few days would likely be some of our longest and most stressful to date.

For the first time in ages, we fell asleep feeling content, certain we'd found El Señor's new hideout. But before we could do anything, we had to run it by Salcedo. We'd all agreed that he, and he alone, would make the final call on whether to proceed with any operation against Miguel. We had to talk to him ASAP—we couldn't be certain he'd be as convinced as we were about the location until we did. It was his life that hung in the balance, and his decision to make.

CHAPTER 27

One Last Shot

"There is nothing wrong with changing a plan
when the situation has changed."

—SENECA THE YOUNGER,
Roman Philosopher and Statesman

The Plan

THE SUN HAD JUST BEGUN to rise when Dave and I left to begin the walk-through of our proposed operational plan. We'd managed to get a little sleep and were ready to focus on our main concern: ensuring that the raiding party would be able to arrive safely at the objective.

Our chosen meet location was a secluded spot outside the city, not far off the interstate. We scouted our intended route of approach all the way to the hillside infiltration point, thoroughly inspected the concrete flood-control channel that led to the edge of the mountain, and, most importantly, surveyed the steep, difficult descent down the mountainside that led to the Hacienda Buenos Aires building. The passage looked treacherous even in daylight, so we could only imagine how it would look when blanketed in total darkness. We started to have second thoughts.

As Dave and I drove south along the Cali River, we spotted the outer ring of cartel security. They were positioned exactly where Salcedo said they'd be, though they appeared to be more substantial than usual. We didn't dare make the right turn leading to the Normandía area, where we'd be sure to encounter Genaro Ángel's men and at least one other ring of security.

Instead, we headed over to the park for a bird's-eye view of the surrounding area from the Belalcázar statue. Dave and I quickly realized that it would be virtually impossible to arrive undetected at Hacienda Buenos Aires via surface streets in military-style transport trucks—cartel security would immediately detect our presence and alert Miguel long before we arrived, giving him plenty of time to disappear into one of his hidden vaults or abandon the apartment entirely. We resigned ourselves to the fact that we had no other choice but to attempt a commando-style raid down the pitch-black mountainside.

We set Monday, August 7, 1995, as the proposed date for the operation. The choice wasn't random: that Monday was a national holiday commemorating the Battle of Boyacá, a decisive victory in the war for Colombia's independence from Spain in 1819. Because it was a holiday, Dave and I hoped that cartel security would be distracted and thus less alert, giving us a chance to use the element of surprise to our advantage.

When Dave and I returned to the safe house, we used the secure telephone to brief our superiors in Bogotá and set our plan in motion. We respectfully requested that General Serrano not travel to Cali—if he did, we'd have no way of preventing his pilot from notifying Miguel. Of course, we didn't mention that we knew the pilot was corrupt, opting to say that it was just too risky with the cartel monitoring the general's every move.

This was a ballsy request on our part. For two American DEA agents to ask the head of almost ninety thousand Colombian police officials *not* to travel to Cali for an operation that would—hopefully—result in the arrest of the world's most wanted drug kingpin and head of the biggest drug cartel in history was audacious at best and arrogant at worst. But General Serrano agreed without giving it so much as a second thought. "Of course," he told Attaché Senneca. "I completely understand."

We requested the same members from Colonel Barragán's team we'd worked with on the Gilberto operation and prior Cali raids, as well as twenty additional members from the elite ANTIN unit. The team also included a handful of Colombian Navy special operators, all of whom had proven to be incredibly effective during our initial surveillance of Mateo.

We knew they'd come in handy when it came time to navigate the rugged mountainous terrain.

One thing was certain: we had to keep the mission completely secret from the police Search Bloc in Cali. We also kept the target location a secret from everyone else—including General Serrano. For additional OPSEC, the raiding party was given a false narrative, told only that they'd be conducting "routine inspections" of several chemical companies outside of Cali. They were to meet me, Dave, Jerry, and Ruben at a clandestine location off the interstate, where they'd be given further instructions.

Attorney General Valdivieso was briefed on the pending operation—that is, everything but the location. Because of the myriad issues we'd had during the Santa Rita raid, we requested to handpick the prosecutor who would accompany us on the op. We also sought forced-entry authorization for Miguel's apartment, the equivalent of a "no knock" search warrant in the US It was critical that we apprehend Miguel *before* he got into a *caleta*. Attorney General Valdivieso approved both requests but made it clear that this was not business as usual. It was, he said, "just an exception to the rule."

So far, so good. Dave and I had gotten everything we'd asked for, with only one thing left on the list: Salcedo's blessing. When we spoke with him later that afternoon and told him our plan to arrest Miguel was already in motion, he was shocked. "What? But how can you two be sure?"

"Well, the intel is as good as it's ever gonna be," I assured him. "The location of perimeter security, the lights, the sighting of the two new maids, the apartment being connected to Claudia—it all adds up."

"It can't just add up. It has to *work*," Salcedo said. "If not, I'm—"

"It will," Dave said. "It *will* work."

Salcedo wasn't convinced. We knew he was terrified, but we hadn't fully grasped how overwhelming the entire situation really was for him. Not only was his life on the line, but if we succeeded and he and his family did get out, they would have to leave everything behind and build new lives—in a foreign country, no less. There would be no time for goodbyes.

Salcedo thought for a minute, then looked at us both and nodded. "Okay. Let's do it." The sighting of the two maids working in the kitchen at 1:00 a.m. had tipped the scales for him, just as it had for us. In any other situation Salcedo may have added that he wouldn't bet his life on it, but in this case, he actually was.

He then began looking for additional cover, since the operation was set to take place sometime within the next seventy-two hours. Just as he had with Sergeant Valencia (and, we still suspected, Major del Vasto), he leaked pertinent information to a military contact of his regarding Carlos Espinosa, the cartel's wiretap guru and point man at the Cali phone company. By eliminating "Pinchadito"—one of the most key cartel facilitators—Miguel's communication infrastructure suffered a massive blow. Then Espinosa dealt another one himself when he joined the ranks of other cartel expats who'd agreed to cooperate with Colombian authorities after being arrested.

But as always, strange forces were at work. After Defense Minister Botero's shocking resignation two days earlier, General Camilo Zúñiga, the head of Colombia's armed forces, was appointed acting defense minister. According to Salcedo, General Zúñiga was Miguel's single most important source in the Colombian military. Complicating things even further, Zúñiga wanted to be briefed on *all* joint counterdrug operations involving the Cali cartel as early as Monday morning.

There was no way the DEA could brief the general on *anything* Cali related. Given that the situation had changed, and in order to counter Zúñiga's mandate, a change of plans was in order. We decided to move the raid up a day to Sunday, August 6.

On Saturday afternoon, the police task force and the prosecutor traveled overland from Bogotá to the meet location outside Cali. Back at the safe house, Dave and I used the same "chemical inspection" ruse when briefing the Colombian Navy team, though I'm sure they suspected something far more important was happening. While we hadn't shared any intel with them, Dave and I had been running around with our hair on fire for the past week, and they weren't blind. Either way, they didn't care. They were just happy to be included in whatever we had planned.

Shortly after midnight on Sunday morning, Dave and I met one last time with Salcedo to gather any last-minute details and discuss the specifics of his extraction from Cali, which was to be immediate, regardless of the outcome of the raid. Salcedo was apprehensive. He wanted to call Miguel to try and confirm his presence in the apartment, something we strongly advised him against. He did it anyway, and Miguel was terse with his responses, offering no discernable clues as to his whereabouts. Also, because of the call-forwarding system, there was no way to be sure that Miguel was even in the Hacienda Buenos Aires building during the call. Miguel recently added a new tech trick to his roster and was now disguising his voice over the phone with the help of a voice-changing machine.

Doubts started to dominate Salcedo's mind, and he began to get cold feet. At one point he suggested that Miguel might even be setting a trap to expose him as the traitor. But we were fast approaching the zero hour, and Dave and I needed to leave to rendezvous with the team that had just arrived from Bogotá. We pressed him for a decision and, finally, he relented. "All right," he said. "Do it. And may God be with you both."

Dave and I were drained as we drove to the meet location about thirty minutes away. We knew we had to pull ourselves together—the pressure was only going to get worse. We didn't want to fail anyone—not our bosses in Bogotá, our Colombian counterparts, the DEA—nobody. And as for Sean—a.k.a. Salcedo—there was no way we could let him down again. The operation *had* to succeed.

When Dave and I arrived at 2:00 a.m., Jerry and Ruben were there waiting for us with the rest of the group, ready to go. Looking them over, we saw just how formidable this combined task force was: a well-trained anti-narcotics and navy special forces assault team, plainclothes officers from Colonel Barragán's special unit, US agents and intelligence officers, and Julieta, our chosen prosecutor.

Julieta was the only one who looked out of place—not because of her gender but because of her attire: a perfectly pressed white jacket, sharp-looking slacks, crisp blue shirt, and high heels. Uh-oh. The shoes, we knew, would not go over well. Of course, she had no idea what was in store for her—then again, no one else did, either.

"I have a warrant approved by the attorney general of Colombia," she said. "We're authorized to use whatever force is necessary to gain entry, and I was told to consult with you regarding the target and the location. So, where is it exactly that we're going?"

Julieta was as impressive as anyone else on the team, if not more so. All four DEA agents held her in very high regard, having conducted several operations with her in the past—especially Jerry, who'd recommended her. Still, despite the fact that she'd always proven to be trustworthy, we couldn't take any chances—not this late in the game. She'd have to find out our destination the same time everyone else did.

"We'll let you know when we get there," I said. It wasn't the response Julieta was expecting. Shaking her head in frustration, she turned and walked away.

A few minutes later Dave and I departed, with the two-truck convoy following closely behind. Neither of us spoke as we traversed the quiet Cali streets in our trusty Chevy Swift, taking the path we'd created for the sole purpose of disguising our intended route and destination. By the time we arrived at the insertion point at the edge of the mountainside it was 3:00 a.m.

Now came the hard part. Ahead of us was a steep, five-hundred-foot climb, followed by the carved-out flood-control channel. Dave and I led the way, grateful that the soft glow of a three-quarter moon reflecting off the grassy hillside made our ascent a little easier. Suddenly, the howls of what seemed like a hundred dogs barking nearly in unison created a cacophony of warnings to anyone within shouting distance. The chorus of wails threatened to alert everyone to our presence, and we tried our best to block it out as we continued upward toward the water duct.

When we arrived at the first plateau and entered the narrow and muddy flood-control channel—which was about eight feet deep, four feet wide, and ran about a quarter of a mile to the edge of the mountainside—Julieta began to get upset.

"Where are we going?" she asked. "I wasn't told we'd be climbing mountains." Though she made every effort to keep the pace, it wasn't long before she was lagging behind. But the deep concrete structure was serving its purpose, which was to mask our approach as we marched onward.

After navigating the channel for what felt like an eternity, we came to the edge of the mountain, and the very top of the white Hacienda Buenos Aires building appeared. It dominated the entire horizon, and the image was so surreal it could have been a mirage—more like an ancient, foreboding pillar than a modern building rising nineteen stories above the ground. We stopped to catch our breath and waited for Julieta and several others to catch up. We still had the steep descent down the mountain

*Flood Control Channel
(Insertion Point)*

ahead—the most challenging part of our mission—and we were already running behind schedule.

I turned to Dave, Jerry, and Ruben. "This needs to go like clockwork," I said. "No mistakes."

Once the rest of the team joined us, I called everyone together. "Okay, everybody, gather around," I said in Spanish. I pointed to the top of Hacienda Buenos Aires and said, "The tenth floor is our destination…and Miguel Rodríguez is the target."

By this point, the entire team knew that this was something of far greater significance than a "chemical inspection." But they hadn't understood just *how* significant, and immediately everyone's excitement tripled. Everyone's, that is, except Julieta's. She was justifiably pissed she'd been kept in the dark—literally. She certainly hadn't signed up to spend her night scaling mountains or trudging through a swampy water duct in a white (not anymore) outfit and heels. Frankly, we didn't have the balls to tell her how much worse it was about to get.

"Minimal radio communication until we reach the objective," Dave added. "I'll maintain overwatch from here, coordinate comms, and provide necessary updates as the operation unfolds."

Dave's job was twofold: call out if cartel reinforcements were deployed to the area (he had a clear view of the roads leading to Hacienda Buenos Aires from his station atop the mountain), and observe and report on any movement from inside the tenth-floor apartment.

Wielding a sledgehammer, Jerry led the raiding party down the mountain, followed by Ruben, while I circled back to the car and drove to a location just outside the outermost ring of cartel security. From there, I could monitor the perimeter security detail and alert our team to their movements or get to the target location quickly should an emergency or anything unexpected occur.

As soon as the group took their initial steps, they encountered the first of a series of steep drops. Julieta fell, breaking one of her heels and getting what was left unsullied of her once snow-white suit covered in dirt. A few others stayed behind to offer her assistance, but she wasn't the only one having trouble. As we'd feared, the daunting descent was doubly demanding in the dark. The team quickly became disjointed, and the mission seemed poised to spiral out of control.

Over forty-five minutes had passed as Dave and I waited at our respective posts for the confirmation that Jerry and Ruben were ready to make their final approach with the assault team. Finally, the quiet was broken by the staticky crackle of Jerry's radio.

"I'm at the bottom of the mountain. We need help!" Jerry said, out of breath. Before Dave or I could respond, he radioed again, "Do you copy? We need help!"

I could barely stop myself from screaming out in frustration. I did, however, bash the steering wheel with my fist a few times before responding: "Roger that. I'll be right there." I forced myself to sound calm. "ETA four minutes."

"Copy," Jerry responded. "Just get here as fast as you can!"

Wanting to keep radio transmissions to a minimum, I didn't engage further. I began to drive slowly down Avenida 4 toward the outer ring of security, hoping that the sight of a lone vehicle on the road at close to 4:00 a.m. wouldn't trigger any alarms. I successfully passed by the outermost ring of security, then a second. The final lookout post was helmed by two operatives parked at a sharp turn in the road, and I tried to drive past them as slowly as possible without arousing suspicion.

After arriving a short distance away from Hacienda Buenos Aires, I parked and then met up with Jerry and what was left of our force in a large, grassy field across the street from the target building. "What happened?" I asked, dreading the answer.

"Only six of us made it," Jerry said. "The rest of the team are still up on the mountain."

"Are you kidding me?" It wasn't exactly Murphy's Law once again, but it *was* the all too familiar feeling that our operation was unraveling.

"We can't stay here," Jerry said, looking around. "We need to move." Dozens of street dogs were barking, accompanied by a backup chorus of stray roosters crowing. Together they sounded absurd, an unlikely duet harmonizing in the middle of a random field in Cali. It felt like someone had clicked their heels together three times and we'd landed on Old MacDonald's farm.

We had a bigger problem, though: we needed more people. There was no way we could storm Miguel's apartment with only seven men, so we waited for a few minutes, eyes glued to the edge of the mountain. No one. And the roosters were relentless—I could barely think straight.

Our combined special operations raid team had now gone from a dream team to a paltry mix of Colonel Barragán's officers, navy commandos, me, and Jerry—hardly the overwhelming assault force we'd envisioned bursting into the secret hideout of the leader of the Cali cartel. But Jerry was determined to forge ahead. "It's now or never!" he bellowed. "Let's go!"

We couldn't stay in our current position much longer without the armed security we suspected was manning the interior of the gated entrance spotting us anyway, so this was it. I gave it a few more seconds—nothing—then radioed Dave that we were good to go. There really was no turning back now.

"Screw it. Let's move," I said to the team, looking upward to the welcoming, outstretched arms of Cristo Rey. Silently, I asked for a little help.

The Assault

We crept soundlessly toward Hacienda Buenos Aires, where we encountered a uniformed armed guard at the gated entrance and quickly immobilized him. We did the same with a second guard as we entered the complex—an auspicious beginning, but now we had a new issue: we couldn't leave the security guards behind for fear they might alert Miguel to our presence.

One of the police officials then volunteered to stay with them until help arrived, and we were now down to six.

We continued on through the lobby and had just reached the elevators when I suggested something that drew strange looks from the group. "Let's take the stairs," I said. I knew the potentially jarring "ding" of the elevator at such an early hour would likely echo off the marble floors and reverberate throughout the entire tenth floor, waking Miguel and everyone else inside. The element of surprise was key, and that meant as little noise as possible.

Double-timing it up ten flights of stairs left us winded, so we paused in the staircase just outside Miguel's front door to catch our breath. "Stand by. We're gonna make entry," I said in a low voice over the radio. Inside, my heart was pounding. Everyone's was.

"Copy that," Dave responded. "All clear, still no movement," he added, after zooming in on the tenth-floor apartment—with *my* binoculars. His KGB superspy specs were still languishing at the bottom of the hill where I'd tossed them.

When we approached the door, Jerry opted to give the honors to one of the navy special operators and handed him the sledgehammer, remembering Ambassador Frechette's unilateral action rant. The operator heaved the sledgehammer behind him, swung it forward, and began to bash the front door.

Thud!

Thud!

Thud!

The noise was deafening.

"Shit!" I whispered to the group. The door was fortified and equipped with extra locking mechanisms and reinforced hinges—it was damaged, but still fully intact and secure.

"Lights are on!" Dave said in Spanish over the radio. "Tenth-floor lights are on!"

"Damn it!" Jerry cried, looking back at the door with pure rage. Turning to the commando, he grabbed the hammer from his hands. "Stand back!" he said, before he leaned in and began to batter the door.

Thud! It caved ever so slightly, just above the handle.

Thud! Better. More serious damage. *Just one more shot,* I remember thinking. *One more.*

Thud! That did it. With the door now broken apart, the six of us entered the apartment and scattered in all directions, desperately looking for lights so we could begin our search.

The apartment was huge, almost four thousand square feet. I found myself first in the kitchen, where I immediately spotted Miguel's signature Panasonic phones along with the elaborate call-forwarding station. I opened the refrigerator and saw that it was fully stocked with fresh fruits and vegetables.

Meanwhile, one of the navy commandos had found two Afro-Colombian employees huddled in a small room off the kitchen, most certainly Miguel's maids.

When I walked into the living room, I saw a man emerging from the back hallway, looking dazed. One of Barragán's plainclothes officers immediately took him to the ground and secured him, and we saw that it was Miguel's assistant, Mateo, the very man Dave and I had followed for an entire week last month when it turned out he was actually on vacation.

We were certain that we were in the right place, but where was Miguel? Had he already managed to hide himself away in a *caleta* this quickly?

I headed farther down the hallway toward the rear of the apartment. Jerry was clearing a bedroom on the left, so I went across the hall to search another. A few seconds later, we both heard a voice cry out in Spanish. We froze.

"*I got him! I got him!*"

Jerry and I exchanged a quick look of shock, then raced together down the hallway. As soon as we entered the master bedroom, we saw Amparo Arbeláez, Miguel's second wife, sitting on the edge of the bed. She was confused, staring at something in a total panic. When we followed her gaze we saw a navy special operator, a massive grin on his face, clenched onto Miguel. The operator—perhaps the biggest man in our group—was holding him in a death grip.

Just behind them in the walk-in closet of the master bedroom was an elaborate, expertly built concrete door that had been partially swung open. The soldier had managed to nab Miguel right as he was rushing to enter the vault, and Jerry and I realized that he'd literally been dragging him away from the *caleta* just as we'd walked in.

The navy commando practically lifted Miguel off the ground as he moved to park him a few feet away from us. Even as we breathed a huge sigh of relief, we couldn't believe we were looking at the actual head of the serpent, decapitated at last. Instead of one of his expensive bespoke suits he wore a simple white T-shirt and boxer shorts—he could have been any one of a million men interrupted from a deep sleep in the middle of the night.

But the darkness of his eyes told a different story. I actually got a chill when he leveled them straight at me—the only identifiable American in the room. I'd never seen eyes so lifeless convey a look so wicked. In Spanish, I told him that it was over: "*Se acabó, señor. Se acabó.*" He didn't blink. No one said anything—it was all too surreal.

When I finally spoke again it was to radio Dave with the news he'd been dying to hear. Even through the static of our radios, I could hear the relief and excitement in his voice.

"Finally!" he said. "I'm on my way!"

One of the officers stood guard over Miguel as he dressed, then handcuffed him and planted him on the living room sofa. The other members of the raid team had already begun to trickle in from outside, each taking in the scene and standing there in awe. A flurry of calls to the officers' respective command staff followed, and the story became official: El Señor had fallen. It was a triumphant, euphoric atmosphere.

A few minutes later, Ruben arrived with Julieta in tow. She'd made it in one piece, and I'm not sure what made her happier: being on solid ground or seeing Miguel in handcuffs. The four DEA agents posed for trophy photos behind the Cali godfather, who still hadn't said a word.

It was impossible not to think of the similar scenario that had played out with Don Miguel's older brother, Gilberto, who'd been so humble during his arrest. ("Don't kill me! I'm a man of peace!") In Miguel, we had a very different kind of personality. He was terrifying to observe.

As I continued to watch him, I realized that he'd gone through three stages in surprisingly rapid succession. The first stage: confusion. He'd been awoken from a dead sleep and had to figure out and process exactly what was happening. The next: wrath. The second he was in handcuffs the

Miguel Rodríguez after his arrest at Hacienda Buenos Aires apartment in Cali. Left to right: *Dave, Chris, CNP Colonel Alejandro Gomez, Jerry Salameh, and Ruben Prieto.*

rage took over. His thousand-yard stare is something I will never forget. Finally: acceptance. Miguel understood the situation, not to mention the gravity of it: he'd been arrested by Colombian security forces, and there wasn't a damn thing he could do about it.

As everyone continued to cluster around Miguel to get their pictures taken, Jerry and I walked back into the master bedroom to inspect the *caleta*. It was a masterpiece—the best we'd ever seen. Roughly three feet deep by three feet wide and eight feet in height, the compartment had been constructed into a preexisting support wall behind a built-in wall unit. The entrance door was located behind four large, file-cabinet-size drawers which had been removed and placed on the floor, allowing for immediate and unfettered access to the compartment.

The door to the vault was three feet wide, five feet high, and made up of eight thick, solid inches of concrete, securely attached with heavy-gauge

Built-in wooden cabinets and shelving in the master bedroom of Miguel Rodríguez's Hacienda Buenos Aires apartment. When drawers are removed (at the right), a highly sophisticated caleta—or a secret hiding spot—is revealed. Miguel was arrested as he was entering the caleta.

steel hinges and bolts. On the inside it was secured with four heavy-duty steel plates or security bars that slid horizontally and locked the door in place from the inside. When closed, there was absolutely *no* indication that the wall had been modified at all, let alone modified to contain a hidden door and secret hiding space. Once the drawers were slid back into the built-in dresser it was impossible to detect the existence of a concealed compartment.

When we inspected the inside of the vault, we found an oxygen bottle and mask secured to the wall, a light with a switch, a folding stool, a gas mask, a couple of two-gallon jugs of water, a can of peanuts, an air-conditioning vent that was bypassed into the compartment from the ceiling of the walk-in closet, and, of course, another briefcase full of incendiary documents.

Jerry and I stood and marveled at the vault's sophistication. We snapped a few photographs and shook our heads in disbelief as we realized just how lucky we'd been. If Miguel had made it in there, we would still be racing around the apartment in a desperate, fruitless search. We could have stayed there *to this day* and never found it.

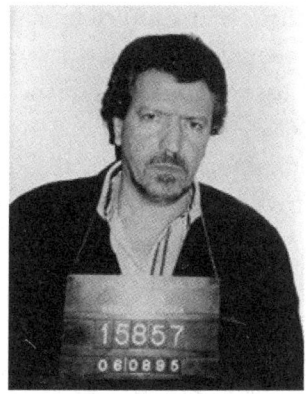

Miguel Rodríguez arrest photographs.

Finally, it came time to wrap things up: concern had already started to mount that the reeling Cali cartel might attempt some kind of rescue operation as Miguel was being taken to Marco Fidel Suárez Air Base about twenty minutes away. At 5:45 in the morning, Miguel Rodríguez and Jesus Zapata were transferred to the air base in a large police convoy, where they awaited the arrival of CNP Director General Rosso José Serrano. The general, of course, would personally escort Miguel back to the capital.

Dave and I stayed behind. We still had the most important call of all to make, and we couldn't wait another minute.

We knew we wouldn't be standing there at all if it hadn't been for Jorge Salcedo. He'd risked his own life on several occasions and was without question the single most critical factor in our success. Salcedo's role as a double agent remained a secret to everyone except me and Dave, and it was time for us to follow through on our promise. His boss was headed to prison, and Salcedo would soon be headed to a new life, free of the clutches of the cartel.

"Sean, we got him!" Dave and I yelled into the phone in unison. "It's over!"

There was a pause, followed by two words: "Thank God," he said.

To our dismay, actually, he already knew about Miguel's arrest—he'd gotten a call just a few minutes earlier from his second in command, Juan Carlos "Dario" Delgado, a former military officer. "We don't know what happened," Dario told him. "No one saw or heard anything!"

Despite our delirium, though, we knew that we had other urgent matters to attend to. Extracting Salcedo and his family from Cali was our top priority now, but as soon as we began to discuss specifics, we were met with a very unexpected response. "No. Not yet," Salcedo told us.

"What?!" Dave and I looked at each other, dumbfounded. "*Not yet?*"

Salcedo was unfazed. "No, not yet. We still have work to do."

CHAPTER 28

The Accountant's Wife

"You can't convince anyone of anything.
You can only give them the right information,
so that they convince themselves."

—EBEN PAGAN,
Entrepreneur and Author

WILLIAM RODRÍGUEZ WAS ALREADY SEETHING by the time he called for an emergency security meeting to try and stop the bleeding. The cartel—what was left of it—was floundering, and the prodigal son was hell-bent on proving his mettle in its time of need.

After the shocking early-morning raid on Hacienda Buenos Aires and subsequent arrest of his father, William took over as the de facto leader of the Cali cartel. His first order of business: identify the spy who'd betrayed them, and do it before they could inflict any further damage. Meanwhile, Miguel and Gilberto's number one priority remained the same: locate and eliminate Guillermo Pallomari. While William was making decisions from the comfort of his own home, his father and uncle were making theirs from the relative squalor of their jail cells.

To Salcedo's relief, most of the initial suspicion surrounding Miguel's arrest revolved around the cartel's head of communications, Carlos Espinosa. Salcedo himself had been the mastermind behind the diversion, setting Espinosa up to take the fall in advance of the raid, but he knew how quickly the blame could shift. It was just a matter of time before the truth got out, and if he had any chance of helping Pallomari he'd have to take immediate action.

Equally urgent was the fact that he had a major confession to make—not to Miguel or Gilberto, but to his own family. He was about to drop two bombshells: first, that he was the one behind the arrest of Miguel Rodríguez and, perhaps more shocking, the fact that they had to leave behind their friends, family, and native country to start all over again in a foreign land. And, he'd have to add, it wasn't a move. It was an escape.

Dave and I traveled to Bogotá to take several meetings and tackle a mountain of paperwork, then returned to Cali the next day to meet with Salcedo. We urged him to reconsider his decision to put off leaving and begged him to leave Cali immediately, but he was adamant. "Not until Pallomari and his family are safe," he insisted. "We must destroy the cartel from within."

If we wanted the three Cali godfathers to remain behind bars, the cartel's entire infrastructure and financial empire had to be completely destroyed. The one man who could make that happen was Pallomari, and we were desperate to find him—but so were the godfathers. It was a mad race to see who could find him first.

Unfortunately for us, Cali still had their deadliest cartel assassin, César Yusti, leading the hunt. The stakes were higher than ever, so the severity of the threat to Pallomari had skyrocketed. Thanks to the pressure applied to Pallomari's turncoat attorney, Jaime Gil, Yusti had finally found the apartment building Pallomari was hiding in: it was in the El Ingenio neighborhood in southern Cali, close to the Fundación Valle del Lili hospital. Although Gil said he couldn't recall the exact floor or apartment number, he did remember that it was directly across from the elevator. That didn't leave much more for Yusti to investigate; all he had to do was narrow it down to the exact apartment. Once he did, he'd get to do what he loved most: murder.

We decided to approach Pallomari's wife, Patricia, at her business in downtown Cali. We'd been avoiding this for the last week since the risks were so high—and not just for Patricia and her family. We'd also be putting ourselves in the line of fire, as the Cali KGB maintained nearly constant surveillance on Patricia, and two obvious Americans walking into her place of business would surely set off every alarm bell possible. But we were out of time and out of options.

At 6:15 on the evening of August 8, Dave and I arrived at Patricia's business, Universal Link. As we pulled up, we spotted two cartel *sicarios* sitting in a parked car down the street from the entrance just waiting for Patricia to leave. Dave and I waited a few minutes for dusk to fall, then made our approach from the opposite end of the street. One at a time we ducked in, eliciting curious looks from a bevy of busy employees in the crowded workplace.

Patricia Pallomari was in her early forties, with long red hair and kind eyes. From what we knew, she was a driven and independent woman who'd been running a successful business for several years. Dave and I took a deep breath as we entered her office, which had her name prominently displayed on the door.

In Spanish, I said, "Hello, Patricia. My name is Chris Feistl, and this is my partner, Dave Mitchell. We're from the American Embassy in Bogotá. I'm sorry to tell you this, but there's a plan in motion by the Cali cartel to kill your husband." It wasn't your typical introduction.

Patricia took the news as if I'd just updated her on the weather. When she did respond, it seemed forced, as if she'd been rehearsing her lines for weeks. "I haven't spoken to my husband in…at least several months," she said. She was calm—nonchalant, even.

Her indifference caught us by surprise, but Dave persisted, explaining to her that we didn't have much time   cartel assassins were outside at that very moment waiting to follow her the minute she left. We revealed that Guillermo's attorney had been helping the cartel locate him and that the sicario had narrowed the location down to the building. All he needed to do was identify the exact apartment.

We offered her and her family immediate protection and assistance in getting them to the US—that is, if Guillermo would turn himself in and cooperate with American law enforcement authorities. If her husband didn't turn himself in, we told her, he was as good as dead. Which was the truth.

Once again, our warnings were received with apathy, if not disdain. Patricia said that she'd suspected the cartel was trying to kill her husband—especially in light of his US indictment two months ago—but that she had no idea where he was hiding.

Dave and I were bewildered, but we weren't leaving until we'd done everything in our power to express the urgency of the situation. We even brought up her children, stressing how their lives were in danger, too.

Eventually Patricia agreed to try and get a message to her husband but repeated that she was unaware of his current whereabouts. We gave her a burner cell phone number to call and made a date to speak the next day at eleven o'clock. When we left her office, we were in a total state of confusion—the conversation with Patricia had been surreal and worrisome. Despite all our warnings, she'd been emotionless the entire time.

Dave and I met up with Salcedo again the next morning, and right off the bat he had bad news to share. Apparently, at some point during the night Yusti had identified Pallomari's exact location and was now just awaiting the final confirmation. It was imperative that he be completely sure before acting, lest he spook Pallomari and drive him further underground.

Dave and I immediately returned to Universal Link to give Patricia the update. She told us that she'd been unable to contact Guillermo but was interested in speaking with someone at the American Embassy—someone, that is, in a higher position of authority—about the severity of the charges against her husband and the possible relocation of her family to the United States. After all, we were complete strangers to her, and it made sense that she'd be wary of trusting us. We arranged for Patricia to speak with Country Attaché Tony Senneca the next day—if she wasn't comfortable with us, certainly she'd be more receptive to the highest-ranking DEA official in all of Colombia.

On August 10, Patricia arrived at the US Embassy accompanied by a family friend, Freddy Vivas Yangua. Over the next two hours there were intense discussions as well as a flurry of telephone calls with various parties at DEA Headquarters, the Department of Justice in Washington, DC, and the US Attorney's Office in the Southern District of Florida. The talks revolved around the nature and extent of the criminal charges against Pallomari, the possibility of his voluntary surrender to US authorities in Miami, and how much prison time he might be facing. For the federal prosecutors, it was imperative that Pallomari cooperate fully and testify as a witness in *any* US court proceeding against the Cali cartel and, additionally, to assist Attorney General Valdivieso in the Proceso 8.000 investigation. Of most importance to Patricia, we assumed, would be the relocation of various family members to the US and their subsequent integration into the Witness Security Program (WITSEC).

But again, Patricia's reaction was not what we expected. Instead of her family's safety, she seemed most concerned about what would become of their furniture and real estate holdings in Colombia, the level of their future quality of life in the US, and exactly how they would exchange their certificates of deposit. We assured her that all of that could be handled later—the most urgent priority was finding a way to warn Guillermo, then getting him and the rest of their immediate family safely to Bogotá.

By that point, it had become obvious that our words were falling on deaf ears. Perhaps she didn't grasp the gravity of the situation, or perhaps she was in denial and deemed the worst-case scenario impossible. But the worst-case scenario wasn't just possible. Without Guillermo under our protection, it was inevitable.

As the meeting drew to a close, Salcedo called me and broke the news that Yusti was positive he'd identified Pallomari's apartment number, and Cali operatives had just wiretapped the landline telephone in the apartment. As soon as Pallomari's presence was confirmed, Yusti would be dispatched.

I hung up and turned to Patricia. "They found Guillermo," I said. "He needs to get out of there. *Now!*"

Patricia and Freddy remained impassive. I'd just told Patricia one of the cartel's most feared assassins could already be on his way to execute her husband, yet they both just sat there, stone-faced. We were astounded.

The meeting continued on with no sense of urgency, finally wrapping up sometime around 1:30. Before she left, Patricia said she'd try again to contact and warn her husband, but it seemed like more of an empty promise than anything. We didn't know what to think.

We escorted her and Freddy out of the embassy, begging them one last time to take immediate action. "There's no time left," Dave said. "Guillermo's only option is to surrender and cooperate. If he stays where he is, he *will* die." Patricia just nodded and looked at us solemnly with her big brown eyes, which now seemed more distant than they did kind.

Patricia asked for Attaché Senneca's direct phone number at the US Embassy in case she had any further questions or an emergency came up, so I gave her the number and also made sure she still had our burner number and my SkyPager. We warned her against using any landline telephones and told her that under no circumstances should she return to Universal Link or stay at *any* house or property connected to her and Guillermo.

When we returned to the embassy, Assistant Attaché Rinehart was just as mystified as we were. "She doesn't understand just how serious this is, does she?" he asked. Aside from denial or indifference, the only other possible explanation was that Patricia was putting on an award-winning act. But if she really *did* know Guillermo's whereabouts and how to contact him, it was a very dangerous game she was playing. Dave and I didn't know what to believe.

With Yusti now fully operational, we needed an immediate plan to slow him down. We discussed possible options with Salcedo, including using the military to establish checkpoints and roadblocks around the area where Pallomari was staying. Mobile checkpoints were ubiquitous in Cali—they were constantly searching for weapons, drugs, or wanted persons. However, we could only use the military; we couldn't risk using the compromised police Search Bloc for anything. Captain Buitrago was still there, eager to report back to William on any enforcement activity or American-led operations.

Fortunately, Dave and I had remained in contact with Major Arango at the 3rd Brigade. Although we hadn't worked much with the army Search Bloc since Colonel Velásquez's transfer eight months ago, we continued to make periodic visits to the base a few times a month. Still, that didn't guarantee the major's help, not least because we couldn't reveal why we needed it.

Somehow, Dave managed to convince Major Arango to flood the neighborhood's key intersections with roadblocks just south of Ingenio Park near Pallomari's apartment building. We needed to put a huge net around the entire area that extended several blocks in each direction. Our hope was that the flashing lights and heavy presence of military soldiers and wooden barricades would prevent Yusti—or his henchmen—from infiltrating the area just long enough for Pallomari to move to another location.

Our heads were spinning. We didn't know where Pallomari was, we didn't know where *Yusti* was—we didn't even know if Pallomari was still *alive* or if Patricia could, or would, attempt to contact him. All we could do now was wait to see how the night played out, and pray that Pallomari survived it.

CHAPTER 29

Defection

"Through conversion of the enemy's spies
we learn the enemy's condition."

—SUN TZU

THREE HOURS HAD PASSED since Patricia and Freddy left the American Embassy, and Dave and I were still mystified by her reaction during our meeting—or lack thereof. Nothing we or Country Attaché Tony Senneca said seemed to make any impact, but the truth was we couldn't tell: she was impossible to read. We told ourselves that we'd done everything we could but hated the fact that it was now out of our control.

Instead, we focused on the fact that it wasn't entirely out of the question that the roadblocks and checkpoints Major Arango had placed around the El Ingenio neighborhood might actually be enough. With Yusti and his band of killers now fully engaged, the roadblocks and checkpoints flooding the area might be the only thing to save Pallomari's life—for this one night, anyway. But Yusti was notoriously persistent, and we'd received no updates from Salcedo. We were also anxiously awaiting any word from Patricia about whether she'd been able to contact Guillermo to have him leave the compromised apartment.

At 4:30 p.m., our Patricia burner phone rang. Dave and I ran back to take the call in one of the embassy's vacant offices.

I scrambled to pick up the phone and immediately heard that it was Freddy, not Patricia. He said that Patricia was finally able to contact her husband and that Guillermo had reacted to the news exactly as Dave and I had hoped.

"Guillermo is willing to do everything you asked. He wants to surrender and agreed to fully cooperate," Freddy said. "He realizes the danger he's in." Pallomari would be turning himself over to us "in the coming days," Freddy continued, but added a troubling caveat: he was still in the same apartment, too terrified to move. So, it was still anyone's guess if he would survive the night.

Dave and I went to brief Attachés Senneca and Rinehart on the development and discuss the complicated legal issues and political ramifications Pallomari's defection would most certainly cause. Aside from being the second most wanted man in Colombia (bested only by Pacho Herrera), Pallomari was someone many people wanted dead. For them, letting him live would be far too risky—he had an untold amount of information regarding Cali's financial empire, the identities of hundreds, if not thousands of corrupt officials on the cartel payroll, and countless damning details regarding the millions of dollars the godfathers had donated to Samper's presidential campaign. He was also a valuable witness in the ever-expanding Proceso 8.000 investigation against the president and key members of his administration.

Since Pallomari had criminal charges against him in Colombia stemming from the July 1994 raid on his downtown office, his legal issues in Colombia took precedent, making things even trickier. The US government couldn't just "remove" him from Colombia without violating Colombian sovereignty, international law, and a number of different treaties. Nor could we expect the Colombian government to just hand him over to us, no questions asked. This was going to be another huge bureaucratic mess and a diplomatic disaster—something Ambassador Frechette and the State Department dreaded.

There was another nail in the political coffin, too: Pallomari's naming in the June 1995 Operation Cornerstone superseding RICO indictment against the Cali cartel. Since he was a Chilean national, an official request for Pallomari's extradition arrived at the US Embassy in Bogotá a few days later, and the sweeping fifty-nine-person indictment received extensive press. Both the cartel and the Colombian government knew that if American agents were able to get ahold of Pallomari, he'd be such a devastatingly effective witness that his testimony would likely finish off the flailing Samper administration. In light of those variables, it was clear that getting Pallomari safely back to Bogotá and then to the US would be a very long shot. No one would put any money on us pulling it off.

Suddenly, the enormity of the whole situation sunk in: Dave and I were field agents working on one of the biggest investigations in DEA history. We didn't concern ourselves with Pallomari's legal and political issues—those were for the lawyers, Ambassador Frechette, and the State Department to contend with. Our job was to devise a comprehensive plan to extract Pallomari from Cali and get him into US custody in one piece. Washington bureaucrats could figure it out from there.

Dave and I discussed a number of different scenarios, but each one shared the same intimidating obstacle: César Yusti. He was the wild card, and it didn't help that he was also the most horrifying cartel operative we might ever encounter.

Yusti's exploits as a cartel assassin were legendary. He was famous for constantly bragging about needing only one shot to kill his marks and about how he'd never failed at *any* mission the godfathers had assigned. It wasn't hyperbole, either—his reputation had reached an almost mythic level. He once famously walked into a popular restaurant in Cali named El Rancho de Jonás at high noon, like a rogue cowboy out for revenge. He spotted his mark from across the restaurant, fired one shot, and killed the unsuspecting man instantly. His target slumped over face-first into his bowl of *sancocho de pescado*.

Afterward, Yusti secured his weapon and walked casually out of the restaurant with zero emotion and zero remorse. It was this combination of skill, nerve, and lust for violence that made him one of Cali's most valuable assets. It wasn't personal. It was just business.

At one point, as we all sat in Senneca's office discussing the numerous Pallomari-related obstacles, Rinehart got frustrated. "Enough already. It's not like any of this actually matters. We'll never get our hands on him— too many people want him dead."

Still, Senneca said he wanted a plan in place for Pallomari's potential extraction from Cali by close of business the following day: August 11. He then left to board a DEA airplane bound for our satellite office in

Barranquilla, on Colombia's north coast, to meet with police and military counterparts.

On Friday afternoon, Salcedo called and gave us an update from Yusti: the roadblocks had worked. But Yusti wasn't deterred. His plan was to try again that evening, sometime after midnight, and this time he had a truly ingenious—if also highly ambitious—plan. To circumvent the military checkpoints, Yusti had recruited several corrupt investigators from the Cali prosecutor's office. Clad in official raid jackets and armed with the arrest warrant for Pallomari—the *actual* warrant—the team would use their official government credentials to bypass the military roadblocks and "arrest" him. Once they had him in their grip, Pallomari would be interrogated, tortured, and killed, his body disposed of like a piece of trash, never to be found.

After we got Salcedo's update, Dave contacted Major Arango and requested that he again saturate the El Ingenio neighborhood with military roadblocks and checkpoints. This time, the major wanted to know the *specific* reason for the continued activity, adding that resources were scarce. Lacking any decent explanation, Dave said, "Honestly, I can't tell you right now. But please, can you do us this one favor?" The major reluctantly agreed, and we bought ourselves another twenty-four hours.

As if things weren't unraveling quickly enough, Salcedo called back and shared another major setback: he'd just been officially dismissed that afternoon from his role as the Cali cartel's head of security by none other than William Rodríguez himself, Salcedo's new boss and not so new adversary. He was summarily relieved of all his duties, and there was no question that any suspicion surrounding Pinchadito—whom Salcedo had set up to take the fall for Miguel's arrest—had landed squarely back on his shoulders. And with Miguel behind bars, William's opinion was the only one that mattered. Worse, we all knew that being fired from the cartel was just the beginning. Once Pallomari was taken care of, Salcedo's name would replace his at the top of Cali's hit list.

About an hour or so later, our Patricia-designated phone rang. *Now what?* I picked up expecting Patricia, or perhaps Freddy again. But it was neither. A panicked voice at the other end of the phone said, "Chris, it's Guillermo. I'm ready to turn myself in. Come and get me!"

I asked Pallomari if he was able to move from his current location, knowing that Yusti had identified the apartment he was in. He told us something along the lines of "not a chance in hell," making it clear that *he* knew Yusti a lot better than we did and was terrified enough just being *inside* the building, let alone outside of it. We told him to stay put and to stay off the landline—Freddy would call him on his cell with the time and place for a rendezvous later that evening where we would collect him and his family. After hanging up, Dave paged Freddy and told him to call us at exactly 5:00 p.m.

Rinehart immediately updated Ambassador Frechette on the recent developments, along with the status of the threat against Pallomari. Frechette granted tentative approval for the DEA to proceed, but he wanted to be *fully* briefed on our extraction plan within the hour, and, to our dismay, *only* Guillermo's exfiltration from Cali was authorized. Patricia, her two children, and any other family members would have to make their own way to Bogotá in the coming days, then depart the country separately from Guillermo. All of them possessed both US visas and valid passports, and none had any pending legal matters in Colombia so, in theory, they shouldn't encounter any issues. The same rules applied to Freddy and his family.

Meanwhile, Assistant Attaché Rinehart wanted to review our plan to extract Pallomari in detail before facing Frechette. He knew that the ambassador would have a *lot* of questions.

I took the lead and laid out our proposed course of action. Along with two other agents, I explained, Dave and I would fly into Alfonso Bonilla Aragón International Airport in Cali aboard our DEA Super King Air— not our first choice, but at this point it was our only one. The Marco Fidel Suárez Air Base imposed strict restrictions on nighttime takeoffs and landings, so we had to modify our initial plan.

After landing, we would give a cover explanation to the small group of police guarding the airport exit, telling them we were in town to pick up a sick colleague. Then, we'd travel to the air force base, where we'd pick up two vehicles (once again, compliments of Mike) and proceed to the El Ingenio neighborhood to recon the area for Yusti and his hit team. If we deemed the area clear, we'd travel the short distance to the Clínica Valle del Lili, our designated rendezvous spot, and retrieve Pallomari.

With the fugitive accountant in tow, Dave and I would then travel back to the international airport, making sure to be on the lookout for any police or military checkpoints. Once there, the four agents would escort Pallomari directly past the police guards and onto the plane. Lastly, on the off chance any police officials confronted us at the airport, Dave and I planned to use the diplomatic *carnet* of fellow DEA agent Tommy Johnson—who, through sheer luck, actually resembled Pallomari—as his proof of identification.

After hearing our plan, Rinehart was at a loss. He buried his face in his hands.

"Please tell me you're joking?" He wasn't amused. "*That's* your big plan? Walk one of the most wanted men in Colombia directly past the police, disguised as Tommy Johnson? And I'm supposed to go to the ambassador with that? With Tommy fucking Johnson's ID?" Rinehart crossed his arms and glared at us, shaking his head in disbelief.

"Um, yes, actually. That's our plan," I said. "Trust us. It's *because* it's so simple that it'll work."

While it wasn't our first option, we'd flown in and out of the Cali airport many times over the past year and knew most of the police officials working there. Also, the area was so dark and dreary that Taylor Swift could've walked by without drawing any undue attention. Handing over a few bottles of soda and some chips would certainly seal the deal.

Rinehart's opinion wasn't swayed, but he had to decide quickly. He knew about most of our shenanigans: straying from the police base, staying in safe houses, working unilaterally, but no matter what, he'd always had confidence in us. It had been Rinehart, after all, who once told us "keep doing what you're doing—just don't get caught" when we were pursuing Gilberto and Miguel Rodríguez in Cali. Even when we got busted and had to face Ambassador Frechette the day after our arrest, detention—whatever the hell it was—Rinehart and Senneca had our backs. They'd always supported us.

When Rinehart discussed the details of our extraction plan with Senneca, he wasn't exactly sold, either. But he trusted in the strength of our experience working in Cali and deferred to our judgment. Rinehart trekked upstairs and briefed Ambassador Frechette, who, much to our surprise, authorized the plan. However, Rinehart had conveniently left out the problematic part—a.k.a. Tommy Johnson and his ID—not to mention the minor detail that Yusti and his hit team would be making another attempt to kill Pallomari later that night.

At exactly 5:00 p.m., Freddy called as instructed. I advised him that we'd received authorization to retrieve Pallomari, but the DEA aircraft was in Barranquilla, and we wouldn't be able to get it to Cali until at least 10:45 p.m. "10:45?" Freddy responded, frantic. "But Guillermo's ready now!" We understood the panic, but with no other means of transportation to Cali, Pallomari would have to sit tight until we arrived. We gave Freddy the meet location—the northwest corner of the Clínica Valle del Lili—and told him to make sure Pallomari wasn't late.

Then, we relayed the news we'd dreaded breaking. We told Freddy that we'd been given authorization to retrieve Guillermo only, and Patricia and her children would have to travel to Bogotá via commercial aircraft the next morning. That went over about as well as expected and Freddy hung up, understandably upset.

At 8:10 that evening, the DEA aircraft landed in Bogotá and by 8:30 four well-armed DEA agents—me, Dave, Jerry Salameh, and Manuel (who'd volunteered to join just prior to departure)—were wheels up and headed to Cali. We carefully reviewed our plan, going over every single possible contingency in case things went bad. We all knew there was a chance we could encounter Yusti and his team of assassins, who'd no doubt be lurking nearby. One by one we each acknowledged the risk that we were taking, then unanimously agreed to proceed.

As soon as we landed, we walked over bearing gifts to the four police guards stationed at the exit—extra drinks, snacks, and our secret weapon: a bottle of *aguardiente* (the national alcoholic drink of Colombia). As we handed out the swag, we casually mentioned that we had a sick colleague we needed to bring back to Bogotá for immediate medical attention, and we'd return in about two hours. As expected, the *aguardiente* sealed the deal, and we left the airport without incident. We caught two of the waiting taxis lined up outside and headed toward the air base.

When we arrived at the air base, we used our official air force–issued credentials to enter and retrieve the car and SUV Mike had stashed at the army intel safe house. We took the extra precaution of choosing a circuitous route to get to Pallomari's location, constantly looking out for any sign of a cartel surveillance. From what we could tell, the coast was clear.

At 10:25 p.m., we arrived just outside the El Ingenio neighborhood and saw the three-ring circus of flashing lights, barricades, and army soldiers posted at the main access roads to the community. Dave and I found a quiet, uncovered back way in a few blocks away, allowing us to completely bypass military security. We radioed Jerry and Manuel and told them to cover the perimeter and maintain a sharp lookout.

Dave and I were on high alert, our thoughts dominated by one all-consuming fear: coming face-to-face with Yusti. But our nerves actually heightened our hypervigilance, and we thoroughly canvased the streets for any sign of him or his henchmen. We did notice a few suspicious vehicles and people that seemed somewhat out of place, but we tried to counter our paranoia with logic. We finished scouring the area, which appeared to be clear.

At exactly 10:45 p.m., Dave and I arrived at the *clínica* while Jerry and Manuel continued to patrol the surrounding area, ready to respond at a moment's notice if needed. We spotted Patricia and Freddy's cars and dimmed our lights.

We cautiously exited our vehicle—we needed them to see us—but were prepared for the worst. We soon saw Freddy and four others emerge from behind a large tree at the end of the street. The second they recognized us, they ran in our direction. Dave and I were ecstatic when we saw Pallomari—then we saw Patricia and their children. This was going to be painful.

As Dave and I collected Pallomari and placed his belongings in the car, his two sons, eleven and fifteen, stuck closely to his side. It was devastating when we had to tell the boys that they couldn't join him. They didn't understand what was happening—how could they? All they knew was that they were being separated from their father—for a second time. Dave and I did our best to stop the tears and assure them they would see their father first thing in morning, but it was agonizing. Patricia then hugged her husband, and they both began to cry as well. It was the first time we'd seen Patricia show any real emotion.

Despite the emotion, we had to break up the tearful goodbyes: Yusti himself might stumble upon the scene at any second. We had to get everyone out of there, immediately.

Dave and I told Patricia that we'd be waiting for her and the boys at El Dorado Airport in Bogotá first thing in the morning, where they'd all be reunited. We reminded her to avoid her home at all costs and to only stay somewhere she was absolutely positive was safe. Patricia hugged us both and thanked us for everything we'd done. She drove off with the children followed by Freddy, while we put Pallomari in the back of our SUV and radioed "the package is secure" to Jerry and Manuel.

Dave and I followed behind the other agents for the entirety of the forty-five-minute ride back to the airport. We didn't test the speed limit: the last thing we wanted to do now was attract any attention. Worn out from so many days and nights of constant terror, Pallomari lay down in the back seat and remained out of sight. We kept a mile or so behind Jerry and Manuel as they kept watch for any police or military checkpoints, and we remained in constant radio contact.

As we approached the airport, we braced ourselves for the final hurdle: getting Pallomari past the police at the airport's side entrance. I handed Guillermo an embassy diplomatic *carnet*. He looked up at me, confused about exactly what he was holding in his hand.

"If anyone asks," I said in Spanish, "your name is Tommy Johnson. We're taking you to Bogotá because you're sick and need immediate medical attention. Understand?"

"*Sí, señor*," Pallomari replied.

With Dave leading the way, the four of us formed a protective huddle around Pallomari and pretended to help our sickly friend while carrying his bags. "We're back," Dave announced to the police officials as we walked through the dimly lit opening in the fence.

"Is your friend okay?" one of the officers asked.

"We think he'll live, but just barely," I joked as we continued toward the DEA airplane. We all laughed (Dave and the rest of our team got that I was really referring to Pallomari's miraculous escape from Yusti), and we passed the officers with ease. Overcome with relief, we boarded the aircraft, stowed Pallomari's belongings, and prepared to depart for Bogotá. None of us would be able to relax until the plane was actually in the air.

Defection

As the twin turboprops of the Super King Air hummed on the runway, we all waited impatiently for the Cali tower to give us final clearance for takeoff. There were no other planes visible, no other activity. The wait was unbearable.

Finally, the pilots received their clearance from the tower, and at 11:40 p.m., we were wheels up. Pallomari raised his arms over his head and shouted, *"Por fin!"* ("Finally!") He became emotional and took his time expressing his gratitude to us. We knew what he'd been through, but it was hard to comprehend the enormous toll it had taken. He'd been in hiding for almost a year by then, frantically trying to avoid arrest from Colombian authorities and, more recently, torture and execution at the hands of one of Cali's top assassins.

I glanced toward the front of the aircraft where we'd stashed all the items Pallomari had brought with him, suddenly curious about the contents. "What's in the bags?" I asked.

"Just the usual necessities…and some other things I was able to take before I went into hiding," Pallomari said. "And I can decode everything. All of it—every single one of the cartel files and ledgers." We could only imagine what Pallomari had managed to get his hands on, given the information he was privy to during his four-plus years working for the godfathers.

After landing in Bogotá early Saturday morning, we accompanied our prize witness to a DEA safe house and placed him under twenty-four-hour security. We still had to figure out how Pallomari would get to the US to provide sworn testimony against the Cali godfathers and the scores of corrupt government officials who'd aided them.

I've always been a firm believer in the principle "Occam's (or Ockham's) razor," which essentially states that "the simplest explanation is usually the best one." The principle has stood the test of time—over 670 years—so I guess you could say that the simplest of principles (about the simplest of explanations) are also the best ones. And when it came to our plan to extract Guillermo Pallomari from Cali that mid-August night, even with all the risks involved, Occam's razor is what I always came back to.

Ultimately, that plan saved his life. Keeping things simple was a lesson I'd learned many, many times before—that and the fact that people rarely, if ever, see what's right in front of them. But I'd learned something else in my career, too: that wasn't *always* the case. Sometimes there was no simple plan. And my gut was telling me that far more complicated times were ahead.

CHAPTER 30

Please Don't Go

"If a blind man leads a blind man,
will they both not fall into a pit?"
—MATTHEW 15:14

IT DIDN'T TAKE LONG for Dave and me to check in with Salcedo after Pallomari's arrival in Bogotá Saturday morning. We called him as we were on our way to El Dorado Airport with Jerry Salameh to pick up Patricia and her two sons, who were scheduled to arrive on a commercial flight from Cali. We told him that we'd successfully exfiltrated Pallomari from Cali late last night and that he was safe and under full DEA protection.

Salcedo said he was happy to hear the news, but his tone indicated otherwise. "So…are you guys all right? Is everything okay?" We heard the concern in his voice—clearly, he was worried. But about what? "Yes, we're fine," I assured him. "Why? Is something wrong?"

"You could say that," Salcedo said. "Yusti's been killed."

"*What?*" For what seemed like the millionth time, Dave and I responded in unison.

Salcedo told us everything he knew: around the same time that we'd been facilitating Pallomari's extraction the night before, someone had shot Yusti, leaving his body slumped over in the front seat of his car—which had been parked disconcertingly close to our own rendezvous site at the Clínica Valle del Lili. There was no question that it wasn't some random crime or robbery gone wrong. He'd been shot in the head, and whoever had fired the shots killing Cali's top assassin knew exactly what they were doing.

We hadn't even processed the news before we got another shock: not only was Yusti dead, but Salcedo assumed we'd killed him. And if not us specifically, then he believed it must've been the handiwork of another US government agency. Worse, he was convinced the cartel would assume the same.

If that was true, we knew they'd waste no time plotting their retaliation—something that would have probably been inevitable once Pallomari's defection was revealed anyway but was still a total disaster. We denied any involvement in Yusti's killing, but Salcedo didn't seem convinced. It went without saying that the cartel wouldn't be, either.

When we started discussing the relocation of Salcedo and his family, the conversation got more uncomfortable. With Cali now spiraling out of control Salcedo was, understandably, more concerned for his safety than ever before. The recent turn of events was astounding: Miguel Rodríguez, the CEO of Cocaine Inc., was in a maximum-security prison in Bogotá; César Yusti, one of Cali's most prolific assassins, had just been gunned down in the street; the whereabouts of their chief accountant, Guillermo Pallomari, was unknown; and Jorge Salcedo, the man who'd spent the last six and a half years deep inside the cartel, had just been, for all intents and purposes, fired. *And* he had every reason to believe that his former employers were currently planning his execution.

Salcedo wanted out. And who could blame him?

But Dave and I had Patricia's escape to deal with first. All the remaining DEA agents in Bogotá were busy providing round-the-clock security for Pallomari, and our resources were stretched to the limit. Salcedo would have to wait another two days for us to coordinate his departure from Cali. Besides, no one else knew or had met Salcedo. Given everything else going on, the two of us could only do so much.

Salcedo was well armed and holed up in a secure, heavily protected apartment building in southern Cali, but he understood the reach and capabilities of the Mafia's military wing better than anyone. Still, he thought it unlikely that the cartel would launch any type of operation to kill him or his family at their home—that would be too high-profile and wasn't how they conducted business. More likely they'd try to lure him out for a meeting or use some kind of other, more subtle ruse. But given the circumstances, did the old rules even apply anymore? No one could predict what choices the cartel might make—especially with an increasingly volatile William at the helm. Salcedo planned to remain in lockdown while we organized their relocation to Bogotá, but as always, he planned for the worst.

When Dave, Jerry, and I got to the Bogotá airport, we waited anxiously at the gate for the arrival of Patricia's Avianca flight from Cali. It had been twelve hours since we'd been in contact with her.

The flight landed on time, and one by one the passengers filed out. We watched them all wind through the jetway and into the waiting area, with no sign of Patricia. Just as we were about to give up hope, we spotted one last burst of stragglers, with Patricia leading the way. She saw us and hurried in our direction, Freddy and the boys rushing to keep pace behind her.

Dave and I relaxed a bit for the first time in hours—they were safe, thank God. For Patricia and her children, the past year had been nothing short of a nightmare, and they'd had to endure it without Guillermo. But now, all that would be behind them. Soon, they'd all be reunited and start a new life, one without constant fear.

We greeted her and Freddy and asked if everything was okay.

"Yes. Everything's fine," Patricia said. That impossible-to-read tone of hers had returned. She was calm, but something seemed off.

She formally introduced us to her two sons—who looked up at us in wonder—and we prepared to leave. "Let's grab your luggage and get the hell out of here," Dave said. "Guillermo's waiting for you."

Patricia didn't move. "Actually, I'm not staying," she said. "I'm returning to Cali."

"What?!" the three of us exclaimed. We were stunned.

I looked over at Freddy, but he just shrugged his shoulders and looked down at his feet.

"You can't go back!" I told her, trying not to raise my voice. "You can't. If you go back, Patricia, I'm telling you with total certainty that you will be—"

I caught myself just in time—her boys were watching my every move. There was no way I could say what I was thinking out loud—but I didn't need to. All the adults knew exactly what was left unsaid.

I turned to Freddy, trying my best to hide my frustration. "Freddy, could you please take the boys and give us a minute?" He nodded and took them away from the escalating drama.

We had to talk some sense into her. There was absolutely *no* way she could return to Cali and expect to stay alive. By now, the cartel likely knew that Guillermo was in the hands of the DEA, which meant an automatic death sentence for him and his family. We had to be rational, reason with her, and keep our cool.

"If you return to Cali, you'll be killed!" I said. So much for the calm and collected approach.

"What about my business?" she fired back.

Her *business*? I told her to forget it. Wasn't her life more important?

But Patricia was adamant. She had real estate and other belongings to sell, she said, along with bank accounts to close and certificates of deposit to redeem.

I turned to Dave, whose powers of persuasion often had more of an effect. He repeated how all those things could be handled later and how the single most important thing was the safety of her and her children. He insisted that they would *only* be safe if they remained in Bogotá under our protection. But the more adamant he became, the more aggravated she got.

"Everything we have and own, not important? Okay, then, you tell me: How are we going to survive in the United States? Where are we going to get money from? *Who* are we going to get money from? And if Guillermo goes to prison? Then what?"

"We'll take care of all that," Jerry said. "We won't just leave you with no money and no way to live!"

It was three against one, but nothing we said made a difference—it was one long, endless debate without a moderator. The back and forth went on for nearly an hour before she told us she'd had enough.

I had to make one final appeal and took her arm, gently. "Patricia, please listen to me. Don't go. I promise you, if you do? The cartel *will* find you, and they *will* kill you. Please, think about what you're doing. I am literally begging you to reconsider."

"Don't make your children grow up without their mother," Dave said. Harsh words, but it was the truth.

Patricia pulled her arm away. "I need to get my affairs in order *before* I leave Colombia. Besides, I need to get my children's passports," she said.

I threw my hands up in the air and turned to Dave and Jerry, defeated. If only we'd had some kind of authority, maybe we could have compelled her to come with us—but we were American agents on foreign turf. There was nothing more we could do.

Patricia called out for Freddy, who brought over her boys. She knelt down and tried to explain what was happening in a way that wouldn't upset them.

"Mommy has some business to finish up in Cali," she said. "But Chris and Dave here are my friends, and you'll be safe with them. They're going to take you to see your father! Mommy will be back in a day or two. Okay?"

The boys were confused. The barely knew us, and they were already uncomfortable. With no idea what to do or think, they clung desperately to their mother and began to cry. They'd already been through this twice before with their father, and now they were living it all over again. The three of us averted our eyes. It was too painful to watch.

Patricia hugged her boys one last time and then, with Freddy's help, gently freed herself from their arms. We all made one final plea for them to stay, but to no avail. The most we could do before Patricia left was to tell her to stay somewhere safe and to make sure she had all of our contact numbers—including Attaché Senneca's direct office number at the US Embassy, just in case she couldn't reach me or Dave.

Patricia and Freddy thanked us and promised they would try and resolve as many issues as they could as quickly as possible so that they could return to Bogotá in two days, three at the most. Patricia looked down at her boys, then over to me and Dave. "Please take care of them," she said to us as she struggled to compose herself.

"I promise you, we will," Dave said. She thanked us again, gave the boys one last look, then turned and walked across the terminal with Freddy. Right before they boarded their return flight to Cali, she turned to wave goodbye. The entire time, we hoped she might change her mind. We also hoped this wasn't the last time we would see her.

The two children were silent and kept their heads down as we walked through the airport terminal. They were confused and upset—truth be told, we all were. Dave, Jerry, and I were having almost as much trouble processing everything that had happened as they were. We tried to console them, but the sympathy of three foreigners was not what they needed. What they needed was to be reunited with their father as soon as possible.

But when we arrived at the apartment where we'd hidden Pallomari, things went from bad to worse. While overwhelmed with relief when he laid eyes on his boys, Guillermo flew into a rage when Dave and I broke the news that Patricia had insisted on returning to Cali with Freddy. He was screaming, crying, and smashing his head and fists against the wall. His outburst was so extreme that the boys burst into tears again, and we had to physically step in and restrain him for fear he might injure himself. At one point, he became so distraught that he threatened to not leave Colombia without his wife. The one thing left unsaid was that in reality, it was probably already too late. He knew what Patricia returning to Cali meant.

Two more days passed before Dave and I heard from Patricia. She told us that she hadn't redeemed their certificates of deposit yet—the current rate wasn't as favorable as she wanted, and she still had some other business matters to attend to. Perhaps the fact that Patricia and Freddy had made it two days without incident had left her feeling invulnerable, who knows, but Dave and I didn't even attempt to understand her thinking at this point. We hit her with a full-on reality check.

"You need to leave, and you need to leave *now!*" Dave told her. "This is not a game. Do you not believe us when we tell you that your lives are in imminent danger? Because I swear to you, it's true. I'm not trying to scare you—actually, I am. I'm trying to make you understand that if you stay there, you will almost certainly die."

Even I held my breath after he said that. But Patricia held her ground. She needed two more days, she told us, and then she and Freddy would meet us in Bogotá on Wednesday afternoon, August 16.

Wednesday morning came and went with no word from either Patricia or Freddy. Day turned to night, and night turned to midnight: still no word.

Pallomari was a nervous wreck. He started making a series of phone calls—all of them leading nowhere—until he finally got ahold of Patricia's housekeeper in Cali, who told him Patricia had left earlier that day and hadn't returned. Several suitcases sat waiting by the front door, exactly where Patricia had left them. And there was something else: a man had called the home a short time ago and said, "We know what you people are up to!" then hung up.

That was it, the confirmation we'd feared. The secret was out. Desperate, Pallomari continued his torrent of calls, begging everyone and anyone he knew for any information. Someone told him that Patricia and Freddy had left Universal Link that evening around seven o'clock in Freddy's red Fiat, but they hadn't been seen since. We already knew they'd never made it home to pick up Patricia's luggage.

Guillermo was half out of his mind by the time he somehow connected with a member of the cartel's military wing, who informed him that Patricia had been kidnapped because he "hadn't followed Miguel's orders." The assassin then made Pallomari an inconceivable offer: cut ties with the DEA and immediately return to Cali, and in exchange they would let his wife live.

In Hollywood, of course, this scenario plays out over and over again. One person—usually the hero—trades their life for another. But in the real world, in the brutal world of the Cali cartel, the script wasn't that cut-and-dried. If Pallomari returned to Cali, it meant certain death. Besides, Pallomari wasn't a hero—he was a distraught accountant, fugitive, and father of two traumatized young boys. There was no way on earth we would have allowed him to take that gamble anyway, even if he'd been foolish enough to try.

It only took a minute for it to finally hit him that his wife was probably already dead—and when it did, Pallomari flew into a rage more violent than the first. In less than a year, he'd lost his job, his freedom, his home, and now he'd most likely lost his wife. Soon he'd be a stranger in a foreign land, with no idea what would become of him or his family.

Like Salcedo, we'd planned for the worst—but now that the worst had actually happened, no amount of planning could have prepared us for how devastating the situation truly was. Eventually Pallomari grew weary, and his fury turned into a state of shock, sadness, and resignation. He could focus on only one thing now: his children. Their lives, he knew, would never be the same again. From this day forward, all the three of them had was each other.

CHAPTER 31

Now What?

"There can be no traceable American footprint."
—MYLES R. R. FRECHETTE,
US Ambassador to Colombia

WITH PALLOMARI NOW SAFE IN BOGOTÁ under US protection, Dave and I shifted our focus to finding a way to get him out of the country without igniting a major firestorm. After all, he wasn't just a high-profile fugitive in Colombia but in the United States as well. He was also a material witness in the Proceso 8.000 investigation, arguably the biggest political scandal in Colombian history and an investigation that had threatened to destabilize the nation for months. Simply put, the entire case was a diplomatic ticking time bomb, and both the Cali cartel and the host of corrupt Colombian officials involved would do everything in their power to prevent Pallomari from making it out alive. Both groups wanted the same thing: to ensure that all the damning secrets he held so close to his vest remained just that: secret.

Within the span of seventy-two hours, things went from bad to worse. On the heels of Pallomari's defection from Cali, Fernando Botero, the former defense minister and manager of Ernesto Samper's presidential campaign, was arrested. He'd resigned as defense minister just two weeks earlier, in the face of rapidly mounting evidence that he'd conspired with the Cali cartel to funnel millions of dollars to Samper's campaign. Things didn't look good for the disgraced politician, especially since the campaign's former treasurer, Santiago Medina, had been arrested three weeks ago and was now divulging damaging testimony against Botero regarding his involvement in the plot. But Colombian authorities were still missing one key piece to the campaign financing puzzle: Guillermo Pallomari. If what he knew were ever exposed, any hope for Botero or the integrity of the Samper administration would fall to pieces.

With that in mind, Ambassador Frechette was adamant that there be *no* direct US involvement or traceable American footprint when it came to Pallomari's departure from Colombia. Relations between the two governments were already shaky, and Frechette was doing everything he could to prevent the diplomatic conflict from escalating. As we awaited further instruction from Washington, Dave and I focused on another urgent priority: getting Salcedo and his family safely to Bogotá.

The Salcedo family had remained barricaded in their fourth-floor apartment for the entire weekend while Dave and I worked on Pallomari's extraction and assisting Patricia and her family. With every minute Salcedo and his family remained in Cali, the threat to their lives increased exponentially. But Dave and I were stretched thin—we couldn't be in two places at once, let alone three. Besides, these weren't the kinds of projects that could be handled with simple multitasking. We were literally in charge of people's lives, and the burden of that responsibility weighed heavily on us.

While Dave and I were hustling to finalize the logistics around Salcedo's departure, he'd been busy making his own arrangements. He'd covertly executed several tasks in advance, starting with the sending off of a van loaded with luggage and other personal items to Bogotá, helmed by a family friend to avoid any suspicion. Over the course of the last six and a half years, he'd also been stockpiling a secret stash of weaponry at a nearby storage facility, in the event of a worst-case scenario. Rather than abandon the arsenal—or, worse, leave it to be found by the cartel's military wing—Salcedo buried it in a field, then drew a detailed map so that we could find it. Along with our ATF buddy Bill, we later recovered two dozen machine guns, several handguns, various boxes of assorted ammunition, and an array of dangerous high-powered explosives.

Dave and I arrived early at the air force base in Cali on August 14 aboard our DEA airplane. We were anticipating a full return flight, with us, Salcedo, his wife, and their children. They weren't expected for several more hours, but we wanted to be there early in case of any unforeseen problems. Dave and I were anxious as we waited inside the base: this had been a long time coming. We wanted to keep our word to the man who'd risked his life to help us deliver a debilitating blow to the once untouchable Cali cartel. It still seemed inconceivable that their twenty-year reign of terror might be coming to an end.

Salcedo and his family arrived at the base at two o'clock sharp. He introduced us to his family, and together we waited for final clearance to depart. The mood was, for once, serene—a far cry from the usual angst we'd felt during most of our past encounters with Salcedo. I reminded him of that first meeting in the sugarcane field, which now seemed like a lifetime ago. "I told you we wouldn't let you down," I said. When Dave and I took turns shaking his hand, we saw that he was fighting back tears. We weren't used to that side of him, and suddenly we felt humbled, as if the significance of what we'd been through was hitting him all at once.

Salcedo was overcome, but still managed a smile. "Thank you," he said. "Thank you for keeping your word. Thank you for believing in me."

It had been a very close call. Just one hour earlier, Andrés Vélez, a.k.a. "El Pecoso" (another one of Cali's lethal assassins, and the man who'd parked the dynamite-laden car bomb outside the Mónaco building in the failed attempt to kill Escobar in 1988), had been calling and paging Salcedo incessantly, asking to meet. The extent of his treachery had officially spread throughout the cartel, and they were coming for him. Had he gone to that meeting, he would never have left alive.

We finally left Cali at 2:30 that afternoon. It was a bittersweet goodbye, and both Salcedo and his wife cried as they looked out the window of the plane and watched their home get more and more distant until all they saw were clouds. They were relieved to escape, but at the same time, their hearts were broken. It wasn't that long ago that they'd been enjoying a happy, prosperous life in Cali, the city they loved. And now they'd likely never see it again.

When we arrived in Bogotá an hour later, Salcedo showed us his pager. Within the past few hours he'd gotten 158 pages, many of them from Pecoso. The cartel was in full panic mode and looking to tie up all loose ends—but of course, it was too late. For the second time in less than a week, we were able to exfiltrate one of their most prized insiders without them having a clue.

After we arrived, we moved Salcedo and his family into a vacant penthouse apartment, replete with round-the-clock security. We arranged for his parents and a few other family members to join them and began the process of coordinating their travel to the US. Two days after his parents arrived at the safe house, cartel thugs broke into their Bogotá home in an attempt to locate Salcedo. It was clear that the cartel was leaving no stone unturned.

Even though we finally had both Pallomari and Salcedo and their families in Bogotá under twenty-four-hour guard, we weren't out of the woods just yet. We constantly worried about keeping the two most critical witnesses *ever* against the Cali cartel alive until they could be relocated to the US and placed into witness protection.

Initially, Ambassador Frechette's plan had called for Pallomari to depart Colombia alone, joined later by Patricia, their two children, and several family members who'd travel separately from Colombia to the US via commercial airlines. Of course, that all changed when Patricia and Freddy went missing.

Patricia's disappearance made an already complicated matter even more so. Since the ambassador still wanted Pallomari to leave Colombia by himself, we scrambled to find a way for his two boys to travel by themselves to the US via commercial airlines accompanied by a DEA escort. That idea was scrapped, however, when we discovered that the scenario was impermissible under Colombian law. Article 111 stated that for children under the age of eighteen traveling outside the country alone or accompanied by *one* of their parents, the authorization of *both* parents or legal guardians with notarial certification was obligatory. The requirement was well intentioned, designed to prevent international child abduction and child exploitation. Colombian immigration (DAS) and US commercial airlines wouldn't allow the children to leave the country by themselves without Patricia's authorization, period.

Pallomari refused to leave Colombia without his children regardless, which everyone understood. He'd resigned himself to the fact that he'd lost his wife, but he still had his boys, and the three would leave Colombia together or not at all.

Meanwhile, Pallomari had grown tired of waiting for Washington to authorize his departure from Colombia. He decided to take matters into his own hands, and after weighing all his options, he made his *own* travel plans—ones that included his children.

Many of the details surrounding Pallomari's "departure" from Colombia have never been revealed. What is common knowledge is that after planning his itinerary, he called the DEA office in Miami and spoke to Special Agent Luis Pérez. He identified himself as a fugitive from Operation Cornerstone and stated his intention to surrender himself to US law enforcement authorities in the coming days. He then chartered a private aircraft to fly him and his children to an undisclosed location in South Florida, covering the cost of the plane and related expenses himself. In anticipation of Pallomari's surrender I traveled to the US to fully debrief him in a secure, less fraught environment once he landed.

On August 18, 1995, Guillermo Pallomari and his two young sons boarded a private chartered aircraft and departed Colombia, without his wife and without any "official" assistance from American personnel.

As soon as Pallomari's charter touched down in the US, he reached out to Agent Pérez, who arranged to have him taken to a safe house under heavy DEA guard. Three days later, Pallomari appeared in federal court in Miami, Florida, for his initial appearance and was subsequently released into DEA custody on the condition that he cooperate fully with the US government regarding his activities and knowledge of the Cali cartel. Pallomari had made his escape, and the worst was over. Now it was Salcedo's turn.

Because of heightened security concerns, Salcedo's departure from Colombia had to be pushed back several days. Dave had already flown to the US along with eight of Salcedo's family members on two separate commercial flights and was focused on getting them situated in a secret location while also helping prepare for Salcedo's arrival. With Dave and I both in the States (I was still in round-the-clock debriefings with Pallomari), we had to rely on Jerry Salameh to ensure Salcedo got out of Colombia safely.

On Saturday, August 26, 1995, three armored embassy vehicles entered the garage where Salcedo was staying. The team moved fast, retrieving

Now What?

Salcedo and swiftly escorting him from the building. The SUVs were airport-bound but had one quick, prescheduled stop to make first.

DEA Attaché Tony Senneca was already waiting in the courtyard when the convoy pulled into the American Embassy. Senneca, on behalf of the DEA and the US government, wanted to express everyone's sincere thanks and gratitude to the man who'd perhaps played the single most pivotal part in crippling the Cali cartel.

It was an emotional exchange, after which Salcedo and the rest of the group got back into the SUVs and resumed the drive to the airport. When they arrived, the caravan headed to an isolated hangar at the airport's far end. Salcedo was ushered into a waiting aircraft, where two pilots were standing by for the final clearance to takeoff.

Dave and I followed every step of his journey and got continuous updates so we could ensure everything went smoothly. And we often wondered: What would have happened, really, had Salcedo not taken that risk to meet us in the sugarcane field that day? It was mainly due to his help and courage that the Colombian and US government brought Cali cartel godfather Miguel Rodríguez to justice and secured Guillermo Pallomari as a witness.

I honestly wasn't sure if I'd ever see him again—once he and his family entered witness protection, there'd be no way of knowing how things would play out. But I knew that Dave would be waiting for him once he landed in the States to reunite him with his family, and, of course, express to him in person how we both felt.

Our in-depth debriefings with Salcedo and Pallomari lasted over a week, and Dave and I were still only scratching the surface. While the majority of our discussions centered around Pacho Herrera, we covered a great deal of ground with both men. Eventually, we were able to compile an extensive list of additional, unexposed, corrupt officials on the cartel payroll, which we subsequently distributed throughout the embassy, the CNP, and the Colombian Attorney General's Office. The list led to the swift firing (or "removal") of dozens more government officials, including our nemesis and primary contact at the police Search Bloc in Cali, Captain Efrén Buitrago, and Juan Carlos, General Serrano's personal pilot. Many other high-ranking Colombian officials ultimately had their US visas revoked.

At some point during those first few days in the States, Salcedo learned exactly what had happened to Patricia and Freddy from his loyal security assistant, Enrique Sanchez. When we heard the full story, we realized that it was as bad as we'd feared.

After leaving Universal Link at seven o'clock in the evening on August 16, Patricia and Freddy were intercepted by Cali assassins as they drove to collect their luggage, then catch their flight to Bogotá to meet me and Dave. The assassins had been patiently staking out Patricia's business for days, waiting to pounce the second she left.

After they were kidnapped, the two were taken to a remote spot and brutally tortured until the cartel was satisfied they'd gotten every single piece of information they could out of them. Once their appetite for information and violence had been satisfied, the heartless captors killed Patricia and Freddy and disposed of their bodies. During their torture they'd learned all about the specifics of Guillermo's defection and that he was now safely in the hands of American agents. The assassins also learned more about me and Dave—though it couldn't have been much more than they already knew from Buitrago and others.

Because the godfathers were as thorough as they were sadistic, it didn't end there. They decided to take another page out of their cartel playbook to help further cover their tracks. On August 21, 1995, DAS immigration records revealed that "Gladys Patricia Cardona de Pallomari" departed Colombia on Aeroperú Flight 613 bound for Lima, Peru—five days after the abduction and murder of the *actual* Patricia Pallomari.

It was a fairly easy endeavor. With the help of corrupt immigration and airport personnel, a female cartel operative bought an airline ticket using Patricia Pallomari's passport, then used it to clear Colombian immigration and create the illusion that Patricia was alive and had left the country. However, when investigators inquired with Peruvian immigration officials, they found no evidence to suggest that "Patricia" had ever arrived. Were it not for Enrique Sanchez and his loyalty to Salcedo, we may never have known the truth about what happened to Patricia and Freddy.

Salcedo again warned Dave about Captain Buitrago's corrupt sidekick "the Shadow," who'd previously been assigned to the Search Bloc. Salcedo didn't know his real name, but he did know that the cartel still saw him as a valuable asset. He gave us a detailed description and even drew us an intricate drawing—right down to the smallest mole on his face. The illustration was so skillfully done you'd think it was drawn by a world-renowned sketch artist, but it was just another by-product of Salcedo's countless hidden skills. With it, Dave and I had no doubt that we'd recognize the Shadow were we ever lucky enough to spot him lurking nearby.

Before wrapping up my lengthy debriefing with Pallomari, I had a few final things I wanted to cover. There was something I wanted to share with him, too—something I thought he needed to know.

Salcedo had always asked me and Dave to *never* reveal to Pallomari his personal involvement in getting him to US soil. The two men weren't friends; in fact, they'd never really liked each other at all. The friction stemmed more from their professional relationship than anything else, and despite that—or perhaps because of it—I thought it was important that Pallomari know the truth behind his newfound freedom. Without Salcedo's help, Pallomari's children would be orphans.

"Guillermo, do you know why you're sitting here today?" I asked.

"Because of you and Dave, of course," he said.

"No, actually. There's much more to it," I said. He looked at me, puzzled. I paused for a second, then hit him with the truth.

"Guillermo, the only reason you're still alive is because of Jorge Salcedo."

His jaw dropped. All this time, Pallomari had been convinced that Salcedo wasn't just a colleague he disliked but also one of the men on the hunt to find and kill him. He didn't know quite what to do with the revelation.

I stood and began to pack up my things. "I thought it was important that you know exactly what he did for you—he's the main reason you're alive and here today. It was his idea for us to approach Patricia to try and get word to you. All of this, everything, is all because of him."

Pallomari was still processing what I'd told him when we shook hands and said our farewells. It didn't feel like a final goodbye; I figured we'd see each other again for future debriefings or the extensive trial prep he'd have to do prior to testifying. His work with the US government was far from over—then again, he was about to go into witness protection. And when that happens, you never know when—or if—you'll ever see someone again.

As it turned out, that was the last time I ever saw Guillermo Pallomari. But to this day, I'm so thankful that I went with my gut instinct and told him the truth about Salcedo.

After that, Dave and I were right back in that familiar *Twilight Zone* state of mind. In just a matter of days we'd watched two men and their families fight for their survival and ultimately leave everything and everyone they knew behind in order to seek refuge and start a new life in a foreign country. It was impossible to comprehend what either family was going through, especially the Pallomari family. That level of suffering was one we couldn't even begin to understand.

After Dave and I wrapped up our debriefings, we reconvened in Colombia, eager to get back to the real task at hand. Armed with a mountain of new intel and leads, we were ready to begin the final phase of our quest: the hunt for the last godfather standing, the elusive and mercurial Pacho Herrera.

CHAPTER 32

A Dangerous Time

*"If you ask me if there are interests outside the country
dedicated to creating instability [in Colombia], I think so, yes.
If you ask me if it's the DEA, I'd say that that rings a bell."*

—HORACIO SERPA,
Colombian Interior Minister

AFTER WE RETURNED TO COLOMBIA, our first order of business was to swap out all our cellular phones and pagers. It was a given that the old ones had been compromised during the Salcedo and Pallomari operations, so everything had to go. Our next task was to replace our SUV and find another well-situated and secure apartment to serve as our new safe house and base of operations.

It wasn't hard to walk away from everything we'd been associated with before—considering everything that had just happened, Dave and I weren't looking to take any chances. We were in it for the long haul, and we knew it wasn't going to be easy. Finding Pacho, we feared, would take much longer than we hoped.

Working in our favor was the fact that the Search Bloc had undergone a transformation and had become something we never expected: potentially trustworthy. General Serrano had excised another wave of compromised officials, and with Captain Buitrago gone, Dave and I decided to give them another shot. We needed help gathering intel regarding Pacho's whereabouts and had identified a number of possible locations throughout the

Valle del Cauca Department we wanted to raid. The Colombian government had also compiled an extensive inventory of holdings, so there was a lot to juggle. We needed all the resources we could muster.

We also wanted to work with the army Search Bloc and Major Arango again. Dave and I still felt very much indebted to him—after all, he was the one who'd provided the roadblocks and checkpoints that had helped keep Pallomari alive. And he'd done it with no questions asked.

Throughout most of September we raided over seventy-five properties related to Pacho with the assistance of the police and military and found absolutely nothing, not the smallest sign that he'd been there—or was even alive, for that matter. "The man is a ghost," Dave said as we crossed target after target off our lists.

Among the places we raided was Pacho's infamous *finca*, El Desierto ("The Desert"). Given its grisly history, a more apt name would have been *The Killing Fields*, the title of the critically acclaimed film from 1984 about Khmer Rouge atrocities in Cambodia. Countless people had been tortured and murdered at El Desierto, with their bodies buried on the property or thrown off a bridge into the Cauca River just a few miles down the road.

Not long ago, Dave and I had learned that Cali transportation specialist Rhadamés Trujillo had been tortured and slaughtered on the *finca* a year earlier, along with three of his associates. We coordinated with the police and Attorney General's Office to bring in specially trained cadaver dogs from the US to aid in the search for human remains on the El Desierto grounds, but the property was too expansive (and the heat too unbearable) for the dogs to work effectively. But we *did* have a witness who'd been there on the day of the murders, and it was through him that we learned exactly what happened.

Our witness was Jorge Salcedo. As he explained, he'd been sent to the ranch in advance to coordinate security matters and help facilitate the ruse that Miguel was coming for a party for his fifty-first birthday. Miguel also wanted him there to question Rhadamés about a recent five-ton cocaine shipment that had been seized in Panama. Salcedo, meanwhile, had no clue what Miguel was planning.

At the time, Rhadamés was in charge of a smuggling operation that routed tons of cocaine camouflaged in coffee from Panama to Miami. Over the past year, US law enforcement authorities had interdicted several cocaine shipments (throughout Central America, Panama, and South Florida) belonging to the Cali cartel. The Rodríguez brothers didn't see these events as a coincidence—especially the most recent Panama seizure—and suspected Rhadamés was cooperating with "the Three Letters," the old cartel code for the DEA. For the record, he wasn't. But Miguel always preferred being safe to being sorry.

When it comes to Colombian drug cartels, suspicion is often all it takes to justify murder. Just the slightest bit of speculation could cost a cartel member their life—no evidence required—and the punishment for simply inciting a shadow of doubt is carried out swiftly and brutally. Any and all collateral damage was irrelevant.

When Rhadamés was invited to attend Miguel's birthday party at El Desierto in mid-August 1994, he saw it as an honor. Rhadamés extended an invitation to a naive young Costa Rican couple, Andrés Cardona Ortega and his wife, Elena Flores Arboleda.

El Desierto was tucked away in the country just north of Cali, not far from the small city of Yumbo. It was a breathtaking ranch in an idyllic location, with massive palm trees stretching almost half a mile along the entrance adding to its grand, stately appearance. The entry led to a large cockfighting arena where guests and spectators would gather to watch and wager on the fights, an imported sand beach led to a lake tailor-made for water sports, and the cool night breeze coming off the water made it the ideal spot for picturesque evening parties replete with roaring bonfires and decadent feasts.

Sometime during the afternoon that horrific day, the four unsuspecting guests arrived at El Desierto for a birthday bash that never actually existed: Rhadamés, his Panamanian bodyguard, his friend Andrés Cardona, and Andrés's wife, Elena. Unbeknownst to the eager revelers, the "party" was nothing more than an elaborate ruse concocted with the singular goal of unmasking a suspected informant at the hands of Memo Lara and several of Pacho Herrera's top assassins. There was only one problem: there was no informant to be identified.

As soon as they walked in the door, the four were separated and dragged into individual rooms. The men were seated in their respective torture chambers, their arms and legs bound to the chairs with duct tape, while Elena was escorted to a back bedroom and told to sit quietly on the bed. They were all shocked and confused, as none of them had anything to atone for. They'd just gotten caught up in the paranoia of a madman.

The Panamanian bodyguard was the first to die. The largest and strongest of the four, he was mercilessly beaten by the assassins during his interrogation. When they decided to finally put him out of his misery, they did so by putting a clear plastic bag over his head and suffocating him until his body fell limp and he stopped breathing.

By then the band of *sicarios* had hit their stride, and from that point on it was just a matter of repeating the exact same process three times over: brutal beatings interrupted only by occasional questions, with rare minutes of silence broken by blood-curdling screams and desperate pleas. Despite repeated denials and proclamations of innocence from all three, one by one they succumbed to their torturers' sadism. All three were innocent, but all three had endured unimaginable pain and died for no good reason. That was because in Miguel's mind, he didn't need a reason. All he needed was a hunch.

To the very end, Rhadamés fought desperately to be heard and believed, to no avail. His last words were something to the effect of, "I am not a snitch!"

Memo Lara and his team of homicidal *sicarios* worked quickly and methodically to dispose of the bodies. It was a routine they'd been through many times before, so it didn't require much thought. The corpses were stripped naked and tossed on their backs atop the tile floor, their bellies cut open with sharp knives, and their entrails removed and dropped in buckets. Large, weighty rocks were tucked inside their stomachs, ensuring that the bodies wouldn't float to the surface and get discovered. Next, the bodies were rolled up in draperies the *sicarios* had torn down from ranch windows, wrapped tightly with duct tape, and driven to the nearby Cauca River. The bodies were then thrown from the bridge and sunk rapidly into the river's depths.

Waiting in the dark waters below were ravenous black caimans, the perfect accomplices to help further dispose of the evidence. Afterward, the *sicarios* burned everything that remained: entrails, clothing, luggage, and any other personal belongings. They kept only passports and airline tickets. It was a crude operation, but a highly effective one.

The next day, four cartel operatives posed as the four victims and caught a flight to Panama (and were documented as arriving safely). Just as the cartel had done with Patricia, the cartel had managed not only to get away with murder, but to successfully engineer a cover-up at the same time. If—*when*—frantic family members and inquisitive authorities came calling, the godfathers could easily prove their lack of involvement. It was an unthinkable but perfect crime, and the many years of practice on Cali's part had made it a seamless endeavor.

In Miguel's mind their hands were clean, and things had gone well, despite the fact that the hunt for their cartel mole had come up empty. But Dave and I knew what they'd done—every sickening detail—and it reaffirmed what we already knew: the Cali cartel would go to any and all lengths necessary to eliminate a perceived threat.

Back in Bogotá, the news of Guillermo Pallomari's defection to the US was officially announced and was fast making headlines throughout the hemisphere. One senior Clinton administration official told the *Washington Post* that "he may turn out to be the biggest witness of international drug trafficking that we've ever had. He was the chief administrator, a man with knowledge of the routes, codes…he knows everything about the operation." The fact that Pallomari's arrival in the US was no longer a secret meant that it was just a matter of time before possible repercussions followed.

Pallomari's most recent statements about the Cali cartel contributing upward of $6 million to Samper's 1994 presidential campaign were soon corroborated by the testimony of Santiago Medina, Samper's former campaign treasurer, who was cooperating with Colombian authorities after his recent arrest. At President Samper's request, a House of Representatives Congressional Accusations Commission had been convened and tasked with investigating the latest campaign financing accusations. Unsurprisingly, Samper hadn't changed his tune. He still vehemently denied any knowledge of the allegations.

On September 27, 1995, Dave and I received an urgent call from Attaché Senneca requesting our immediate return from Cali. He also had shocking news: President Samper's personal attorney, Antonio José Cancino, had been shot in Bogotá earlier that day.

Apparently, Cancino had just dropped off his son at a downtown university and was en route to a local radio station for an interview when gunmen intercepted his vehicle. A second car in Cancino's motorcade was also riddled with bullets, killing two of his bodyguards.

It was a miracle that Cancino survived the assassination attempt. Somehow, he emerged relatively unscathed from the ordeal, save for two minor gunshot wounds to his right hand and arm. A third bodyguard—who'd been sitting next to Cancino—was seriously wounded.

Horacio Serpa, Colombia's outspoken interior minister, suggested that the DEA may have orchestrated the attack on Cancino. "If you ask me if there are interests outside the country dedicated to creating instability [in Colombia], I think so, yes," Serpa told reporters. "If you ask me if it's the DEA, I'd say that that rings a bell."

At best his words were foolish, at worst they were reckless. For a Colombian minister—a cabinet-level official, no less—to make such a dangerous statement was appalling. The Colombian presidential palace wasn't done with their character attacks yet, though, and issued another statement claiming the attack on Cancino was carried out in order to prevent Samper from clearing his name and that it had most likely been supported by "national and foreign" interest groups.

It was obvious that many in the Colombian government were convinced the US was trying to destabilize Colombia and help collapse the shaky Samper administration. That, or they knew better and simply wanted to deflect blame. Regardless, for anyone looking for someone to condemn, the DEA was always an easy target.

Washington brass might have considered the comments laughable if they weren't so thoroughly enraged. Defiant, categorical denials immediately followed from DEA Headquarters, the Justice Department, and the State Department. In addition to rejecting Serpa's remarks, Washington officials declared that they held the Colombian government responsible for the security of its nationals in the country. It was also suggested that Colombia was simply trying to divert attention away from the serious political crises it was currently facing, not least the credible allegations of drug corruption.

Sparring aside, the DEA and American Embassy thought it better if Dave and I were back in Bogotá, as opposed to our safe house in Cali two hundred miles away, alone, with no backup or protection. Soon after, all embassy travel was put on a temporary hold. Relations between Colombia and the United States had quickly turned sour after Minister Serpa's misguided declarations, but things would get far worse the following week.

While driving to the embassy in Bogotá on the morning of October 4, I thought I heard a familiar voice on a Colombian radio station. When I recognized it as Attaché Tony Senneca's, my interest was piqued. As I continued to listen, I realized that it was more than just a familiar voice— even the comments sounded familiar. I knew it wasn't a vague sense of déjà vu: I was *positive* I'd heard those words before. And, as it turned out, I definitely had.

What I thought was an interview wasn't an interview at all. What it was, I now understood, was a telephone conversation between Senneca, Robert "Bobby" Nieves, chief of DEA's international operations, and Mary Lee Warren, deputy assistant attorney general in the Criminal Division. And not only did I *know* the exact conversation, I knew it because Dave and I had been there for it.

When that fact hit me, my first thought was *Oh, shit*. I then realized that not only had someone wiretapped the office of the head of the DEA at the US Embassy in Colombia but that those tapes were also now being aired, live, on the radio.

It took me a minute or so, but I finally figured out what was happening: Carlos Alonso Lucio, a former M-19 leftist guerrilla who became a member of the Colombian House of Representatives, was airing select parts of the (illegally) intercepted telephone calls, as well as gleefully reciting various passages of the calls from transcripts. Even worse, it was also airing live on television. The final blow: it was all going down *during an actual session of Parliament*.

My anger overtook my shock, though, when I learned that the American flag was later burned in the background during the Colombian legislative session as the tapes aired. Somehow, this made things feel much more…personal. I sincerely hoped that, at some point in my life, I would have the opportunity to *discuss* it with Lucio. In person.

Lucio had become a member of Congress after the government struck a deal with the M-19 guerrillas to give them representation in the government in exchange for renouncing violence and their affiliation with the rebel group. According to Salcedo, he later established close ties with the Rodríguez Orejuela brothers and became the perfect conduit to carry their water. As Lucio played the tapes, he made sure to voice his belief that the DEA was conducting unilateral antidrug operations in Colombia and, for added effect, implied that we were also conspiring to destabilize the government and ultimately remove President Samper from office.

One of the conversations Lucio chose to air was about our operation to use cadaver dogs to help detect human remains at El Desierto ranch. Even though the search had been coordinated in advance with Colombian officials, Lucio attempted to spin the call, making it seem as if the DEA was conducting unilateral operations.

Ambassador Frechette and other Clinton administration officials were quick to denounce the illegal wiretapping of a US diplomat. "This episode suggests another disturbing attack against the United States government, possibly aimed at deflecting attention away from ongoing investigations into charges of narcotics corruption," said Nicholas Burns, then spokesperson for the US State Department. "We continue to be highly disturbed and displeased by a number of the allegations and unfounded rumors that have been made by prominent people in Colombia."

As embassy officials searched for answers as to who could have authorized such a brazen act, Néstor Humberto Martínez, Colombia's justice minister, denied any government involvement in the wiretapping of the head of the DEA. When Dave and I met with Senneca in his office to discuss the mess, the answer hit us both at the exact same time: Patricia Pallomari.

The telephone line that had been illegally intercepted—Senneca's direct office number at the US Embassy—was the same number that Dave and I had given to Patricia during our meeting at the embassy two months ago.

There was no doubt that Patricia's captors had learned everything about her husband's defection during her "interrogation"—including Senneca's private office number. In a desperate attempt to prove the DEA's involvement, the cartel used one of their corrupt contacts in the telephone company to intercept Senneca's line. Once they succeeded, they gave the tapes to one of their loyal puppets—Lucio—and instructed him to play them in an attempt to further embarrass and discredit the DEA and US government.

We knew without a doubt who was behind it. The cartel, like a cornered and wounded wild animal, had become much more impulsive. They were well known for their carefully constructed façade of dignity and restraint—remember, "the Gentlemen of Cali"—but now their actions had become careless. This, in turn, made them a more fearsome adversary, since their recklessness caused them to be even more dangerous and unpredictable.

Back in the US, debriefings of Salcedo and Pallomari by American agents continued, with the resulting intelligence reports disseminated to the US Embassy in Bogotá. One report, a memorandum sent by Miami Special Agent Morgan Holley, caused considerable consternation to DEA management in light of recent events.

In it, Salcedo said he was "very concerned for the safety of Bogotá agents David Mitchell, Chris Feistl, and Jerry Salameh." It was literally the last thing we wanted to hear.

Up until the arrest of Miguel Rodríguez, Cali's policy was to "avoid committing any acts of violence against DEA agents in Colombia, especially those agents operating in Cali." The "policy" was essentially just a PR strategy, designed to strengthen the cartel's fictionalized reputation for preferring peace and gentility to violence and disrespect.

With Salcedo and Pallomari in the US and Yusti dead, Salcedo was concerned that the cartel might actually retaliate, this time making no exceptions for agents. He said, "It was only reasonable that with the large number of corrupt government officials on the payroll, the cartel knew of the direct participation of the three agents in the operations to arrest Gilberto and Miguel." He also pointed out that because of our many trips to Cali and interaction with Captain Buitrago and others, "The cartel was familiar with their appearances." And, lastly, "If these agents continue to travel to Cali, their lives may be in danger." Great.

We knew Salcedo was just looking out for us, but in doing so he'd created a host of security concerns within the DEA. Among other things, DEA Headquarters now wanted to restrict our travel to Cali *and* assign the three of us temporary protection details. It took some work, but eventually we were able to convince Headquarters that this was more about Salcedo's genuine concern for us personally than about any viable threat. After all, no specific information about any direct threats had been presented.

We should have known better. It didn't take long—early November, to be exact—for us to be reminded that Salcedo was rarely, if ever, wrong. Over the course of several days, I received four messages in Spanish on the answering machine in my Bogotá apartment, all of them death threats. Left by a man and woman, the threats were vulgar, explicit, and made most terrifying by their directness. "When you leave your house, you will die. You are dead. You know you will die. Death to all gringos. We are going to get you." Message received, loud and clear, thank you. But I wasn't going anywhere.

I reported the threats to Diplomatic Security Service Special Agent Patrick Durkin in the mission's Regional Security Office (RSO) and provided him with copies I'd made of the tape from my answering machine. DEA Headquarters reacted as you'd expect and recommended my immediate evacuation from Colombia. I pleaded my case to stay, and, thankfully, DEA Attaché Senneca stepped in and proposed alternative security measures instead.

Willing to do pretty much anything but leave, I agreed to be relocated to a vacant embassy apartment and assigned round-the-clock security to accompany me wherever I went. All travel outside of Bogotá was restricted, and I made sure to constantly vary my departure times and travel routes to and from the embassy.

A two-week investigation by the RSO determined that none of the threats referenced me by my name or even acknowledged the fact that I worked for the DEA. Furthermore, the investigation couldn't confirm the threats originated from the Cali cartel. So, to my relief, I was authorized to return to full duty, with no further restrictions. To this day, I owe Pat an enormous debt of gratitude!

I was more than ready to get back to our primary objective—Pacho—but I'd be lying if I said that I didn't have a lingering worry in the back of my mind after everything that had happened over the past two months.

But by the end of November, Dave and I were back in Cali and back on our game. We continued to follow our daily ritual—wearing our nondescript baseball hats and sunglasses and taking turns on who started the SUV we kept in the garage of our safe house in case of a potential car bomb, the same routine we'd put in place a little over a year ago. Back then we'd joked about it, but now we had a lot more cause to be nervous about something as mundane as turning the keys in our vehicle.

This was an unfamiliar role for us: potential targets. We didn't live our lives in fear, but our perspectives had definitely changed. Each day brought a heightened sense of suspicion and uncertainty, and Dave and I were well aware that our number one focus now was to exercise extreme caution. The indelible images of what had happened to Patricia and Freddy were always with us. But in a way, that pushed us forward. We were going to do everything we could to help find Pacho, we were going to bring him to justice, and no one was going to convince us otherwise.

CHAPTER 33

The Shadow

*"Everything that we see is a shadow cast
by that which we do not see."*

—MARTIN LUTHER KING JR.

WITH THE END OF 1995 APPROACHING, we were still no closer to finding Pacho Herrera. Along with the police and military we'd literally torn up the Valle del Cauca Department searching for him, and Dave and I were wiped. We felt stunted and had absolutely no clue as to his whereabouts. For all we knew he was busy cutting to the front of the Space Mountain line at Disneyland.

By this time, Jerry Salameh had begun to accompany us more frequently on our trips to Cali. After the recent trifecta of close calls—the attack on Samper's attorney, the illegal wiretapping incident at the US Embassy, and the death threats made against me—DEA brass decided it was best if any trips to Cali consisted of three agents, rather than two, whenever possible.

As for the godfathers, imprisonment wasn't stopping them from running their multibillion-dollar criminal enterprise, it was just an inconvenience that slightly slowed them down. And when it came to their lifestyle, they weren't exactly roughing it. Their quality of life in prison would qualify as a major upgrade for many Colombians—aside from the fact that they couldn't leave. They had a slew of daily visitors who relayed messages to their operatives in the exterior and full access to cell phones to use for meetings and to facilitate cartel business decisions. Their accommodations were comfortable, and they had everything they needed—including their very own chefs.

The DEA and the IC kept Colombian authorities informed about the Cali leaders' ongoing, flagrant engagement in criminal activity from behind bars, but the reports were largely ignored. When the US Embassy and Washington officials pressed the Colombian government on the matter, they had to ask: How secure, *really*, was La Picota prison? Could the US actually trust the fact that the godfathers couldn't leave of their own volition if they chose to? Just because it was a maximum-security prison didn't mean that US officials didn't have their doubts.

Amidst our trips to Cali, Dave, Jerry, and I were tasked with a special assignment by DEA Headquarters: to help design and implement the first ever DEA-sponsored Sensitive Investigative Unit (SIU), an endeavor that was long overdue. If there was one thing we'd learned while operating in Cali, it was that the DEA desperately needed their own vetted unit in order to effectively target the growing horde of sophisticated transnational organized crime groups.

The specialized unit was to consist of a dozen or so polygraphed Colombian police officers, who would serve as a critical component in supporting US counterdrug initiatives in the country. Dave, Jerry, and I had witnessed firsthand just how effective Colonel Barragán's police unit and the vetted navy intel and commando teams were during our operations targeting Gilberto and Miguel, so we knew exactly what we were looking for.

Over the course of two months, we narrowed down candidates, conducted background checks, and administered drug and polygraph examinations in conjunction with the CNP. Finally, we got to the point where we needed only a few more selections before DEA's inaugural SIU would be ready for their initial two-week training program, scheduled for mid-February in Quantico, Virginia. Jerry and I were chosen to accompany the team to Quantico to assist in the overall training and instruction, a diverse curriculum that included firearms, complex conspiracy investigations, wiretaps, and covert surveillance, among other things.

If 1995 had ended with a whimper, 1996 started off with a massive bang. Former defense minister Fernando Botero was now directly accusing President Samper of taking—*knowingly* taking—Cali cartel drug money during the 1994 presidential election. The evidence was piling up, along with witnesses: Santiago Medina, Guillermo Pallomari, and now, Fernando Botero.

What's more, the attorney general's exhaustive Proceso 8.000 investigation would ultimately discover a staggering total of 36,925 checks (originating from ninety bank accounts) that moved $500 million between 1989 and 1996 for the cartel. As much as $400 million of that money corresponded to deposits made at thirteen thousand bank and corporate accounts connected to countless politicians, sports-related figures, journalists, and other corrupt officials.

The chorus of calls for President Samper's resignation seemed impossible to ignore, but Samper did just that. True to form he remained obstinate, never wavering from his declarations of total innocence. He also continued to call for a rapid conclusion to the comprehensive investigation that was already well underway in Congress.

For the most part, Dave and I ignored the political drama and focused instead on finding Pacho Herrera. In early January, we received credible intel from a trusted asset that Pacho was planning to attend the wedding of a fellow trafficker in Villavicencio, in the department of Meta, seventy miles southeast of Bogotá. He was set to arrive at an isolated airstrip near Puerto López, flown in on an aircraft helmed by one of his pilots, Fernando Gaitán. From there, they would drive to Villavicencio for the reception. It was the first solid lead we'd gotten on Pacho in well over six months.

Along with a handful of presumptive candidates from our newly formed SIU, Dave, Jerry, and I traveled to Villavicencio to coordinate the operation. The mission would be the units' first deployment, and the team members were eager to prove themselves.

As usual, things didn't exactly go as planned. At the last minute, our asset reported that Pacho was no longer set to attend the reception but was expected to join the after-party at the Hotel del Llano later that evening.

The hotel's picturesque setting made it the perfect venue for an outdoor party, and the guests quickly overtook the grounds. The drunken chaos made it simple for two SIU members posing as an invited couple to breeze in alongside the crowd and check out the attendees. They identified a number of high-ranking military officers, as well as Fernando, but there was no sign of Pacho.

Outside, Dave and I watched the front entrance from our SUV, anxiously waiting for any sign of Pacho. We'd just teamed up with one of the new prospective SIU candidates, Oscar Arias, whom we'd met for the first time just moments earlier. We were surprised to see him, since he hadn't yet undergone the rigorous vetting process. He was a last-minute addition to both the group and operation, having been recommended by a high-ranking national police official.

After a few minutes, Dave leaned toward me from the back seat, cast his eyes toward Oscar in the driver's seat, and whispered, "Does he look familiar to you?" I was on the passenger side, staring intently toward the hotel lobby directly to my right. It was dark, so I waited for the headlights of an approaching vehicle to illuminate the interior of our SUV before sneaking a glimpse. As soon as the SUV was temporarily flooded with light, I casually glanced over and took a careful look at the man to my left. *Son of a bitch*, I thought. "Look familiar" was an understatement.

The driver looked exactly, and I do mean *exactly*, like the sketch Salcedo had drawn for us five months earlier. I leaned back and pretended to stretch and as I did, I looked over at Dave and subtly mouthed the words *"the Shadow."* Dave grinned back at me and nodded in agreement.

We couldn't believe we were finally seeing the Shadow in person, the elusive corporal from the Search Bloc who'd first come on our radar while assisting Captain Buitrago in spying on the DEA for the Cali cartel. Salcedo had come up with that perfect nickname and repeatedly warned us to keep an eye out for him.

The jolt we got from seeing him in person was immediately followed by our realization—and subsequent anger—over the fact that our new addition was obviously here to keep tabs on the DEA and our efforts to target Pacho. Successfully placing Oscar into our clandestine crew was no easy feat. We were floored—who even had that kind of authority to pull it off? It could only have stemmed from the highest levels of the CNP.

At that point, we knew our operation against Pacho was compromised. So, with nothing to lose, we had SIU members stop Fernando's vehicle when he finally left the party in the early morning and question him anyway. We held out hope that he might decide to cooperate and lead us to Pacho, but in the end, he gave us nothing, going so far as to deny even knowing Pacho.

Before leaving Villavicencio later that morning, Dave and I decided to take a photo of the entire SIU group during breakfast. We wanted to send the picture to Salcedo—now officially in witness protection—to confirm our suspicions. We didn't really *need* to—we were certain the man we'd seen was the Shadow—but we wanted it for the official record.

As we expected, Oscar was wary of taking part in any pictures. As soon as Dave and I suggested the idea, he jumped up and offered to take the photo—a savvy way to get out of actually being *in* it. Still, Dave and I persisted. We needed to commemorate the DEA's first joint operation with our new, *entire* SIU, we said, if only for posterity's sake! Oscar knew he didn't really have a choice (aside from literally taking off and running), so ultimately we were able to snap a few photos of him, which we sent to Salcedo care of the US Marshals Service.

After our return to Bogotá, we brought Oscar in and administered a polygraph test. Not only did the results find him to be deceptive, but they were also incomplete: halfway through, he got up and walked out of the examination before the polygrapher had even finished his questions. When Dave and I confronted him about his relationship with Captain Buitrago and the Cali cartel, he denied everything. Furious, he stormed out of the embassy.

Soon after, Oscar was transferred out of the SIU and subsequently removed from the CNP. Two weeks later Dave and I got word back from Salcedo, with the confirmation we knew was coming: Oscar Arias was, indeed, the Shadow.

Dave and I never were able to identify the person behind the attempted infiltration into our new vetted unit, but only someone at the very top of the power chain could have finagled it—at the very least a full bird colonel, if not a general. But if there was one good thing that came out of the fiasco, it was the reminder that despite all the blows the cartel had taken, they still had friends in the highest of places.

The hourglass was fast running out of time, and the level of urgency had gotten to a point where it was all-consuming. Our pursuit of Pacho was becoming infinitely more difficult with each passing day, and if we had any hope of seeing this through to the end, any hope at all, we needed to make something happen, and we needed to make it happen now.

CHAPTER 34

The Great Escape

*"One cannot escape their fate, but their path may be altered,
potentially resulting in a different outcome."*

—A. C. HELLER,
Author

ON JANUARY 11, THE SAME DAY Oscar Arias was dismissed from the SIU, Chepe Santacruz decided he was done with incarceration. Mind made up, he walked out the front door of his Bogotá-based maximum-security prison and went directly into hiding.

Earlier that day, Chepe had been sitting in a prison interview room, enduring a litany of questions posed by a "faceless" judge. The glass in the adjacent room was blacked out, a regular security precaution taken to protect the identity of judges and prosecutors. Not even prison officials were allowed to see their faces, nor were they privy to their true identities.

This wasn't uncommon in Colombia, where the discovery of a government official's identity could lead to a barrage of cartel-driven threats, intimidation, or even death. Numerous judges and prosecutors were, in fact, targeted and murdered during the treacherous Escobar era.

At some point during the interview, Chepe managed to pull off an "escape" worthy of any cinematic thriller. After removing the glass in the interview room, Chepe crawled through and casually changed his clothes. He then posed as one of the faceless judges, walked directly past several guards, and made it past a number of locked doors before waltzing right through the exit doors. Waiting for him outside was his getaway car, an SUV with tinted windows resembling a government vehicle. Chepe got in, and they sped off without so much as a look back.

Needless to say, this wasn't some kind of caper or daring prison bust pulled off by an *Ocean's Eleven*–style team of criminal experts. It was so flagrant, so obvious, that no one ever questioned the fact that prison officials *had* to have aided the godfather in his escape. And the men on the other side of that blacked-out glass never really needed their identities disguised or their faces hidden—Chepe knew exactly who they were. They were part of his own crew.

The exact logistics of *how* it happened wasn't of much concern to me or Dave. But the fact that we now had to look for Chepe *again*, and in addition to our hunt for Pacho, no less, was an infuriating setback.

Incensed, the Colombian government immediately declared a state of emergency, followed by the offering of a massive reward for Chepe's capture. The reward was the equivalent of well over two million US dollars, one of the largest ever offered. The amount wasn't all that shocking, though. Chepe had embarrassed the government yet again, and they wanted to track him down quickly—no matter how much money it took.

It was then that Dave and I realized just how unlikely it was that Chepe would be taken alive. We knew several criminal factions in Colombia who'd no doubt view the offer as the ideal chance to settle some old scores they had with the Cali Mafia. Others would simply want to help diminish the increasingly fragile and flailing cartel for their own financial benefit. Some, meanwhile, didn't need any reason other than just wanting Chepe dead. For those people, the reward would just be an added bonus.

He'd been in prison for only six months, but Chepe had pined for his old existence from day one. He'd always been larger than life, with an insatiable appetite for the finer things and a carpe diem approach to each day. So, when it came to quality of life inside La Picota, not least the cuisine— well, it wasn't winning any Michelin stars in Chepe's book. He had lofty standards, and he wasn't willing to slum it any longer.

Dave and I once heard a story from someone in Chepe's inner circle that summed up his approach to life perfectly. One afternoon, Chepe announced that he was heading out for a jog around his Cali neighborhood. He was all decked out in a sleek new sweatsuit, and as he stepped out into the sweltering heat he called over to his wife, Amparo Castro de Santacruz, and told her he'd be right back. He was gone before she had a chance to answer, and she found herself standing alone in their luxurious mansion, bewildered. Chepe was hardly in the best of shape—unsurprising, given his affection for decadent dinners and fine wines—so she couldn't imagine what had prompted this sudden urge for exercise. Nor could his security detail, who waited patiently on the front grounds of the residence for their boss to return.

Fifteen minutes passed, followed by another fifteen, and everyone assumed that Chepe was still out on his jog. But after another half an hour passed, Chepe's wife and bodyguards began to panic. Being the wife—or employee—of a drug baron made for some justifiable worries as to his whereabouts: Had he been arrested by the police? Kidnapped by FARC guerrillas or rival drug traffickers? Or was this unrelated to the cartel, and he'd had an accident—maybe a heart attack, or a stroke?

Hours turned into days, and still there was no word and no leads at all as to where Chepe had vanished. Frantic, his security team scoured the city day and night, all to no avail. In just a few days, they'd gone from worry, to panic and, now, desperation.

Finally, almost one week later, Chepe's bodyguards were standing guard in front of the mansion and spotted him coming from the exact same direction from which he'd left, lumbering back home at a leisurely pace. He looked like he was just cooling down after a brisk walk: composed, calm, and wearing the exact same sweatsuit he'd left in.

His security detail rushed out into the street, weapons drawn, thinking he must have escaped potential captors or been abandoned on the side of the road by rivals. Hearing the commotion, Amparo also ran out of the house, crying and screaming at the top of her lungs. I have no idea what excuse Chepe ultimately went with, but I *do* know where he'd actually been.

Apparently, halfway through his impromptu jog, Chepe had run into one of his former flames. Opting for a far more preferable type of exercise, he went back to her place—not for the day, or the night, but for the entire week. He simply didn't feel like calling anyone (including his wife) to let them know where he was, so he didn't. And that is exactly what people referred to as "typical Chepe," and why the other godfathers coined the nickname "Mil Amores," or "a Thousand Lovers" just for him. He was both a thug and a Romeo and, above all, lived by his own rules. So the idea of him behind bars, with no autonomy at all? The actual miracle is that he made it six months before calling it quits.

Following Chepe's escape, we coordinated with the police Search Bloc in Cali to raid scores of properties we'd previously linked to him. The hunt was all hands on deck, with the national police and all of Colombia's security services in hot pursuit. Chepe was rumored to own over two thousand properties throughout Colombia, so the list was vast. Countless sources hungry for the huge financial windfall that would come with his capture inundated the DEA and CNP with a nonstop torrent of leads.

In an ironic twist, our focus eventually narrowed down to several locations in Medellín, the very city that had once been forbidden for members of the Cali cartel because of its longstanding conflict with Pablo Escobar and the Medellín cartel. The losses sustained during that bloody six-year war were devastating on both sides, and many of Escobar's close friends and associates were either killed or sent to prison. Chepe himself was implicated in a 1989 car bombing there that killed seven people, including Antonio Roldán Betancur, then the governor of Antioquia.

In other words, Medellín was still very much enemy territory. As one major drug trafficker once told me, "Never, ever leave your base of power." And in Medellín, Chepe barely had any power to begin with, let alone after six months in prison.

At the time, Medellín was still in a state of transition and unrest. It was the center of operations for right wing paramilitary death squads— groups that had spun off from the infamous remnants of Los Pepes (People Persecuted by Pablo Escobar), who'd openly terrorized Escobar and his family throughout the last year of his life. The Pepes had forged a close alliance with Cali during the war against Escobar and, in addition to hunting Pablo, had killed scores of his associates. After Escobar's death, there was a shift of power, with Carlos Castaño, one of the founders of Los Pepes, emerging as a major underworld figure. He eventually founded and led a powerful national paramilitary movement called the Autodefensas Unidas de Colombia (United Self-Defense Forces of Colombia), or AUC.

After leaving La Picota prison, Chepe traveled to Medellín to try and establish new drug-trafficking alliances with left-wing guerrilla groups.

Needless to say, the ideologies of left-wing guerrillas and right-wing para-militaries were (and always will be) on completely different ends of the spectrum. They were sworn archenemies and continually fought over strategic drug corridors in Colombia. Chepe's attempts to forge new part-nerships were certain to provoke Castaño.

As always, Chepe was traveling in style and was rumored to be toting a briefcase holding north of $2 million—roughly the same amount as the reward for his capture. One might also call it his literal get out of jail free card (or get out of jail free *again* card). Should he be detained by the police or military, he had the prerequisite bribe right there with him. But when word of Chepe establishing ties with guerrilla groups reached Castaño, that wasn't a problem he could solve with cash. Castaño devised a plan for Chepe's kidnapping while also taking note of the huge reward for his capture. He made it clear that he wanted Chepe with all his belongings intact—most importantly his coveted briefcase.

Just before midnight on March 5, 1996—fifty-three days after Chepe's escape—his dead body was found sprawled on the side of the road a short distance from the InterContinental Hotel, in the upscale Las Palmas section of Medellín.

The official story of what happened that night was that the CNP received an "anonymous" call saying that Chepe had been spotted driving a red Suzuki Samurai in the area. A group of police special operators were dispatched, located the vehicle, and began to follow it. When the police attempted to intercept Chepe's SUV, he resisted and fled the scene. A gun battle ensued, and amidst all the chaos Chepe was shot and killed.

A few days after the incident, Dave and I attended a meeting at CNP headquarters where we were briefed on the operation along with other DEA and embassy officials. We were shown photographs of Chepe's body and the crime scene and heard exactly how everything unfolded—accord-ing to the CNP, anyway.

After reviewing everything, it became apparent that the information police officials had given us didn't even come *close* to matching the actual evidence found at the crime scene. Based on the photographs, where Chepe's body was found, where police vehicles were positioned, and the breakdown of how events had unfolded, we saw that their explanation was logistically impossible. Some of the contradictions (what appeared to be bruising on Chepe's body, marks on his hands consistent with signs of them being bound, etc.) were hard to miss. The evidence was speaking to us, and it was telling a very different story.

Within days, we talked to two high-level assets who filled us in on what really happened. Unlike the sloppy storytelling we got from the CNP, their version actually made sense.

After reportedly being lured to a meeting by Castaño, North Valley cartel leaders and a group of Castaño's paramilitary loyalists (aided by Danilo González, a corrupt police colonel assigned to the Medellín Search Bloc during the hunt for Escobar) made a surprise appearance and Chepe was subsequently beaten and interrogated. The motley crew wanted information regarding Pacho Herrera's whereabouts (also rumored to be in Medellín), Chepe's newfound guerrilla alliances, and the whereabouts of his so-called $2 million briefcase. When his captors felt they'd taken everything Chepe was ever going to give, they shot him, tossed his body on the side of the road near the InterContinental Hotel, and vanished.

Afterward, someone (believed to be Colonel González) called the police and told them where to find Chepe's body. The police then rushed to the location and quickly staged the crime scene (poorly) to make it appear as if Chepe's death was just a casualty of a shoot-out with police, who were attempting to capture him.

After the dust settled, more rumors began to swirl. Castaño and his cronies were said to have received at least a portion of the reward, and it appeared that Chepe had indeed been making his rounds in Medellín while carrying the most expensive briefcase in Colombian history. True or not, it only added to Chepe's larger-than-life legacy.

While an ongoing debate still exists regarding the details of Chepe's death, Dave and I don't harbor any doubts. We saw the evidence for ourselves, first of all, and we knew of several other high-level assets who corroborated our initial source's reporting. Regardless, the exact details of Chepe's death were no longer relevant to us. As far as we were concerned, the book on José Santacruz Londoño was officially closed as of March 5, 1996.

Chepe's death did remain relevant to the top brass back in Washington, however. On March 1, 1996, the Clinton administration decertified Colombia as a partner in its antidrug efforts for the second consecutive year. "This is a decertification not of Colombia, but of President Samper," said Marc Thiessen, then spokesperson for Senator Jesse Helms. Mounting evidence corroborated by credible witnesses left little doubt with many Washington officials that Team Samper had, without question, knowingly accepted cartel money. "There is no doubt at this point that the Samper campaign received significant financing from drug lords," then Assistant Secretary of State for International Narcotics Matters Robert Gelbard stated.

While US officials had lost all faith in Samper, they remained steadfast in their support for CNP Director General Serrano and Attorney General Valdivieso, citing their joint efforts in the pursuit of the Cali cartel leaders and their work toward rooting out corrupt officials. Of course, Chepe's January 11 escape from La Picota (along with the suspected involvement of several corrupt Colombian prison officials) certainly didn't help when it came to the certification process.

Chepe's death remains a hotly contested topic to this day. It's unlikely that the truth will ever come out or that one single explanation will be universally accepted, so for now it remains a matter of personal opinion.

With Chepe finally out of the picture—permanently, this time—we could resume our quest to find Pacho. We had our newly trained SIU eager and waiting, and we were more than ready to finish what we'd started.

CHAPTER 35

The Last Don

"The ghosts you chase you never catch."
—JOHN MALKOVICH

ON FRIDAY, MARCH 8, I left my apartment in Bogotá to meet with Dave and an asset who'd promised us some new intel regarding Pacho. We'd just returned from Cali, where we'd been conducting a series of enforcement operations targeting Pacho and Juan Carlos Ramírez Abadía (a.k.a. Chupeta), a young, filthy rich, up-and-coming Cali trafficker for whom the Colombian government had recently issued an arrest warrant.

It was almost 5:30 p.m. when I left my apartment and drove into the early-evening rush hour to begin my surveillance detection route (SDR). I immediately noticed a woman in a gold Mazda follow me into traffic and begin to shadow me. I kept one eye on her and watched as she used a car radio to (I assumed) communicate with other surveillance vehicles. As I approached a major intersection, I saw a white Ford Explorer followed by another vehicle fall in behind me. Suddenly we were a party of at least four, and there was no doubt that I was being followed. But why? Was this a hostile government surveillance or just another attempt by the Cali cartel to try and identify a DEA asset? I radioed Dave and told him to cancel the meeting with our source but, more importantly, to be on high alert until we could figure out exactly what was unfolding.

After talking to Dave, I continued with my SDR to gather as much intel as I could on my new adversaries. While I managed to glean the license plate and a good physical description of the driver of the Mazda, I couldn't get anything on the Explorer or other possible shadows. After about ten minutes, the tails lost me in the heavy Bogotá traffic.

Their surveillance skills gave me pause. It was highly unlikely that the surveillance was being conducted by cartel operatives—Dave and I had seen them in action before, having been followed many times by the Cali KGB, and we knew the extent of their capabilities. But this time, everything seemed off: the vehicles, the car radios, the surveillance tactics, using a female operative—if anything, I would have classified it as a government surveillance operation, most likely DAS (Department of Administrative Security). But if so, there was still the question of who'd authorized it. Was the cartel somehow using corrupt DAS agents to follow us, or was the surveillance ordered by high-level Colombian government officials?

I reported the incident to embassy security officers, who did as much as they could with what little information I'd given them. Unsurprisingly, they came up empty—no registration on file for the gold Mazda, nothing at all to indicate who might be pulling the strings.

The next night, Dave was sound asleep when his doorman woke him with a call at 2:00 a.m., explaining that three visitors had just pulled up in a taxi and were waiting outside to speak with him. The men asked for Dave by name (first and last), and one of them—gruff-looking, holding a briefcase—looked particularly out of place. A briefcase, at 2:00 a.m.?

It wasn't just unusual to have visitors at such a late hour, it was unheard of—not least a surprise visit from strangers in one of the most dangerous countries in the world. Thanks to my brush with the mysterious surveillants just twenty-four hours earlier, Dave was already on high alert. He told the doorman that he would not be coming downstairs under any circumstances and instructed him to ask the men for their identification. Surprisingly, two of them *did* hand over their IDs but became angry while they were kept waiting. When Dave repeated that there was no way in hell he'd be meeting them—or anyone else—outside at this hour, the three men piled back into the taxi and left, visibly fuming.

The second they left, Dave instinctively reverted to his 82nd Airborne days, retrieving his M4 carbine and guarding the front door for the rest of the night. Once the sun began to rise, he called me and Jerry, and the two of us drove over to Dave's place, picked him up, and headed straight to the embassy to report the incident. When police officials checked on the names the men had given, they turned out to be false. Opting to err on the side of caution, Dave was relocated to another embassy apartment, but he wasn't happy about it. The three men had messed with his sleep, and now they'd messed with his home life.

We didn't know what to make of the back-to-back incidents, let alone who might be responsible. It could have been a warning message being delivered, or maybe it was connected to Chepe's death. Then again, maybe it had to do with Pacho? Chupeta? The NVC? With no way to find out and no semblance of control, Dave and I grew more and more anxious.

One week later, the thirty-three-year-old Chupeta walked into the Colombian prosecutor's office in Cali, accompanied by two attorneys, and peacefully surrendered to authorities on outstanding drug-trafficking and money-laundering charges.

Like many of his peers, Chupeta had taken note of what was happening within the cartel inner circles in Colombia and wanted to take full advantage of the considerable benefits afforded to traffickers who voluntarily surrendered and cooperated with government officials. If he seized the opportunity while he still could, he stood to reduce his jail time down to five or six years—perhaps even less. He'd be free to return to his extravagant lifestyle before turning forty, with his fortune fully intact and the rest of his life ahead of him.

The Cali cartel was now universally viewed as being down but not out. Colombian authorities still saw them as a formidable adversary and knew better than to become complacent. They continued their offensive against Pacho and initiated another series of seizures and the forfeiture of ill-gotten assets from the four godfathers and their *testaferros* (straw men). This further sapped the Mafia's strength, depriving them of potential cash sources and options.

But there were others who no longer felt intimidated and had begun viewing the cartel as a severely weakened entity. Two of their once nearly omnipotent leaders were behind bars, and a third had just been shot to death. The last don left was on the run and in hiding, fighting for his life. The four tyrants who'd once ruled with an iron fist, who'd attained nearly mythic reputations and limitless strength, were now viewed as frail and, frankly, not just old but old news. It was as big a fall as Mike Tyson losing his heavyweight title fight to Buster Douglas in Tokyo in February of 1990: the champion had been toppled. Tyson was never the same indestructible force he once was, but with him there would be future battles. With the Cali cartel, there would be no more chances for redemption, let alone world domination.

While major decisions were still being made by Miguel and Gilberto from behind bars, William Rodríguez continued to manage day-to-day operations for the cartel on the outside. But despite his last name, William was most definitely not a godfather. These were uncertain times in Cali, and while he may have seen himself as the new king wearing the crown, the power dynamic was unsteady and his leadership untested. If there's one constant in the drug business, it's that there's nothing quite as dangerous—or inviting—as instability.

In any line of business, there's always the next generation of hungrier, greedier, more enterprising up-and-comers just waiting for the right moment to strike. Unfortunately for William, a group of North Valley traffickers had decided that their time was now, and they were ready to take over as the most powerful drug cartel in Colombia. They were poised to seize the throne before William had fully settled into it.

On Friday, May 24, William was enjoying a late lunch at Río D'Enero, a Brazilian restaurant in northern Cali, when six heavily armed gunmen burst into the restaurant and opened fire with automatic weapons and silenced pistols. The assassins were disguised as plainclothes police officials—replete with official credentials—and had even pulled up in a van near identical to those belonging to the national police. It was a well-orchestrated operation with one goal: take out the prodigal son and, with that, put the final nail in the coffin of the Cali cartel.

William was struck no fewer than eight times during the onslaught, suffering gunshot wounds to his arms, legs, and abdomen. Although he was grievously wounded, he somehow managed to survive the attack. But five other men did not, including cartel assassin Nicol Antonio Parra, who was shot thirty-two times while trying to protect William during the ambush, as well as Dario Delgado, Salcedo's former deputy chief of security. In total, almost one hundred rounds were fired during the attack.

While the hit team took the lives of five men of critical importance to William, the attack failed to take him down. It was a miracle that he emerged from the assault still breathing, but it was a very close call. He spent the next month in the hospital recovering from his injuries, followed by another month at home.

When Dave and I heard about the shooting on the radio, we were in Yumbo scouting out possible locations where Pacho was rumored to be hiding. We immediately headed to the upscale Santa Mónica neighborhood where the restaurant was located, and the first things we saw were the pools of blood still spreading along the sidewalk and in the street—they were impossible to miss. It was yet another reminder of the unparalleled level of ruthlessness within the drug trade and the high stakes behind the battle for control over the Cali corridor and strategic Port of Buenaventura.

Meanwhile, the political drama surrounding the cartel campaign-finance investigation (Proceso 8.000) of President Samper—a crisis that had dragged on for nearly two years—was finally drawing to a close back in Bogotá. In May, the Accusations Committee recommended to the Colombian Congress that no formal charges be filed against Samper. That wasn't surprising—the Liberal Party controlled much of the special committee and voted along party lines—but, to their credit, Congress decided to pursue the investigation anyway. So there was still a sliver of hope left that Samper might eventually be held accountable.

But in a resounding show of support, the Colombian Chamber of Representatives voted 111 to 43 to absolve President Samper of any political or criminal wrongdoing in regards to any cartel-related contributions during his 1994 presidential campaign. The fact that he'd emerged unscathed from the scandal despite the staggering amount of evidence was astounding. Samper was free to finish out his term without fear of impeachment, and even better, no further investigations into the matter would be conducted. He truly had lived up to his reputation as the Colombian version of a Teflon President Reagan.

Naturally, Conservative Party officials and Colombian citizens alike openly questioned the integrity of the chamber—as it stood, nine of its members were already in jail for accepting Cali drug money, with many more still under investigation. But the matter was settled, at least legally. Samper could keep his title *and* claim vindication.

The decision—not to mention Samper's smug demeanor—essentially amounted to a middle finger aimed directly at Washington officials.

Furious and stunned, they responded by threatening economic sanctions and ultimately revoked Samper's US tourist visa, along with the visas of several other high-ranking Colombian officials suspected of being on the Cali payroll.

As usual, the political spectacle held no interest for me and Dave, nor did it affect our mission—we just wanted to keep focused on Pacho. The DEA didn't have any hidden agendas. We weren't in Colombia to investigate President Samper or to try and topple his government, contrary to the belief of the president, Interior Minister Horacio Serpa, and other senior Samper administration officials. We were there to help Colombian authorities bring the four Cali godfathers to justice and to dismantle the cartel, period. As for Samper, I can't say we were surprised.

Throughout the summer of 1996, we debriefed one asset after another while also conducting countless raids with Colombian security forces, all fruitless. Our momentum began to wane, and I kept thinking about what Dave had said to me almost one year ago: when it came to Pacho, we were chasing a ghost. I had to consider the possibility that even after everything we'd been through, we might never actually catch him. Months had passed, and we didn't even have a good *photograph* of him. Maybe we were just spinning our wheels.

I considered passing the torch to fellow agent Jerry Salameh or one of the other new agents who'd arrived in Bogotá—why not let the new guard take over and finish the job?—but Dave wouldn't let me. To this day, I'm indebted to him for that. He reminded me of the vow we'd made shortly after we arrived in Colombia: that we would remain in the country until all four Cali godfathers were either in handcuffs or dead. At any cost.

"Whatever it takes. Remember that?" He was repeating my own words back to me, pushing me to get my head back in the game. He was right, and either way, I knew I couldn't stop. Not now. We *had* to finish what we'd started and what we'd been sent to Colombia to do. By then, I'd come to understand that our pursuit of the godfathers had become something much more than a simple goal: it had become an obsession. I had to see it through—I was just exhausted, that's all. We all were.

On September 1, Dave and I were in Cali with several members of our SIU following up on new intel we'd received from a reliable asset regarding Pacho. At about 12:30 that day, I left our DEA safe house with two SIU officers to go check out a couple of remote ranches in Yumbo we'd heard Pacho was traveling between.

An hour later, Dave called and told me that rumors were circulating throughout the police that Pacho was planning to surrender to Colombian authorities in Cali later that day. For the past few weeks, we'd been hearing variations of this particular rumor from our assets, but for the most part we'd dismissed them. There'd been talk for years of Pacho being on the brink of surrender, but of course nothing ever came of it. We didn't expect anything to change now.

Then again, if I'd ever add a fourth rule into the mix, it would be to always expect the unexpected. While Dave and two SIU officers headed over to the Search Bloc to check on the information, my team and I continued to navigate through the mountains in search of Pacho's *fincas*.

As soon as Dave arrived at the Search Bloc, he knew something was happening. The typically calm compound was in a frenzy, with police officials and members of the media racing around in all directions. CNP Deputy Director Montenegro, who'd just arrived from Bogotá, was mustering the troops near the soccer pitch. It was pandemonium.

General Montenegro pulled Dave aside and briefed him on an operation that was already underway: a police helicopter had just picked up Pacho from a church in Yumbo and was currently en route to the Search Bloc in Cali.

Dave was still processing the news when a helicopter began circling over the garrison. He looked up and watched it slowly descend onto the pitch—the very same pitch where Dave and I used to play pickup games with Colonel Serna and his officers after first arriving at the base over two years ago. Ironically, soccer had always been one of Pacho's greatest passions.

Dave, and a contingent of police officials and journalists, waited for the helicopter to shut down as armed soldiers swept in and surrounded the area. The entire scene was so dramatic that it almost seemed staged. Which, of course, it essentially was.

Finally, a small, impeccably dressed man emerged and made the grand entrance everyone had been waiting for. He wore a dark double-breasted suit, pressed white shirt, and colorful tie, and he took a minute to adjust his round wire-rimmed glasses as he stepped off the helicopter. He had the air of a gentleman who'd made this kind of entrance a million times before, and he could easily have passed as a dignitary, diplomat, or Fortune 500–level CEO. And in fact, he was a gentleman—the fourth and final of the Gentlemen of Cali, to be exact. He was Francisco Hélmer Herrera Buitrago, a.k.a. Pacho, the most violent and elusive of the four horsemen of Cali. By his side was General Serrano, Gustavo Salazar (one of Pacho's many attorneys), and several police special operators.

As Pacho was escorted past a slew of Colombian journalists and reporters, they all snapped photographs of his arrival as if they were lining a red carpet. It was clear his surrender was a well-choreographed event that had been in the works for days, if not weeks. He was then taken to an administrative office at the Search Bloc, where he was fingerprinted and photographed so his identity could be positively confirmed. For the record, Pacho looked nothing like any of the photographs the DEA or police possessed.

After being processed, Pacho spotted Dave through the large crowd at the base and asked to speak with him privately. Dave assumed Pacho knew exactly who he was, thanks to Captain Buitrago, the Shadow, or any one of the countless spies in his employ.

"Hello, Dave," Pacho said as he reached out to shake Dave's hand. Even though Dave towered over him, the far more diminutive Pacho was more commanding than anyone else present, with his deep, authoritative voice. Dave was taken aback by the disparity between reputation and reality: the man who'd always been justifiably described as violent and vicious was, in person, calm and cordial. He told Dave that he was tired—tired of running, tired of hiding—just tired in general. The relentless efforts by the national police had taken their toll, and he'd had enough. He knew that government forces were closing in on him, and he wanted to take full advantage of every possible benefit available by voluntarily surrendering. He was also worried that North Valley assassins would make him their next target—they'd played a key role in Chepe's murder and had attempted to kill William Rodríguez just three months earlier. There were just too many external forces working against him, and he knew it.

Despite Pacho's courteous manner, when Dave asked him about Chepe and how he was *really* killed, Pacho's demeanor changed completely. He took a look around the room before telling Dave he couldn't answer. Then

Surrender of the last godfather, Pacho Herrera, at the CNP Search Bloc in Cali. Left to right: Pacho Herrera, Dave, and a CNP officer.

he leaned in and took on a conspiratorial, almost protective, tone. "Stay away from those types of questions," he told Dave. "They could lead to problems you wouldn't want to have." Dave took it as an unsubtle warning from the godfather, though he couldn't be sure. A Cali drug lord making a sincere attempt to protect a DEA agent—during his surrender, no less—was about as surreal as it gets.

Before leaving, Pacho posed for a photograph with Dave and some of the SIU officers and was then taken to a maximum-security prison in nearby Palmira. By the time I arrived at the Search Bloc to get my own glimpse of the youngest godfather, he was already gone.

To say that his surrender was anticlimactic would be inaccurate. It was just as surreal as the others, if not more so, and a perfect reminder of what the cartel had always been about: business. In the end, it was just another transaction.

Still, it was almost incomprehensible that the Cali cartel had officially crumbled. As the Colombian government rejoiced, President Samper took a predictable victory lap. "And now, there are none," he said, proudly. There had been only one remaining leader of the Cali cartel left to be captured, and that man was now behind bars.

Fifteen months after Gilberto Rodríguez was arrested and twenty-seven months after Dave and I first stepped foot in Colombia, the Cali cartel was officially declared dead. With Pacho's arrest, the Colombian government had essentially all but dismantled the biggest, most powerful drug cartel in history.

For me and Dave, it was a momentous occasion for many reasons. We'd persevered, stuck it out, fulfilled our vow, and finished what the DEA had sent us to Colombia to do. Along with Jerry and Ruben, we'd done everything in our power to aid Colombian authorities in their quest to bring down the Cali cartel. But we weren't ready to leave the country, not yet. We still had some loose ends we needed to tie up.

Even though Miguel, Gilberto, and Pacho were in prison, they were still desperately trying to salvage what remained of their dying empire. Dave and I sought to obtain additional evidence and witnesses against them and other cartel operatives for American and Colombian prosecutors to use in upcoming trials and continued to help identify and seize assets owned by the Cali leaders and their front men. Together, the four godfathers had amassed more than a few billion dollars in assets, and both governments wanted to ensure that not one single penny would ever be available to them or their families.

Along with several other government entities, prosecutors from the Colombian Attorney General's Office had embarked on a massive operation begun a year prior to seize and forfeit assets the godfathers had illegally acquired during their more than two decades of drug trafficking and illicit activities. In October 1995, President Bill Clinton signed Executive Order (EO) 12978, which declared a national emergency with respect to significant foreign narcotics traffickers based in Colombia.

EO 12978 named each of the four Cali cartel leaders as "Specially Designated Narcotics Traffickers," allowing economic sanctions to be levied against the Cali cartel. The US Treasury Department's Office of Foreign Assets Control (OFAC) worked in conjunction with the DEA, host-nation counterparts, and other US agencies to help identify potential assets derived from narcotics trafficking for subsequent seizure by Colombian authorities. With literally thousands of properties and assets, the process would take years to complete.

A few weeks after Pacho's arrest, Dave and I were having an early dinner at Salerno, one of our favorite Cali pizzerias. I happened to glance outside and saw two SUVs come to a screeching halt in the parking lot. Four armed men jumped out of the vehicles, then moved into the restaurant. They took a careful look around, scoping out the restaurant and all its patrons, then left. "Somebody big is about to crash the party," I said to Dave.

Moments later, four SUVs pulled alongside the restaurant and a young man hopped out, strolled to the front door, and sauntered into the pizzeria with several bodyguards in tow.

"Holy shit. That's William Rodríguez," I said. As the group sat down, they looked briefly in our direction, then resumed their conversation.

"I'm going to go over and say hello," I told Dave.

"I wouldn't do that," Dave said. "You know his bodyguards have to be on high alert, considering everything that's happened." He was right—the assassination attempt that had almost taken William's life was only four months ago.

"Well, here's the thing," I said, taking a moment to try and put together my most convincing argument. Dave, meanwhile, was giving me his "here we go again" expression.

"Hear me out. We have to let them know that *we* know exactly who *they* are. Otherwise, they'll just think we're a couple of clueless American agents. And you *know* they already pegged us as agents." I was sure about that, because Carlos Millán—a semi-obscure driver, assistant, and friend of William Rodríguez, known within the cartel by his nickname, Mario—was sitting with William. Dave and I had crossed paths with him before, most recently during the raid on Solomon Prado's town house fifteen months earlier.

Dave rolled his eyes but nodded his approval. As I got up to head over to William's table, Dave took out his Glock 17 and placed it in his lap, under the table and well out of view. He was ready to react should my visit be misinterpreted—but I wasn't anticipating any drama. I felt confident that the group wouldn't be alarmed by one slowly approaching, lanky, surfer-looking dude—even if they did know I was DEA. Besides, there weren't any outstanding criminal charges against William in Colombia at the time.

When I walked up to the table, the group fell silent. Addressing them in Spanish, I said, "Hello, William. Hello, Mario." Mario, who'd looked up at me as if ready to greet an acquaintance or old friend, quickly took on a shocked expression. He clearly recognized me but was stunned by the fact that I'd used his nickname, the one used only by his cartel colleagues. With that name drop alone, my mission was accomplished. He understood that I knew exactly who he was.

I asked William how he was coping since the assault and said he looked well, considering what he'd endured. "I'm doing much better, thank you," he replied. He was relaxed, affable, not at all on edge. Before leaving, I told him that should he need any additional or specialized medical care in the US, we'd be happy to assist. William smiled and nodded his head at the gesture, as did the rest of his entourage. Then he did something that surprised me: he leaned over and waved to Dave, a thank-you of sorts. "I appreciate the offer," he said, "but I think the worst is behind me." We chatted for another minute, then I wished him well again and headed back to our table. Visibly relieved, Dave reholstered his weapon, took a deep breath, and returned to his pepperoni pizza. Priorities.

For me, I was happy I'd gotten the chance to do what I did. Acknowledging William and Mario served a dual purpose: it revealed that we knew *exactly* who they were, and it gave me the chance to sincerely extend our offer of medical assistance. If William were to ever travel to the States—which was unlikely—he could be arrested on any outstanding US indictments against him, something he was surely already aware of. Either way, it was a genuine offer on our part.

As 1996 was drawing to a close, so too was our time in Colombia, and Dave and I spent many hours thinking about what the future had in store for us. We'd accomplished our mission, and we were ready for the next chapters in our DEA careers, and lives, to begin.

Shortly after the new year, Dave and I were having a few beers in Bogotá's Zona Rosa. "So, now what?" Dave asked.

"How about we stick around and go after the North Valley cartel?"

"*What?*" Dave looked at me like I was crazy, and not for the first time. "Are you being serious?"

"Yeah. Very serious," I replied.

"I'll think about it," he said, laughing. "But I'm gonna need a pretty damn long vacation first."

We raised our bottles of Club Colombia, toasted, and took a swig. It went without saying that the toast was to our accomplishment, but it was also to something else that had gotten us through everything: our partnership.

Ruben, Jerry, Dave, and I all left Colombia for new assignments in the United States in mid-1997. Of the four, I was the only one who returned to Colombia to help host-nation counterparts go after the rising North Valley cartel and continue the DEA's investigation into the Cali Mafia's vast financial empire.

When I did return, I didn't think anything could match my time taking down the Cali cartel—but I was wrong. Regarding the NVC, and exactly how they fell, well, that's another story for another time.

After Cali

"What was suffered was more than what was enjoyed."
—MEMBER OF THE RODRÍGUEZ OREJUELA FAMILY

Gilberto and Miguel Rodríguez Orejuela

IN 1996, THE BROTHERS STRUCK a deal with the Colombian government. They both pled guilty to drug-trafficking and money-laundering charges, in the hopes that doing so would prevent any possible future extradition to the United States, and were both subsequently sentenced to fifteen years in prison. In November 2002, after serving less than half his sentence, Gilberto was shockingly released from his Colombian prison thanks to a controversial judicial order citing his good behavior and participation in a work-study program. Four months into his newfound freedom, Gilberto was recaptured by Colombian authorities in Cali.

In mid-1997, Colombia reinstated its extradition treaty allowing the extradition of Colombian nationals to the US for crimes committed *after* December 17, 1997, and evidence obtained by US investigators revealed that the Rodríguezes had continued to run their criminal empire from prison. They were indicted on drug-trafficking and money-laundering charges in the Southern District of Florida and the Southern District of New York and subsequently extradited from Colombia to the US: Gilberto in December 2004 and Miguel in March 2005. Per the Florida indictment, the brothers were responsible for the importation of over two hundred thousand kilograms of cocaine from Colombia into the United States. I was there, in person, to see them both off.

Gilberto and Miguel pled guilty to both indictments and were sentenced to thirty years in federal prison each. They also agreed to a final judgment of forfeiture in the amount of $2.1 *billion* to be levied against their drug-related assets and businesses found anywhere in the world.

Gilberto Rodríguez died in custody at a federal prison medical center in Butner, North Carolina, on May 31, 2022, at the age of eighty-three. Miguel Rodríguez, eighty-one, continues to serve out his sentence at the Federal Correctional Institution, Loretto (FCI Loretto), in Pennsylvania.

José Santacruz Londoño

After Chepe's early exit from prison followed by his murder, Colombian authorities never wavered from their story that his death was just the result of a spontaneous shoot-out sparked by Chepe's resistance to arrest. But rumors about the details of his death—and his $2 million briefcase—persist.

Francisco Hélmer Herrera Buitrago

Pacho surrendered to Colombian authorities on September 1, 1996, and was initially sentenced to six years and eight months in prison. Due in large part to increased US pressure, in October 1998 the sentence was increased to fourteen years. On November 5, 1998, Pacho was shot and killed in prison by North Valley cartel assassin Rafael Ángel Uribe Serna during a game of soccer (which is probably how Pacho would have wanted to go). Uribe, who'd entered the prison by posing as a lawyer, shot Herrera seven times.

Pacho's murder ignited a vicious war between the Herrera family and the NVC, and a slew of vendetta killings followed. One week after the prison assassination, José Orlando Henao Montoya, one of the powerful NVC's leaders, was shot and killed in a Bogotá prison by Pacho's disabled half brother, José Manuel Herrera Moncada. The NVC responded by murdering a staggering number of the Herrera clan, including several key associates and operatives, along with Pacho's brothers: José Manuel, Álvaro Herrera, and William "Tony" Herrera.

William Rodríguez Abadía

Miguel's son continued to manage day-to-day operations for the cartel, even after the attack that almost took his life. In 2002, William was indicted in the Southern District of Florida on drug-trafficking and money-laundering charges. He went into hiding in Colombia, successfully avoiding prosecution for the next three and a half years until he eventually agreed to surrender to Immigration and Customs Enforcement (ICE) agents in Panama in January 2006. He was subsequently taken to Miami, where he pled guilty and agreed to cooperate and testify—even against his father and uncle if necessary, a move that shocked many. He also agreed to forfeit roughly $300 million in worldwide assets and helped US prosecutors identify tens of millions more belonging to the Cali cartel.

William was initially sentenced to twenty-one years and ten months in federal prison, but after providing substantial assistance to the US government, his sentence was reduced to five years. He was released in June 2010 after serving just four and a half years. William and his family were allowed to remain in the United States, where they still reside today.

Juan Carlos Ramírez Abadía

After surrendering in Colombia in 1996, the up-and-coming Cali trafficker known as Chupeta was sentenced to twenty-four years in prison for a combination of drug-trafficking and money-laundering crimes. Thanks to his voluntary surrender and cooperation with the Colombian government, he was given considerable benefits and released from prison in 2002. Soon after his release, he aligned himself with the NVC and resumed his drug-trafficking activities. In 2004, he was indicted on RICO charges in the District of Columbia, and subsequently in the Eastern District of New York in 2004, and again in 2007.

In January 2007, enforcement operations targeting Chupeta in Cali—spearheaded by the CNP—led to the seizure of over $80 million in US dollars, euros, and gold ingots. The cash and gold were found in hermetically heat-sealed plastic bags that had been concealed within enormous floor vaults, covered in concrete, and tiled over. The stash was also hidden behind walls in several different houses throughout the city, stacked from floor to ceiling. At the time, it was the largest drug cash seizure in the world, and in all my twenty-six years with the DEA I'd never, ever seen anything like it. Two months later, Mexican authorities would seize over $200 million in US currency from drug traffickers in Mexico City.

As a result of the ensuing hunt for him, Chupeta underwent extensive plastic surgery and fled to Brazil. Despite the makeover, he was arrested on August 7, 2007, in São Paulo by the Brazilian federal police and extradited to New York, where he pled guilty and cooperated with US authorities, eventually testifying in the 2019 trial of Joaquín "El Chapo" Guzmán Loera. He initially received a twenty-five-year sentence, but his sentence was reduced to twenty years after he testified against Guzmán. He was released from federal prison in December 2024.

Guillermo Alejandro Pallomari González

The cartel accountant chose to plead guilty to a negotiated plea agreement and cooperated with the US government. Pallomari provided the majority of the most damning testimony regarding Cali and the inner workings of their financial empire, becoming one of the DEA's most significant witnesses ever in the process. He provided testimony in a number of US court proceedings, gave sworn declarations to Colombian prosecutors, and assisted several other governments with independent investigations concerning the Cali cartel. Because of the breadth of his knowledge and evidence, hundreds of police, military, and political officials were arrested or removed from office in Colombia, and tens of millions of dollars in assets were identified and seized. Pallomari entered witness protection with his two sons and now lives in an undisclosed location in the US

Gladys Patricia Cardona Cáceres (Pallomari) and Freddy Vivas Yangua

To this day, the bodies of Patricia Pallomari and Freddy Vivas have never been found.

Captain Efrén Buitrago and Oscar Arias, a.k.a. the Shadow

The two corrupt Cali Search Bloc officers were removed from the CNP after being exposed for their roles in the aiding and abetting of the Cali cartel. According to Jorge Salcedo, after Buitrago helped Miguel Rodríguez escape (following the failed Santa Rita raid in July 1995), Miguel gifted him with a bonus of $50,000. On Buitrago's behalf, Salcedo deposited the money into two bank accounts: one in the name of Buitrago's sister, the other in the name of his mother. Dave and I later turned the information over to CNP officials, who were able to recover some of the money, as well as additional monies from a search of a residence associated to Buitrago.

Enrique Sanchez

Jorge Salcedo's most loyal security operative's safety was put at risk after Salcedo's betrayal was exposed. Sanchez was deemed a liability due to his close association with Salcedo, and as a consequence, the cartel placed him atop their kill list.

When Dave and I learned of the threat against Enrique, we were able to contact and warn him with Salcedo's assistance. Enrique agreed to cooperate with the DEA and testify against the godfathers and other Cali operatives, despite the fact that doing so would almost certainly lead to him spending a significant amount of time in a US prison.

During a debriefing in Bogotá in late February 1996, Enrique outlined his seven and a half years of service in the cartel. He shared details regarding Cali's financing of Ernesto Samper's 1994 presidential campaign, as well as cartel-sanctioned murders, government corruption, and other key information.

Dave and I both vehemently urged Enrique to accept our offer of US protection while the consular section processed his parole entry into the States, but he refused. Confident that he could evade the cartel assassins hot on his trail, he chose to return to Cali instead. On March 21, 1996, Enrique Sanchez was shot and killed in Cali by one of the ruthless cartel *sicarios* who'd been contracted to kill him.

César Yusti

After being tasked with executing Guillermo Pallomari, one of Cali's most notorious assassins was gunned down in the street the very same night we extracted Pallomari from his hideout in Cali. While many theories were (and still are) put forth regarding his murder, no evidence has linked anyone directly to his killing, and the mystery behind his death remains unsolved.

Hernando Camilo Zúñiga Chaparro

According to Jorge Salcedo, General Zúñiga, the former Colombian Army general, commander of Colombia's armed forces, and acting defense minister, was one of Miguel Rodríguez's most secretive and coveted assets within the Colombian military. In January 1995, Miguel ordered Salcedo to conduct an electronic sweep of Color Stereo, a broadcast station in Cali owned by Haydée Rodríguez, Miguel's sister.

As Miguel explained it to Salcedo, US intelligence officials had somehow managed to plant a covert listening device in a bookcase in Haydée's downtown office. During a sweep of the office, Salcedo discovered a tiny, exceptionally well-hidden transmitter built *into* the shelf of the wooden bookcase. Without the help of electronic countermeasures, the device would have been undetectable. Salcedo was intrigued by how precise Miguel's information was. When he asked Miguel for more details, he was told that the information had come from his best source in the Colombian military: General Camilo Zúñiga.

Subsequent information provided by Guillermo Pallomari set a process in motion to revoke the US visas of at least six senior Colombian officials due to suspected ties to the Cali cartel. One of the names listed, allegedly, was Zúñiga's.

Predictably, Zúñiga denied any allegations that his visa had been canceled and even denied ever meeting Miguel. His denials were largely dismissed, however, and in January 1996, CIA Director John Deutsch refused to meet with General Zúñiga during an official visit to Colombia. Zúñiga was never able to distance himself from his alleged ties to the Cali cartel, and he retired from the Colombian Army in March 1996.

Ernesto Samper Pizano

Colombia's former president was absolved of all charges by the Colombian Chamber of Representatives in June 1996, but Washington officials remained convinced that Samper knew—and always had—about the Cali drug money that helped him win the presidency. In July 1996, the State Department revoked Samper's tourist visa, marking the first time the United States barred a democratically elected leader in nearly a decade. He later admitted that there *was* "serious evidence" to support the allegation that money from the cartel had been accepted by his campaign but doubled down on his claim that he had never been aware of it. Samper finished out his four-year term in 1998 and went on to serve as the secretary general of the Union of South American Nations from 2014 to 2017.

Santiago Medina Serna

President Samper's former campaign treasurer was arrested on July 27, 1995, and chose to cooperate with Colombia authorities. He was sentenced to five years and four months in prison after pleading guilty to illicit-enrichment charges but served barely five months before requesting to serve the remainder of his time under house arrest. Because of his ongoing cooperation and rapidly declining health, the request was granted. He moved back into his mansion in northern Bogotá, Casa Medina, where he lived under house arrest until his death in January 1999 from chronic kidney failure.

In June 1996, I was contacted by an associate of Medina's who informed me that Medina wanted to secretly meet with DEA agents. Medina sent a middleman to give me a list he'd compiled of the people and topics he wanted to discuss, including Medina's personal manuscript, *El Pacto de Recoletos*.

Perhaps Medina knew his time was running out and he wanted to atone for the part he played in certain things that had happened, or perhaps he just wanted to ensure that others were held accountable. If I had to guess, I'd say it was both.

Since Medina was already under house arrest at the time of his request, any meeting would have to have been conducted in total secrecy, and from the relative safety of his home. But pulling that off would have been almost impossible, as Casa Medina was watched round the clock by both government entities and the Colombian media. Medina proposed that I be smuggled past the residence gates in the trunk of a car, then ushered into the home, where we could speak privately.

I jumped at the chance to take the meeting, of course. It was clear that Medina had amassed a bounty of highly sensitive and damaging material involving a number of controversial issues—enough to ruin more than a few political legacies. Unfortunately, my proposal was resoundingly denied by the US Embassy and Washington officials, and I never got the chance to meet with him. But I was able to obtain a copy of Medina's manuscript (through the same middleman), which contained significant details about the Proceso 8.000 investigation and other topics. The manuscript was sent to DEA Headquarters and used to help US analysts and investigators piece together the incestuous relationships between the Colombian government, the Cali cartel, and corrupt officials that permeated its institutions.

Fernando Botero Zea

As a result of Santiago Medina's allegations, President Samper's former campaign manager and defense minister resigned from his post as minister on August 2, 1995, and was arrested by Colombian authorities two weeks later. Medina claimed that Botero had solicited drug money–sourced donations from Cali for then presidential candidate Samper, an allegation that was confirmed with the seizure of the stacks of documents from Miguel's desk during the Santa Rita raid and, later, further corroborated by other witnesses, including Guillermo Pallomari. Botero was sentenced to five years and three months detention at a military base in Bogotá after pleading guilty to illicit enrichment and falsifying campaign document charges. He was released from prison on February 12, 1998.

Andrés Pastrana Arango

The Conservative Party candidate went on to succeed Ernesto Samper (to whom he lost in 1994) and served as Colombia's thirtieth president from 1998 to 2002.

Colonel Carlos Alfonso Velásquez Romero

In December 1994, the colonel was transferred out of his role as commander of the elite army Search Bloc in Cali and reassigned to the position of second in command and chief of staff of the army's 17th Brigade in Urabá, Antioquia. In May 1996, Velásquez filed a report against his new commanding officer, accusing him of having ties to paramilitary forces operating in the area. In response, a disciplinary investigation was opened against Velásquez, ultimately leading to his retirement in January 1997. He left the army after nearly thirty years of service, ending his lifelong dream of one day becoming a general. However, he continued to thrive, taking on the roles of professor of political policy and theory at the Universidad de la Sabana in Bogotá as well as political analyst. In May of 2024 he announced his candidacy for the presidency of Colombia in 2026.

Ruben Prieto, Jerry Salameh, Dave Mitchell, and Chris Feistl

The four DEA special agents whose collective efforts helped bring about the demise of the Cali cartel went on to receive numerous accolades from both the US and Colombian governments, including the DEA's highest award (the Administrator's Award of Honor) and two Distinguished Service Medals from the Colombian National Police.

Ruben Prieto was laterally transferred in mid-1997 and assigned to DEA Headquarters, Office of Domestic Operations. He later served as the DEA country attaché in the Dominican Republic and retired from the DEA in 2003 after almost thirty years of federal service. Ruben passed away in November 2019.

Jerry Salameh was promoted in April 1997 and assigned to DEA Headquarters, Office of International Operations, with oversight for Colombia. He was later assigned to posts in Florida and the Bahamas and retired from the DEA in 2015 after twenty-eight years of federal service. Jerry currently serves as a consultant to a diverse group of clients, specializing in security and investigative interests in the US and abroad.

Dave Mitchell was laterally transferred in July 1997 and assigned to Tampa, Florida, then promoted two years later and assigned to Miami. Dave retired from the DEA in 2020 after thirty-three years of federal service and currently provides personal protection services to select clientele in the US and around the world.

Chris Feistl was promoted in April 1997 and assigned to DEA Headquarters, Mexico and Central America Section. After being sent back to Colombia in mid-1999 and serving as a group supervisor, he left in 2002 and spent seventeen months serving in the States before being promoted in 2004 and returning once again to Colombia as an assistant regional director for the Andean Region. In 2014, Chris retired from the DEA after twenty-six years of federal service as an assistant special agent in charge. In total he spent over twelve years in Colombia, one of the longest tenures ever served by a DEA agent in the country. Chris currently serves as a consultant and special advisor on television and film projects, including Season 3 of Netflix's widely acclaimed hit series *Narcos: Rise of a New Empire, The Cali Cartel*, which chronicled Chris and Dave's efforts against the cartel.

During subsequent assignments in Colombia, Chris helped direct DEA's financial efforts, in coordination with Colombian and US counterparts, to identify additional cartel assets for subsequent seizure by Colombian authorities.

Below is a partial list of assets seized by the Colombia government over the years relating to the four Cali godfathers:

The Rodríguez Orejuelas

In September 2004, a total of 432 Drogas La Rebaja stores in twenty-eight cities throughout the country were seized and taken control of by Colombian authorities. The drugstore chain had over 4,200 employees and was conservatively valued at between $220 and $300 million. The seizure was Colombia's largest ever of properties tied to drug traffickers.

José Santacruz Londoño

In total, more than 1,076 properties and businesses were seized from Chepe. With an estimated conservative value close to $100 million, the rumor that Santacruz owned over two thousand different properties isn't so far-fetched. Without question, there are still hundreds more properties owned by Santacruz and his *testaferros* in Colombia and elsewhere that have never been identified.

Francisco Hélmer Herrera Buitrago

More than 1,751 properties and businesses were seized from Pacho, conservatively valued at well over $100 million.

In total, over $2.8 billion in Cali cartel assets were seized and/or agreed to be forfeited through forfeiture agreements by the Colombian and US governments.

Jorge Salcedo Cabrera

The former head of security for Miguel Rodríguez and the Cali cartel pled guilty to a negotiated plea agreement for one count of racketeering in October 1998. Because of his significant cooperation with the US government and the critical role he played in the dismantling of the Cali cartel, he received probation and served no time. He also received over $1.7 million in reward money from the Colombian and US governments. Salcedo and his family entered witness protection and currently live in an undisclosed location in the United States.

Author's Note

OVER THE PAST THREE DECADES, both Dave and I have been on the receiving end of the occasional call from Salcedo, always shown as coming from an obscure area code (likely routed through the US Marshals Service) or a blocked number. He's also sent holiday cards to our respective DEA offices, never with a return address (in typical Jorge fashion, he had our addresses, but we don't have his). Neither Dave nor I know anything about the new name or identity Salcedo has assumed since entering witness protection, but to us it doesn't really matter. We'll always know him as Sean.

In 2012, I was contacted by producers from National Public Radio's acclaimed program *This American Life*. After reading William Rempel's riveting book *At the Devil's Table*, which chronicles Jorge Salcedo's life while in the employ of the Cali cartel, they asked us to participate in a discussion to further delve into our stories (*This American Life* 469: "Hiding in Plain Sight, Act Three: Seven Year Snitch"). After traveling to California to be interviewed for the show, I met up with Bill Rempel (also a longtime friend), and to my great surprise, Salcedo was there as well. It had been almost seventeen years since we'd last seen each other in Colombia, right before he'd left to start a new life in the US with his family.

Four years later, I was reunited with Salcedo once again, this time during the making of Season 3 of *Narcos*. The two of us were brought together for a special Q&A with the talented *Narcos* production crew and equally talented Netflix executive staff at one of their off-site facilities in California. In so many ways, it seemed as if no time had passed at all. Rehashing all the details of our times together—even the ones most fraught with danger—felt effortless. I've never met anyone like him, and don't think I ever will. It was the last time I ever saw him.

Bibliography

Books

Aguilar, Hugo. *Así Maté a Pablo Escobar*. Barcelona, Spain: Planeta, 2014.

Bowden, Mark. *Killing Pablo: The Hunt for the World's Greatest Outlaw*. New York: Atlantic Monthly Press, 2001.

Cédilot, André, and André Noël. *Mafia Inc.: The Long, Bloody Reign of Canada's Sicilian Clan*, Chapter 9—Operation Compote. Canada: Random House, 2011.

Chepesiuk, Ron. *The Bullet or the Bribe: Taking Down Colombia's Cali Drug Cartel*. Westport, Conn.: Praeger, 2003.

_____. *Drug Lords: The Rise and Fall of the Cali Cartel*. Lytham, U.K.: Milo Books, 2007.

Duque Daza, Javier. *Políticos y Militares en Colombia*. September 29, 2020. Cali, Colombia: Universidad del Valle, 2020.

Grosse, Robert E. *Drugs and Money: Laundering Latin America's Cocaine Dollars*. The Santacruz Londoño Organization, 1988-90, Chapter 9, (Jurado). Westport, Conn.: Praeger, 2001.

Rempel, William C. *At the Devil's Table: The Untold Story of the Insider Who Brought Down the Cali Cartel*. New York: Random House, 2011.

Richards, James R. *Transnational Criminal Organizations, Cybercrime, and Money Laundering: A Handbook for Law Enforcement Officers, Auditors, and Financial Investigators*. U.K.: Routledge, 1998, p. 17-20. *Figures courtesy of *The Wall Street Journal Almanac 1988*, (Random House 1997) P. 36.

Rodríguez Abadía, William. *Son of the Cali Cartel*. Liverpool, U.K.: Gadfly Press, 2002.

Bibliography

Magazine and Newspaper Articles: (WEB) Documents

"Abatido José Santacruz en Medellín." *El Tiempo*, March 6, 1996.

"Accountant Says Cali Cartel Gave Millions to Help Samper." *The Spokesman-Review, Associated Press*, July 23, 1997.

"Agents Seize Seven Tons of Cocaine Among Vegetables." *UPI*, April 29, 1992.

Ambrus, Steven. "Colombia Arrests Brother of Cali Drug Cartel Chiefs: South America: Suspect has also been Charged in US Officials Hope Leaders Will Feel Pressure to Surrender." *Los Angeles Times*, March 4, 1995.

Amoruso, David. "The Canadian Connection: Flooding the US with Dope." *Gangsters Inc.*, October 16, 2014.

Anderson, Brian. "The Cartel Supercomputer of 1994." *Vice*, September 9, 2014

Anderson, Curt. "Drug Trafficker Gets Big Cut in Sentence." *The Ledger— The Associated Press*, January 4, 2007.

Anderson, Jack, and Michael Binstein. "Drug Cartels' Big Planes are Big Problem." *The Washington Post*, February 6, 1995.

"Application of the Mansfield Amendment to the Use of United States Military Personnel and Equipment to Assist Foreign Governments in Drug Enforcement Activities." US Department of Justice, September 18, 1986.

Britt, Ran. "The Infamous…José El Chepe" Santacruz Londoño." Blogger, June 1, 2017.

Brocklehurst, Steven. "The Scottish Mercenary Hired to Kill Pablo Escobar." *BBC*, March 28, 2004.

Bullmore, Joseph. "If You Thought Pablo Escobar was Bad, You Should Meet the Cali Cartel—Meet the Cali Cartel—Pacho Herrera & Net Worth." *The Gentleman's Journal*.

Butt, Shelby. "A New Era for US-Colombia Extradition Policy? Only Time Will Tell." *Columbia Journal of Transnational Law*, October 8, 2022.

"Cae Santacruz en un Restaurante." *El Tiempo*, July 5, 1995.

"Caen Sospechosos de la Masacre de Cali." *El Tiempo*, July 30, 1991.

"Cali Cartel Drug Kingpins Plead Guilty." *CBS News*, September 26, 2006.

"Cali en la Mira? *Semana*, December 6, 1992.

"Cali Money-Launderers Sentenced in NY." *UPI*, June 28, 1996.

"Cali Pachanguero." *Semana*, April 2, 2005.

"Capturado Extraditable en Cali." *El Tiempo*, March 17, 1995.

"Casi me Desmayo." General (r) Recuerda la Captura de Gilberto Rodriguez Orejuela. NoticiasRCN, June 1, 2022.

Cavelier Castro, Andrés. "Otra Dura Advertencia de EE.UU." El *Tiempo*, October 6, 1995. (spacing)"Cayó Pacho Herrera." *El Tiempo*, September 2, 1996.

Cervera Moreno, César. "Así Fue la Muerte de Pablo Escobar, Según los Agentes que lo Acorralaron." ABC Historia, August 9, 2022.

"Chantajes Ocultos del Cartel de Cali al Bloque." *El Tiempo*, April 9, 1996.

Coll, Steve, and Douglas Farah. "Panama Still a Conduit for Cocaine Profits." *The Washington Post*, September 20, 1993.

Collett, Merrill. "Colombia's Drug Lords Waging War on Leftists." *The Washington Post*, November 14, 1987.

"Colombia Allegations Have US Fuming." *DesertNews*, by *Associated Press*, October 6, 1995.

"Colombia Arrests Cartel Leader." *Tampa Bay Times*, March 4, 1995, updated October 3, 2005.

"Colombia Busts Store Chain for Cocaine Links." *NBC News*, September 17, 2004.

"Colombian Drug Figure Surrenders." *Tampa Bay Times*, June 25, 1995. Updated October 4, 2005.

"Colombian Governor Slain in Medellín." *The Washington Post*, July 5, 1989.

"Colombia Police Chief Denies Drug Link." *UPI*, July 13, 1994.

"Colombia Sentences Former Samper Aid." *UPI*, October 5, 1996.

"Colombia Ties US to Attack on Lawyer Defending President." *The Washington Post*, September 28, 1995.

"Colombia Update: Relations with US Strained, Political Fallout Continues, Another Arrest Made." *Ndsn.org*, November 1995.

"Condenado a 64 Meses de Cárcel Santiago Medina." *El Tiempo*, July 12, 1996.

Bibliography

"Condenan a Cinco Años a Mayor (r) Luis del Vasto." *El Tiempo*, February 27, 1997.

"Confusión por Visas de Militares." *El Tiempo*, January 26, 1996.

Cooper, Michael. "US Indicts a Fugitive Over Drugs." *The New York Times*, June 8, 1995.

"Cuentas Pendientes." *Semana*, August 29, 1999.

"DAS Ocupó la Casa Blanca de Santacruz." *El Tiempo*, May 16, 1997.

"Delatar Si Paga." *Semana*, March 2, 1997.

"Del General Camilo Zúñiga." *Semana*, February 18, 1996.

den Held, Douwe. "Spain: The European Base for Latin American Organized Crime." *InSight Crime*, February 9, 2021.

Dermota, Ken. "Drug Cartels Benefit From NAFTA." Special to *The Christian Science Monitor*, August 2, 1995.

"Desaparecida." *Semana*, August 31, 1997.

Deshawn. "How Pablo Escobar Died 28 Years Ago." *24 News Recorder*, December 3, 2021.

Dillon, Sam. "Drug Plane Lands in Mexico and is Unloaded, Possibly by Police." *The New York Times*, November 30, 1995.

"Doing the Wash: Inside a Colombian Cartel's Money-Laundering Machine." *The Free Library by Farlex*. *Harper's Magazine*, February 1, 1997.

Dragosin, Maria. "The Cali Cartel or The Cali KGB." Centuria Study Association, May 25, 2022.

"Drug Cartel Leader Escapes From Colombian Prison." *The Washington Post*, January 12, 1996.

"Drug Lord's Son Hurt, 5 killed in Colombia." *Desert News*, May 24, 1996.

"Drug Scandal Implicates Colombian President." NewsBriefs, October 1995.

"Drug Suspect Surrenders in Colombia." *Desert News by Associated Press*, June 24, 1995.

"Economic Sanctions Against Colombian Drug Cartels." Office of Foreign Assets Control, US Department of the Treasury, March 2007.

"Edificio Mónaco." *El Colombiano*.

"El Amor Pudo Más." *Semana*, August 24, 2012.

"El Coletazo del 8.000." *Semana*, August 18, 1996.

"El Coronel, La Dama y el Video." *Semana*, September 11, 1994.

"El DAS Capturó a Extraditable en Cali." *El Tiempo*, February 25, 1995.

"El 'Dossier' Mestre." *Semana*, May 28, 1995.

"El Maletin de Miguel Rodríguez." *Semana*, August 20, 1995.

"El Regreso del Coronel Velásquez." *El Espectador*, August 6, 2013.

"El Señor." *Semana*, January 2, 2000.

"El Ventilador de Pallomari." *Semana*, November 5, 1995.

"El 8.000, Dia a Dia." *Semana*, January 7, 1996.

"En Atentado Resultó Herido Hijo de Miguel Rodríguez." *El Tiempo*, May 25, 1996.

"Ernesto Samper." Britannica, September 27, 2023.

"Escenas Intimas no son Publicables: Tribunal." *El Tiempo*, October 13, 1994.

"Extradition Treaty with the Republic of Colombia (From Handbook on Drug Control in the United States …)" US Department of Justice, Office of Justice Programs, 1990.

Farah, Douglas. "The CrackUp." *The Washington Post*, July 21, 1996.

_____. "Criticizing US, Samper Concedes 'Serious Evidence' of Drug Money." *The Post*, March 7, 1996.

_____. "Rival Colombian Groups Battle Over Heroin Trade." *The Washington Post*, January 18, 1992.

_____. "Snaring Cali Cartel Tiger, Officials Found a Pussycat." *The Washington Post*, August 28, 1995.

_____. "US-Bogotá: What Went Wrong? This is a Decertification not of Colombia, but of President Samper." *The Washington Post*, March 3, 1996.

_____. "US to Revoke Colombian's Visas." *The Washington Post*, January 25, 1996.

Farah, Douglas, and Don Podesta. "Jailed Drug Lord Said to Order Killings." *The Washington Post*, July 20, 1992.

Farah, Douglas, and Molly Moore. "Mexican Drug Traffickers Eclipse Colombian Cartels." *The Washington Post*, March 30, 1997.

Bibliography

"Final de un Capo que Empezó Como Mandadero." *El Tiempo*, November 6, 1998.

"Fiscalía Investigará a Agentes de la SIJÍN Cali." *El Tiempo*, February 22, 1995.

Finemand, Mark, and Craig Pyes. "A Plane is Buried in Baja—and Drug Ties Unearthed." *Los Angeles Times*, November 18, 1995.

"Former Colombia Defense Minister Testifies." *UPI*, August 16, 1995.

"Former Defense Minister Released From Prison." *AP Archive*, February 14, 1998.

"Frechette, Myles R. R." *The Association for Diplomatic Studies and Training*, Interviewed by: Charles Stuart Kennedy, September 4, 2001. P. 144, 150-170.

Gaffey, Conor. "Colombia Just Seized $360 Million of US-Bound Cocaine, but What are the Biggest Drug Busts in History?" *Newsweek*, November 9, 2017.

García, Maria Isabel. "Detenido el Hermano del Jefe del Cartel de Cali Cuando iba a la Pitonisa." *El Pais*, March 3, 1995.

García-Roberts, Gus. "Cocaine Drug Cartel Leader's Interior Designers Took the Fall for the Cali Cartel." *USA Today*, November 6, 2019.

Gardiner, Sean. "Heroin: From the Civil War to the 70s, and Beyond. *City Limits*, July 5, 2009.

Gaynor, Tim, and Tiemoko Diallo. "Al Qaeda Linked to Rouge Aviation Network." *Reuters*, January 13, 2010.

"General Hernando Camilo Zúñiga Resigns." *Reuters*, March 11, 1996.

"Gilberto Rodríguez Orejuela, alias 'The Chess Player.'" *InSight Crime*, June 15, 2022.

"Gilberto Rodríguez Orejuela Biography." *History and Biography*.

"Gilberto Rodríguez Orejuela Once Ran 80% of the World Cocaine Market." *The Economist*, June 30, 2022.

Golden, Tim. "Tons of Cocaine Reaching Mexico in Old Jets." *The New York Times*, January 10, 1995.

Green, Peter, S. "The Ever-Changing Logistics of Drug Smuggling." *The Wall Street Journal*.

Greenhouse, Steven. "Dispute Over Tapes Further Sours US-Colombian Relations." *New York Times*, October 7, 1995.

"Guillermo Villa Alzate." *Semana*, October 1, 1995. "Guerra Entre FARC y Cartel de Cali." *El Tiempo*, November 20, 1992.

Gutkin, Steve. "Colombia Arrests Leader of Top Drug Cartel." *The Washington Post*, June 10, 1995.

_____. "Colombian President Elect Accused of Taking Cocaine Cartel's Fund." *The Washington Post*, June 23, 1994.

_____. "DEA Agent Attacks Colombia as 'Narco-Democracy.'" *The Washington Post*, October 1, 1994.

"Habla Mestre." *Semana*, November 23, 1997.

"History of Drug Trafficking – Colombia, US & Mexico." *History Channel*, June 10, 2019.

I. de Roux, Gustavo, and César Chelala. "Colombia's Violent Culture." *The Christian Science Monitor*, September 13, 1993.

"Interviews-Jorge Ochoa | Drug Wars | Frontline." *PBS*.

Isikoff, Michael. "Federal Officials Seize 12-Ton Cocaine Shipment." *The Washington Post*, December 3, 1991.

Jaramillo, Ana Maria. "Guillermo Pallomari Penso en el Suicidio." *El Tiempo*, July 29, 1997.

_____. "Señor Juez, Imploro Su Perdón." *El Tiempo*, December 16, 1998.

_____. "The Cartel of Cali, Inc." *El Tiempo*, July 20, 1997.

"Julian Murcillo Captured by Police." *AP Archive*, July 8, 1995.

Kaldina. Mariela Ibarra Piedrahita. "Especial de Policía y Corrupcíon— Primera Parte." *Hechos y Noticias*, February 21, 2016.

Kryt, Jeremy. "The Sicario's Tale, Part 4: The Cuckold Who Brought Down the Cartels." *The Daily Beast*, December 29, 2018.

"King's College Men's Basketball Program History." King's College Athletics, October 1, 2008.

"La Guerra Entre Carteles y la Oscura Historia de Drogas La Rebaja, Cadena de Farmacias que Apoyará Reforma a la Salud." *Semana*, June 13, 2023.

"La Hora Cero." *Semana*, April 2, 1995.

"La Hora del Cartel de Cali." *Semana*, January 15, 2005.

"La Red del Mayor del Vasto." *El Tiempo*, April 9, 1996.

"La Siniestra Vida de Gilberto Rodríguez Orejuela." *Infobae*, July 1, 2022.

Bibliography

"La Tragedia del General." *Semana*, September 18, 1994.

La Trampa del Cartel de Cali al Coronel (r) Carlos Velásquez que Case Acaba con su Carrera y con su Familia. *Semana*, September 3, 2001.

"La Ultima Entrega." *Semana*, October 6, 1996.

"Las Primeras Huellas." *Semana*, June 2, 1996.

"Las Razones del Atentato al Hijo de Miguel R." *El Tiempo*, October 13, 1996.

"Las 9 Condiciones de la DEA." *El Tiempo*, June 1, 1995.

"Laundering Money: Obscuring the Link Between the Criminal and the Crime." *vlex*, June 1998.

Lawrence, David Aquila. "Colombia Drug-Fighter Learns Hazard of Blowing the Whistle." *The Christian Science Monitor*, February 14, 1997.

"Liberada la Hermana de José Santacruz Londoño." *El Tiempo*, January 21, 1993.

"List Shows Cartel had an Elite Payroll." *Desert News, by Associated Press*, July 23, 1995.

"Los Allanamientos Claves." *Semana*, May 1, 1996.

"Los Cambios no Pueden Esperar." *El Tiempo*, September 3, 1994.

"Los Otros Enemigos de Pablo Escobar, El Cartel de Cali." *Steemit*.

"Los Secretos de Pallomari." *Semana*, October 22, 1995.

Lozano, Pilar. "Dimite el Jefe del Ejército Colombiano por Presunta Vinculación al Narcotrafico." *El País*, March 11, 1996.

"Manuel de Dios Unanue." *Heroism.org*.

"Manuel de Dios Unanue Killed." Committee to Protect Journalists, March 11, 1992.

Martínez, Antonio. ¿"Mojaron" La Mano Derecha de Samper?" *Hoy.Tawsa. com*, August 17, 1995.

"Mas Cheques del 8.000." *Semana*, August 30, 1998.

"Massive Indictment Charges Former Justice Official and 58 Others with Racketeering." *NDSN.org*, September 1995.

Matheson, Mary. "The World's Most Wanted Man Captured, but His Cartel May Live." *The Christian Science Monitor*, June 12, 1995.

_____. "Colombia Faces Its Own Watergate." *The Christian Science Monitor*, August 4, 1995.

McDermott, Jeremy. "Colombia Elites and Organized Crime: 'Don Berna.'" *InSight Crime*, August 9, 2016.

McGee, Jim. "Ex-Prosecutors Indicted in Cali Case." *The Washington Post*, June 6, 1995.

_____. "From Respected Attorney to Suspected Racketeer: A Lawyer's Journey." *The Washington Post*, June 18, 1995.

"Meet Miguel Ángel Félix Gallardo, "The Bill Gates of Cocaine" Who Put Mexican Narcotrafficking on the Map." *All That's Interesting*, March 28, 2022, Updated October 19, 2022.

Moody, John, and Pablo Rodríguez Orejuela, and Tom Quinn. "A Day with the Chess Player." *Time*, July 1, 1991.

"Murió Santiago Medina. *El Tiempo*, January 16, 1999.

Noguera Montoya, Susana, Patricia. "Edificio Mónaco, la Huella de Pablo Escobar que Dejó de Existir en Medellín." *Anadolu Agency*, February 23, 2019.

Ortiz, Nieves Jesus, and Francisco Celis. "Cambio de Gobierno, Cambio de Estilo." *El Tiempo*, October 9, 1994.

Ospina, Clara Elvira. "Cayó Anoche Jorge Rodríguez Orejuela." *El Tiempo*, March 3, 1995.

Ospina, Jaime Andrés., "Excomandante de las FF.MM. Niega Haber Conocido a los Rodríguez Orejuela." *W Radio*, April 11, 2011.

"Paramilitaries." *Yali.Imodules.com*.

"Patterns of Homicide—Cali, Colombia, 1993-1994." Centers for Disease Control and Prevention, October 6, 1995.

Pérez B., Juan Pablo, and Daniela Garzón. "De Héroes a Villanos." *La Silla Vacía*, November 26, 2016.

"Principales Hitos en la Lucha Contra el Cartel de Cali: Cronología de la Persecucion." *El País*, June 1, 2022.

"Relevan a Comandante del Bloque de Búsqueda." *El Tiempo*, February 18, 1995.

Rempel, William, C. "A Daring Betrayal Helped Wipe Out Cali Cocaine Cartel." *The Seattle Times*, February 25, 2007.

_____. "The Man Who Took Down Cali." *Los Angeles Times*, February 24, 2007.

Bibliography

"Report on International Extradition Submitted to Congress Pursuant to Section 3203 of the Emergency Supplemental Act, 2000 as Enacted in the Military Construction Appropriations Act, 2001, Public Law 106-246 Relating to Plan Colombia. United States Department of State, January 17, 2001.

"RG-8A Condor Schweizer SA2-37B." *GlobalSecurity.org.*, July 28, 2011.

Risen, Clay. "Gilberto Rodríguez Orejuela, Colombian Drug Lord, Dies at 83." *The New York Times*, June 2, 2022.

Risen, James. "US played Key Role in Arrest of Drug Lord, Sources Say: Law Enforcement: CIA, DEA provided Colombian Officials Intelligence on Rodríguez's Whereabouts." *Los Angeles Times*, June 13, 1995.

Robberson, Tod. "Panama Probes Unfreezing of Funds." *The Washington Post,* November 28, 1992.

Ruiz, Albor. "The Death of a Journalist." *Al Día*, March 18, 2020.

Salazar, Salvo Manuel. "The War of the Cartels" (Excerpt From 'Mafia Connections') *Interferencia*, January 19, 2021.

Salcedo, Jorge. "What I Saw Inside the Cali Cartel." *CNN*, January 18, 2012.

"Sale Zúñiga y Asume Almirante Holdan Delgado." *El Tiempo*, March 12, 1996.

"Salida en Falso." *El Tiempo*, October 1, 1994.

Schemo, Diana Jean. "Rightist Avengers Become the Terror of Colombia." *The New York Times*, March 26, 1997.

"Second Cartel Leader Surrenders in Colombia." *Greensboro News and Record*, June 25, 1995.

"Se Entregó Arizabaleta." *El Tiempo*." July 9, 1995.

"Sepultado Hijo de Director de la Policía Nacional." *El Tiempo*, August 20, 1994.

Selsky, Andrew. "Drug Cartel's Bookkeeper Could Topple Government Evidence Details Corruption in Colombian Presidency." *The Spokesman-Review*, September 24, 1995.

_____. "Tapes: DEA Goes Solo in Drug War—Colombia Shut Out of Some Operations." *The Seattle Times*, November 1, 1995.

Serena, Katie. "How Pablo Escobar's Medellín Cartel Became the Most Ruthless in History." *AllThat'sInteresting.com*, September 28, 2021 | Updated October 6, 2021.

Serrill, Michael, S. "Rocked by Scandal, Samper's Presidency is in Peril as an Aide Says His Boss Took Campaign Contributions from DrugLords." *Time*, August 14, 1995.

Shannon, Elain. "The Cali Cartel: New Kings of Coke." *Time*, July 1, 1991.

Sheridan, Mary Beth. "Phone Taps Fray US-Colombia Relations." *Chicago Tribune*, October 8, 1995.

Smyth, Frank. "A New Kingdom of Cocaine." *The Washington Post*, December 26, 1993.

Speck, Mary. "Kidnapping has Become a Thriving Industry in Colombia-Abductions have Quintupled since 1987. 1,400 people held for Ransom in 1991." *The Baltimore Sun*, May 13, 1992.

"Summary of Guillermo Pallomari's testimony in the 1997 Operation Cornerstone Trial of Michael Abbell and William Moran." *ResearchGate*, September 13, 2017.

"Tapes Say US Agents Led Colombian Drug Raids." *Deseret News*, November 1, 1995.

"Terrorismo a la Carta." *Semana*.

"The 3 AML Stages: Layering, Placement, & Integration Explained." *Unit21*, May 16, 2022.

"The Cali Cartel: The New Kings of Cocaine—Drug Intelligence Report." Office of Justice Programs, November 1994."

"The Cali Cartel: The Takedown of History's Biggest Drug Mafia." *Gangsters Inc.*, April 6, 2017.

"The Drug Enforcement Administration (DEA) 1985-1990." Drug Enforcement Administration.

"The Drug Enforcement Administration (DEA) 1990-1994." Drug Enforcement Administration.

"The Real Life of José Santacruz Londoño." *TheDrugLords.com*.

"The Story Behind Norman's Cay: Original Home of the Frye Festival." *Impulsive Wanderlust*, March 8, 2019.

"Thirty Years of America's Drug War—a Chronology." *PBS*.

Thomas, Pierre. "Informant's Revelations on Cali Cartel Implicate Colombian Officials." *The Washington Post*, January 28, 1996.

Thomas, Pierre, and Thomas W. Lippman. "Top Cali Aide Surrenders to US Officials." *The Washington Post*, September 22, 1995.

Bibliography

"Timeline: Key Events in US War on Drugs in Latin America." *Reuters*, January 14, 2010.

Torchia, Chris. "Another Cali Cartel Leader Surrenders." *Lewiston Morning Tribune*, June 25, 1995.

"Tras Las Rejas El Genio del Lavado de Dólares." *El Tiempo*, July 29, 1991.

"United States v. Jurado Rodríguez, 907 F. Supp. 569 (E.D.N.Y. 1995)." *Justia*, November 15, 1995.

"Un Nuevo Casete." *Semana*, September 3, 1995.

"US Cocaine Seizure is 2nd Biggest." *Los Angeles Times*, December 3, 1991.

"Vea los Lujosos y Billonarios Bienes Incautados a Testaferros de Pacho Herrera en el Valle." *El País*, February 5, 2020.

Velásquez, Vásquez, John Jairo—Popeye. "Se Arma el Cartel (1980-1987)." *Facebook*, December 31, 2014.

Volckhausen, Taran. "'I think' Gaviria Knew Tapes Linking Cali Cartel to Samper: Former US Ambassador." *Colombia Reports*, December 3, 2013.

Wilson, George. "How Pablo Escobar Died 28 Years Ago and 3 of the Theories about Who Shot Him." *24 News Recorder*, December 3, 2021.

Woody, Christopher. "Pablo Escobar was Gunned Down 29 Years Ago—Here are 3 Theories About Who Took the Kingpin's Life." *Yahoo! Finance UK*, December 2, 2022.

"Y Como Es El." *Semana*, April 3, 1995.

"Yo Acuso." *Semana*, October 30, 1994.

"Zúñiga Habríapedido la Baja." *El Tiempo*, February 23, 1996.

"3 Tons of Cocaine Found in Chocolate." *The Washington Post*, July 2, 1988.

Press Releases

"Cali Cartel Leaders Plead Guilty to Drug and Money Laundering Conspiracy Charges—Rodríguez Orejuela Brothers, Other Family Members Agree to $2.1 billion in Forfeiture." Press Release, US Department of Justice, September 26, 2006.

About the Authors

Chris Feistl was a DEA Special Agent for twenty-six years, serving in diverse assignments throughout the US as well as twelve years in Colombia, South America, where he investigated major drug cartels that were supplying tons of cocaine and heroin destined for the US. Starting as a new agent in Miami, he finished his career as an Assistant Special Agent in Charge in Phoenix in 2014.

Chris has been a frequent guest on television documentaries and true crime podcasts regarding the Cali cartel. He was portrayed in eighty episodes of a Spanish-language series entitled *En la Boca del Lobo*, as well as in Season 3 of Netflix's hit series *Narcos*. He has also appeared in several other television projects, shows, and radio programs.

Chris has been the recipient of numerous awards, including the DEA Administrator's Award of Honor (DEA's highest honor), and four Distinguished Service Medals from the Colombian government.

Dave Mitchell is a retired DEA Special Agent with thirty-three years of service, where he played a crucial role in numerous high-profile cases targeting major drug cartels, including the Cali cartel. He began his career in Miami during the era of the Miami Cocaine Cowboys, and later conducted cocaine interdiction operations in the jungles of South America and led drug investigations throughout South Florida, the Caribbean, Central and South America, and Europe. He retired in December 2020 after receiving numerous awards, including the DEA's highest award, the Administrator's Award of Honor, and two Distinguished Service Medals from the Colombian government.

Dave currently resides in the Fort Lauderdale area and owns ClearPath Investigative Solutions, LLC, which provides investigative services and personal protection to a select group of high-profile clients.

About the Authors

Jessica Balboni is a Boston-based writer and editor with a diverse background in media that spans artistic, academic, corporate, and nonprofit sectors, including roles held with the Food Network, The Rockefeller Foundation, and ESPN.